CIRCULATION

WRITTEN BY
JOHN WOOD

BookLife PUBLISHING

©2019
Book Life
King's Lynn
Norfolk PE30 4LS

ISBN:978-1-78637-462-2

Written by:
John Wood

Edited by:
Holly Duhig

Designed by:
Amy Li

A catalogue record for this book is available from the British Library.

All facts, statistics, web addresses and URLs in this book were verified as valid and accurate at time of writing. No responsibility for any changes to external websites or references can be accepted by either the author or publisher.

All rights reserved. Printed in Malaysia.

Nottinghamshire Education Library Service

E220197708

Askews & Holts	Feb-2020
612.1	£12.99

PHOTO CREDITS

Images are courtesy of Shutterstock.com. With thanks to Getty Images, Thinkstock Photo and iStockphoto.

Front Cover – Ismagilova, Phonlamai Photo, Crevis, Creative Mood, Magic mine, mikeledray, Master Images – Incomible, Andrew Rybalko (Seymour), AIZhi, newelle, Yuii (vector embelleshments), Andry Frith (header texture), Petkowicz (textbox texture), Ismagilova, Crevis, Andry Frith (background images), Flas100 (paper scrap vectors), 4 – altanaka, wavebreakmedia, 5 – eranicle, rumruay, 6 – MDGRPHCS, UGREEN, NelaR, 7 – MoreVector, Pavel L Photo and Video, Jorge Salcedo, 8 – Africa Studio, Liya Graphics, 9 – pablofdezr, Studio BKK, 10 – wacomka, Rawpixel.com, NatchaS, 11 – charnsitr, extender_01, 12 – Magic mine, GraphicsRF, 13 – Liya Graphics, Sebastian Kaulitzki, 14 – Oksana Telesheva, Incomible, joshya, Robert Kneschke, 15 – Africa Studio, Sebastian Kaulitzski, samunella, 16 – Magic mine, ballemans, 17 – BlueRingMedia, UGREEN 3S, 18 – Mopic, nobeastsofierce, Rvector, 19 – NotionPic, vitstudio, New Africa, 20 – Vector Tradition, Matej Kastelic, Anton Nalivayko, Andrew Rybalko, 21 – Incomible, Milkovasa, Daria Serdtseva, 22 – Gunraya Ums, pedalist, 23 – Jingjits Photography, Kalamurzing, Sebastian Kaulitzski, 24 – AVIcon, Sebastian Kaulitzski, Kateryna Kon, 25 – Magic mine, Nerthuz, kmls, 26 – ARTSIOM ZAVADSKI, somersault1824, Din Mohd Yaman, 27 – Juan Gaertner, 9Thanaphon, 28 – Tewan Banditrukkanka, Barb Elkin, 29 – Ralwel, Mykola Komarovskyy, 30 – Sebastian Kaulitzki

CONTENTS

PAGE 4 — The Most Amazing Machine
PAGE 6 — What Seems to Be the Problem?
PAGE 8 — Start at the Heart
PAGE 10 — Round and Round behind the Ribs
PAGE 12 — Loop the Lungs
PAGE 14 — Travel down the Trunk
PAGE 16 — Straight through the Stomach
PAGE 18 — Go past the Guts
PAGE 20 — Left at the Legs
PAGE 22 — Back up the Back
PAGE 24 — Look, It's the Liver
PAGE 26 — All Aboard the Arms
PAGE 28 — Head Back to the Heart
PAGE 30 — All Better
PAGE 31 — Glossary
PAGE 32 — Index

Words that look like **this** can be found in the glossary on page 31.

THE MOST AMAZING MACHINE

There is a machine that can solve difficult problems. It can learn complicated things. This machine can move around and jump up high. If the machine gets a **virus**, it can often cure itself – and if the machine gets broken, it can often fix itself. It is made up of **billions** and billions of parts, and it even grows bigger.

THIS MACHINE... IS THE HUMAN BODY.

YOUR BRILLIANT BODY

Every day, your body does incredible things to keep you alive. You are probably not even aware of what it is doing most of the time. However, under your skin, all the parts of your body are working together to keep you healthy and ready for the day ahead. Do you ever think about what happens to your food after it disappears down your throat? Or why your body becomes so snotty, sweaty and sick-y when you are ill? What about how you can breathe without thinking? Your body does a lot of things **automatically.**

YOUR BODY IS ALWAYS LOOKING OUT FOR YOU AND HELPING YOU OUT.

EVERY BODY NEEDS A BRAIN

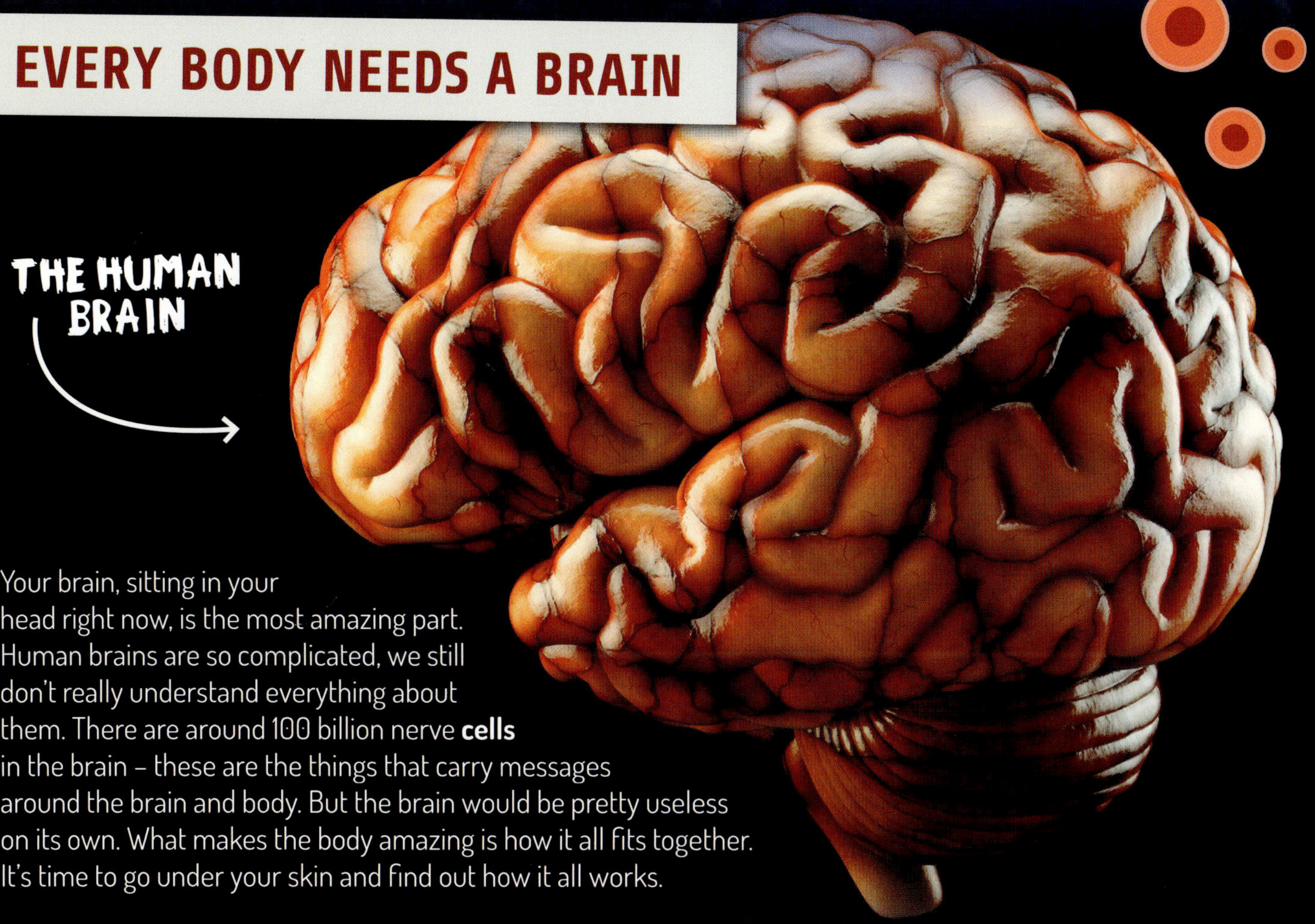

THE HUMAN BRAIN

Your brain, sitting in your head right now, is the most amazing part. Human brains are so complicated, we still don't really understand everything about them. There are around 100 billion nerve **cells** in the brain – these are the things that carry messages around the brain and body. But the brain would be pretty useless on its own. What makes the body amazing is how it all fits together. It's time to go under your skin and find out how it all works.

THE DOCTOR IS HERE

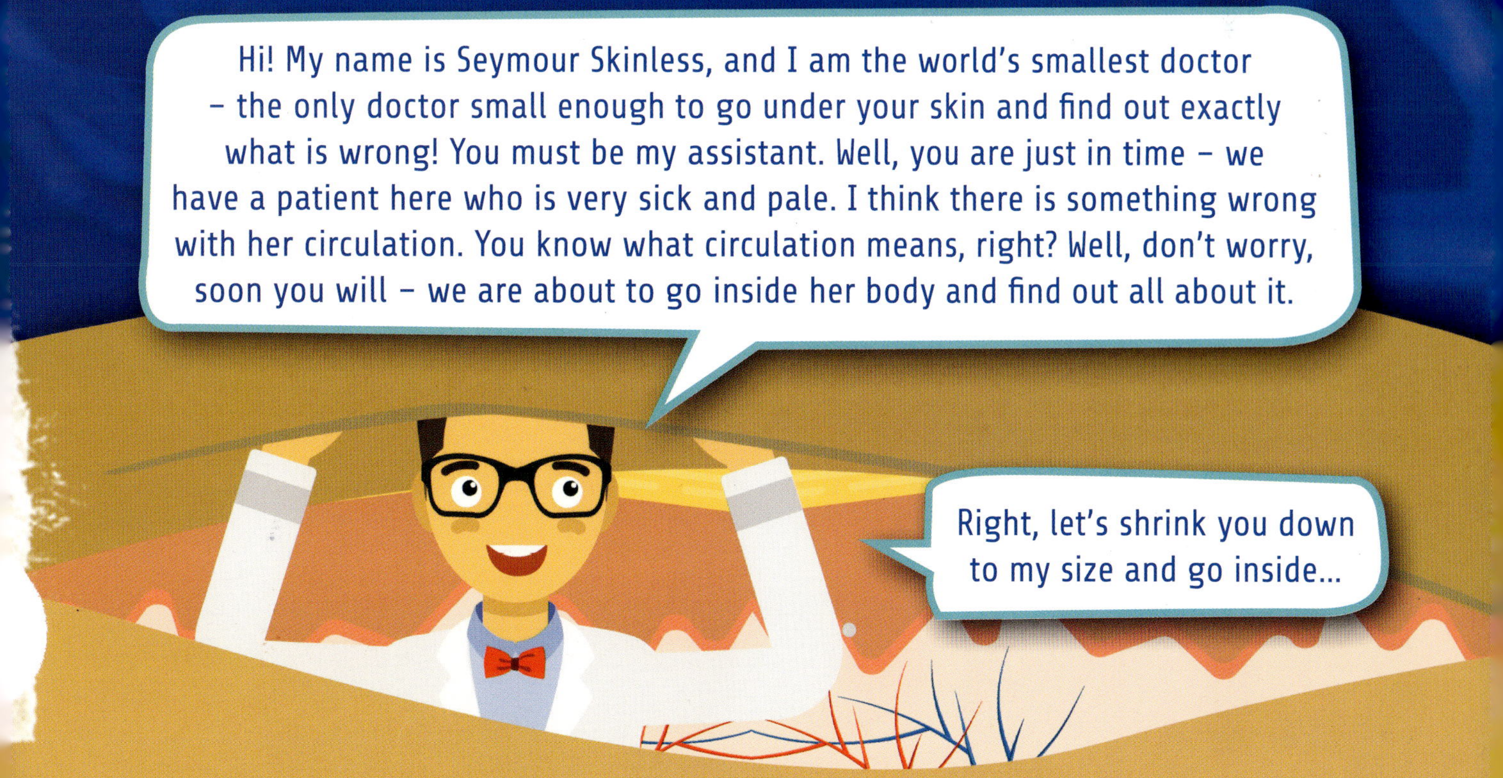

Hi! My name is Seymour Skinless, and I am the world's smallest doctor – the only doctor small enough to go under your skin and find out exactly what is wrong! You must be my assistant. Well, you are just in time – we have a patient here who is very sick and pale. I think there is something wrong with her circulation. You know what circulation means, right? Well, don't worry, soon you will – we are about to go inside her body and find out all about it.

Right, let's shrink you down to my size and go inside...

WHAT SEEMS TO BE THE PROBLEM?

THERE WILL BE BLOOD

When we talk about circulation in the human body, we are talking about something called the circulatory system (say: ser-cue-LAY-tory sis-tum). This is the system that pumps blood around the body. It's called the circulatory system because it is a circuit – a bit like a race track or a running circuit on a sports field. The blood goes round and round the circuit in one direction. The system is made up of blood, the heart, and tubes such as **veins** and **arteries**.

THE HEART IS THE CENTRE OF THE CIRCULATORY SYSTEM.

WHAT HAS THE CIRCULATORY SYSTEM EVER DONE FOR US?

The circulatory system has a very important job: it carries blood to different parts of the body. The blood is like a delivery driver, carrying important stuff that keeps the body working. There are tubes of different sizes in the circulatory system; they are like the roads for the delivery driver.

IF YOU STRETCHED OUT ALL YOUR BLOOD VESSELS IN A STRAIGHT LINE, THEY WOULD BE AROUND 96,000 KILOMETRES LONG.

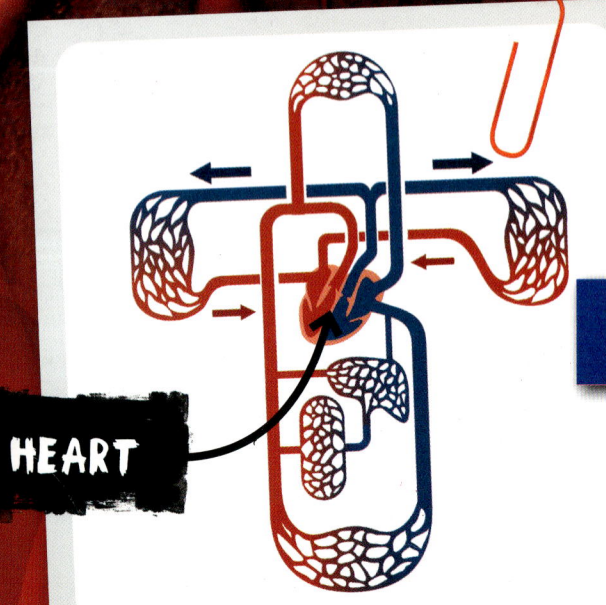

HEART

TWO CIRCUITS

The circulatory system is actually made up of two circuits, connected by the heart. The first one goes from the heart to the lungs. The second one goes from the heart to the rest of the body. We will learn about both of these circuits more later on in the book.

To start with, we are going to go round the circulatory system and help with the deliveries. It is going to be a bit like delivering the post! We've even got our own red van. Well, it used to be white, but blood is very hard to clean off.

Anyway, looks like our main delivery today will be something called oxygen. You say it like this: OX-EE-JUN.

WHAT IS OXYGEN?

Oxygen is a **gas** that is part of the air we breathe. It is stored in the lungs, and collected and carried by the blood. It is used by our body to create **energy**. Energy is needed so that our bodies can do all the things they need to do to keep us alive. However, as we will find out, the blood carries many important things, not just oxygen.

WITHOUT THE ENERGY THAT OXYGEN GIVES, YOU WOULDN'T BE ABLE TO MOVE YOUR MUSCLES.

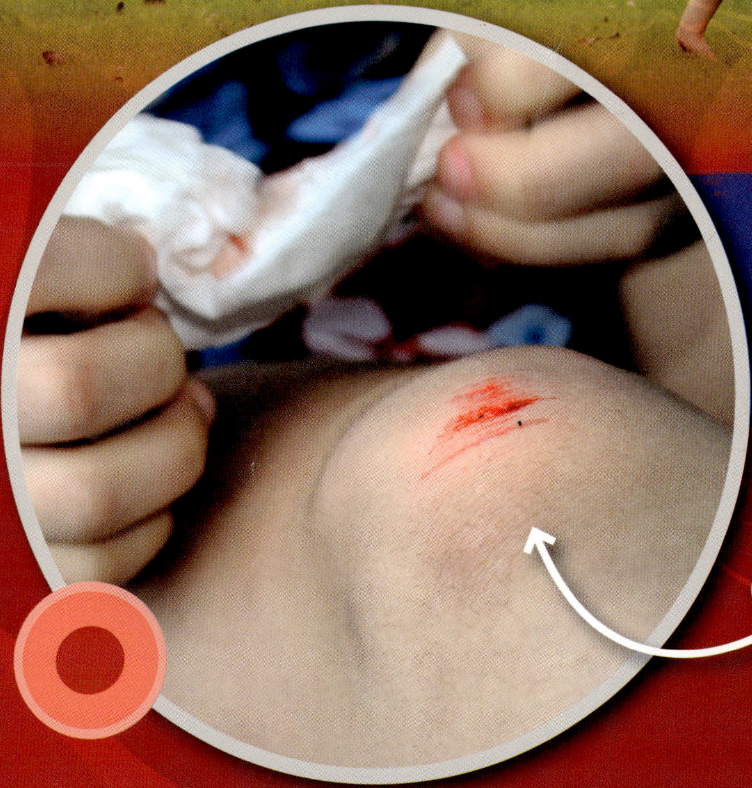

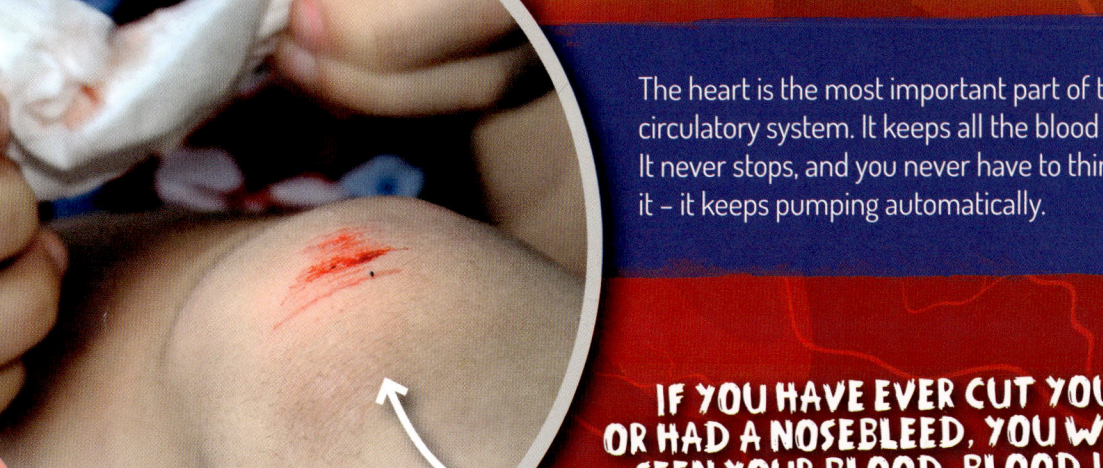

The heart is the most important part of the circulatory system. It keeps all the blood moving. It never stops, and you never have to think about it – it keeps pumping automatically.

IF YOU HAVE EVER CUT YOURSELF OR HAD A NOSEBLEED, YOU WILL HAVE SEEN YOUR BLOOD. BLOOD IS RED.

START AT THE HEART

A HUMAN HEART

Your heart can be found in your chest, slightly to your left. It is about the size of your fist. If you put your hands against the right spot in your chest, you might feel it beating. This is what the heart does all day long. It beats in a steady rhythm, like a drumbeat going BUM BUM... BUM BUM...BUM BUM. The heart beats faster when you exercise, or when you are scared, angry or excited. This is because the body needs more oxygen, so more blood needs to go round the circuit.

THE HEART BEATS AROUND 60-100 TIMES A MINUTE WHEN YOU'RE RESTING. THAT'S AROUND 100,000 TIMES A DAY OR 35 MILLION TIMES A YEAR.

SUPER STRONG

Your heart is a muscle. A muscle is something that is made out of **body tissue** and can be squeezed so it becomes smaller. This is called contracting. When muscles contract, parts of the body move.

When the heart contracts, it squeezes blood through itself, and around the whole circulatory system. However, the whole heart doesn't contract at once. It is more like a wave that starts at the top and spreads to the bottom.

UNLIKE EVERY OTHER MUSCLE IN THE HUMAN BODY, THE HEART NEVER GETS TIRED. IT NEVER STOPS BEATING FOR YOUR WHOLE LIFE.

HEART PARTS

THE HEART HAS TUBES GOING INTO IT, AND TUBES COMING OUT OF IT.

1. On the right side of the heart are the venae cavae (say: vee-nee cay-vee). These are the tubes that bring blood into the heart.

A HUGE ARTERY CALLED THE AORTA TAKES BLOOD FROM THE HEART TO THE REST OF THE BODY.

2. The heart has four spaces inside it, called chambers. The first chamber, on the top-right, is called the right atrium. Atriums are chambers of the heart that take blood in.

4. The blood is then sent to the lungs through tubes called the pulmonary (say: pull-mun-ree) arteries.

5. The blood comes back from the lungs and enters the left side of the heart through tubes called pulmonary veins. The top-left chamber is called the left atrium.

3. The blood is then pumped into the bottom-right chamber, called the right ventricle. Ventricles are chambers of the heart that pump blood out.

6. The blood is pumped into the bottom-left chamber, called the left ventricle.

THE HEART ALSO HAS FOUR VALVES. VALVES STOP THE BLOOD FLOWING BACKWARDS THROUGH THE BLOOD VESSELS AND HEART.

> Wow, the heartbeat is much louder up close! I wish this sound would just stop for just a minute! Actually, no, that would be very bad indeed. Ah, let's just get out of here.

ROUND AND ROUND
BEHIND
THE RIBS

The first circuit we will explore is called the pulmonary circuit. This is the one that goes between your heart and your lungs. But before we get to the lungs, we need to find out what blood really is.

WHAT IS BLOOD?

Blood is mostly made up of red blood cells. Cells are the tiny building blocks that make up all living things. You are made up of trillions of different cells that all join together to create your body. Each type of cell has a different job.

BY THE TIME YOU ARE AN ADULT, YOU WILL HAVE AROUND 4-6 LITRES OF BLOOD IN YOUR BODY.

RED BLOOD CELLS

Red blood cells have a special shape: they are mostly flat, but the middle is pushed in a little bit. These cells are made in our bones, and they usually last for around 120 days. Red blood cells are made to join up with certain gases, such as oxygen. They are emptier inside than most other cells, so they have more room to carry gases.

RED BLOOD CELLS

IS BLOOD ALWAYS RED?

Yes, our blood is always red. Most of the time, it is because there is a lot of iron in our blood. When the iron and oxygen join together, it creates a bright red colour. If you have ever seen some rusty iron metal, you might notice it is an orangey-red colour. This is for the same reason – when iron and oxygen join together, it creates a reddish colour.

OUR BLOOD IS ALWAYS RED, EVEN THOUGH OUR VEINS LOOK BLUE.

SICKLE RED BLOOD CELL

DIFFERENT SHAPES

Some **diseases** change the shape of the blood cells. For example, sickle cell disease makes the blood cells into a sickle shape, which looks a bit like a crescent moon. Red blood cells with this sickle shape break down and die faster than normal, until there are fewer red blood cells in the body than usual. This can cause someone to feel tired and out of breath. They might get ill more often too. Sickle cell disease is passed on from parent to child.

AROUND TWO MILLION RED BLOOD CELLS DIE EVERY SECOND. LUCKILY, AROUND TWO MILLION RED BLOOD CELLS ARE MADE EVERY SECOND TOO.

Oh no, I'm bleeding! I'm dying! This is the end! This is... this is not my blood, is it? I forgot that we were in the blood vessels...

LOOP THE LUNGS

WHAT ARE THE LUNGS?

The lungs are a pair of **organs** in your chest which help you breathe. They are like two bags that get bigger as they take air in, and smaller as they push air back out. Your lungs are connected to your mouth by a tube called a windpipe. This is how the air gets in and out of the lungs. They are controlled by the diaphragm (say: die-ah-fram), which is a stretchy sheet of muscle underneath the lungs.

THE LUNGS

MORE TUBES

As the air travels down the windpipe, it branches out into two tubes called bronchi. Each bronchus leads to a different lung. The left bronchus leads to the left lung, and the right bronchus leads to...

Oh! Oh! I know this one. The right bronchus leads to... hmm, it leads to... Nope, I lost it. No idea.

... the right lung. Inside the lungs, the bronchi split into even smaller tubes, called bronchioles. At the end of the bronchioles are very small, spongy sacs called alveoli.

WINDPIPE

BRONCHI

BRONCHIOLES

ALVEOLI

12

You might know that the lungs are one of the largest organs in the body. However, did you know that they are not the same size? The right lung is slightly wider but shorter because the liver is squashed beneath it. It has three parts, called lobes. The left lung is slightly thinner because it has to fit in the chest along with the heart. It only has two lobes.

THIS PICTURE SHOWS THE LOBES OF THE LUNGS.

YOUR LUNGS HAVE TO BREATHE A LOT OF AIR. PEOPLE TAKE AROUND 20,000 BREATHS EVERY DAY TO GET ENOUGH OXYGEN.

THE HEART WANTS WHAT IT WANTS (OXYGEN)

When the air we breathe gets to the alveoli, it is ready to be passed to the blood and sent back to the heart. The blood vessels from the heart also split into smaller and smaller blood vessels. These tiny blood vessels are wrapped around the alveoli. The walls of the alveoli and the blood vessels are so thin that gases can pass through them. Oxygen from the alveoli is passed into the blood, which is then sent back to the heart, ready to be pumped out into the rest of the body.

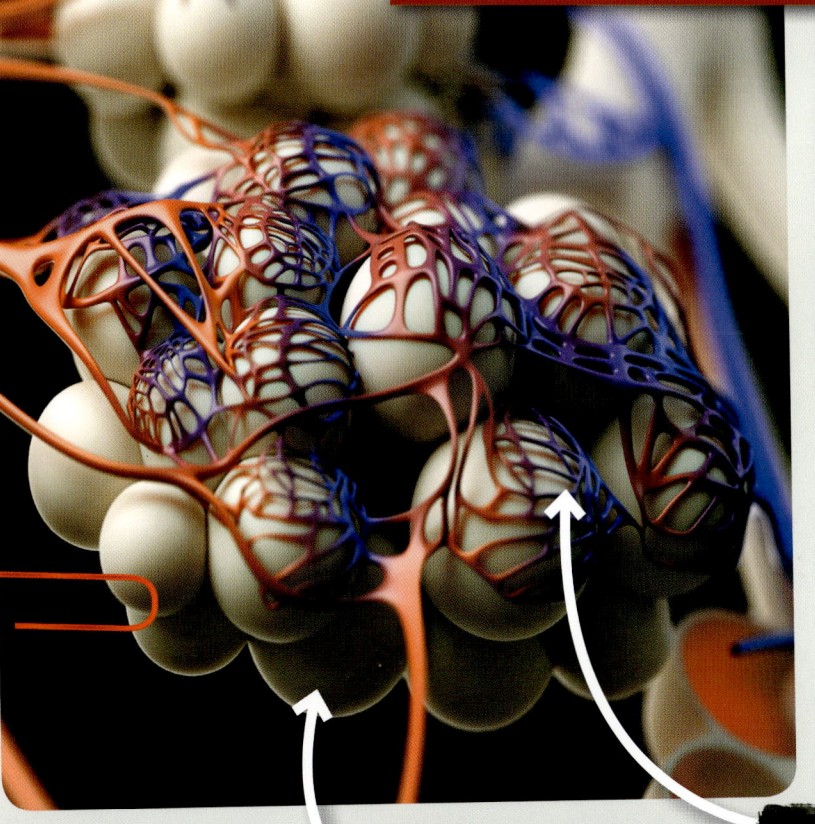

ALVEOLI

BLOOD VESSELS

TRAVEL DOWN THE TRUNK

Ok, fine, we are lost! But it's not my fault. There are millions of blood vessels in the body! Wait, these walls look pretty thick. Does that mean we are in the arteries?

THAT DOES MEAN YOU ARE IN THE ARTERIES

The large tubes that carry blood away from the heart are called arteries. Arteries usually carry blood that is full of oxygen. This means the blood inside an artery is a bright red colour. Arteries have thick outer walls. Inside, they are made of many **elastic** layers of muscle. Blood vessels have to be elastic so that they can stretch wider as blood is pumped through them.

YOU CAN FEEL YOUR BLOOD VESSELS BECOME WIDER AS BLOOD GOES THROUGH THEM. IT IS CALLED YOUR PULSE.

AORTA

The main artery in the body is called the aorta (say: ay-or-ta). It is the strongest and thickest of all the blood vessels. The aorta starts at the top of the heart's left side. After a few branches come off it (which go up the body), the aorta snakes downwards. As it travels down the body, more and more branches come off the aorta, leading to other body parts.

THE AORTA

UNDER PRESSURE

Arteries have to be much thicker and stronger than other blood vessels because there is a lot of blood **pressure** from the inside. Blood pressure is the amount that the blood is pressing on the walls of the blood vessels. With every beat of the heart, a swell of blood is pushed through the arteries, which creates more blood pressure. The walls stretch to let the swell pass through. Let's have a look at some of the biggest arteries in the human body.

THE WALLS ON THE LEFT SIDE OF THE HEART ARE ALSO THICKER AND STRONGER THAN THE RIGHT. THIS IS BECAUSE OF THE PRESSURE.

CAROTID ARTERIES

The carotid arteries are a pair of blood vessels that carry blood to your neck, face and brain. It is very important that the brain gets enough blood and oxygen because it controls the whole body. If it doesn't get enough blood, cells in the brain can die off. This is sometimes called a stroke.

FEMORAL ARTERIES

The femoral arteries are big arteries found in your leg. There is one in each leg. They are found alongside the femur, or thighbone, which is the longest and strongest bone in your body.

STRAIGHT THROUGH THE STOMACH

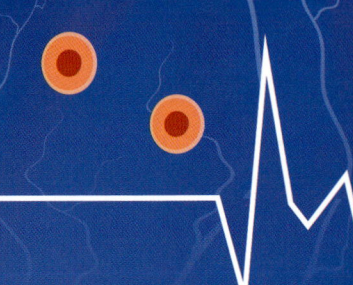

Like all other parts of the body, the stomach is given oxygen by the blood. It needs the oxygen so that it can keep churning up our food, as well as moving the food to the other parts of the body after it has been broken down. But how does the oxygen get from the arteries to the cells in the stomach, without blood getting everywhere? The answer is this: different kinds of blood vessels.

LIKE THE OTHER ORGANS, THE STOMACH GETS ITS BLOOD FROM BLOOD VESSELS WHICH HAVE BRANCHED OFF FROM THE AORTA.

ARTERIOLES

Arteries branch into smaller and smaller arteries. Soon, they begin branching into smaller blood vessels called arterioles. Just like arteries, arterioles have thicker walls because of the pressure. They both also have muscles around them which make them wider or thinner, depending on how much blood is pumping through. We can't control the movement of these muscles – it happens automatically.

BLOOD VESSELS BECOME SMALLER AND SMALLER AS THEY BRANCH OFF.

I hope these blood vessels don't get any thinner. I wish I'd eaten a smaller lunch.

16

CAPILLARIES

The arterioles branch into even smaller vessels called capillaries. Capillaries are the smallest type of blood vessel. They are joined together in big groups called capillary beds. Capillary beds run alongside all the body's tissues. Capillary beds are much too small to see, but if we could see them, they would look a bit like a net of blood vessels.

CAPILLARY BED

DELIVERY TIME

Capillaries have very thin walls. The walls are so thin that they let gases through. As the blood travels through the capillaries, it lets go of its oxygen. The oxygen travels through the walls and is taken in by hungry cells. However, the blood still has a job to do. It also picks up a different gas, called carbon dioxide. Carbon dioxide is a waste gas produced by our bodies – this means that we don't want to keep it in our bodies. Carbon dioxide travels through the walls of the capillaries and is picked up by the blood. The blood will then take this all the way back to the lungs to be breathed out.

IF YOUR CIRCULATORY SYSTEM WAS LIKE A TREE, THE ARTERIES WOULD BE THE BRANCHES, THE ARTERIOLES WOULD BE STICKS, AND THE CAPILLARIES WOULD BE TWIGS.

GO PAST THE GUTS

Row, row, row your boat, gently past the spleen... wait, I don't like the look of this place. It looks diseased and scary. But don't worry, there is another type of blood cell that should show up any minute now. They're called white blood cells, and they will know just what to do!

YOUR OWN ARMY

White blood cells protect you from illnesses. They are like your own personal army, going to fight any dangerous-looking invaders that enter your body. White blood cells spend most of their time in blood tissue, getting rid of diseases. However, they use the circulatory system to quickly travel to parts of the body where they are needed.

THIS IS A WHITE BLOOD CELL. THEY ARE MADE INSIDE OUR BONES. SOME DON'T LIVE VERY LONG—MAYBE ONE TO THREE DAYS.

THE ENEMY

Things that cause diseases are called pathogens (say: path-oh-jens). For example, bacteria are tiny pathogens which can make you ill. Viruses are even smaller pathogens that sneak inside your cells. Once inside, viruses make more and more of themselves until the cell bursts, and the virus spreads further through your body.

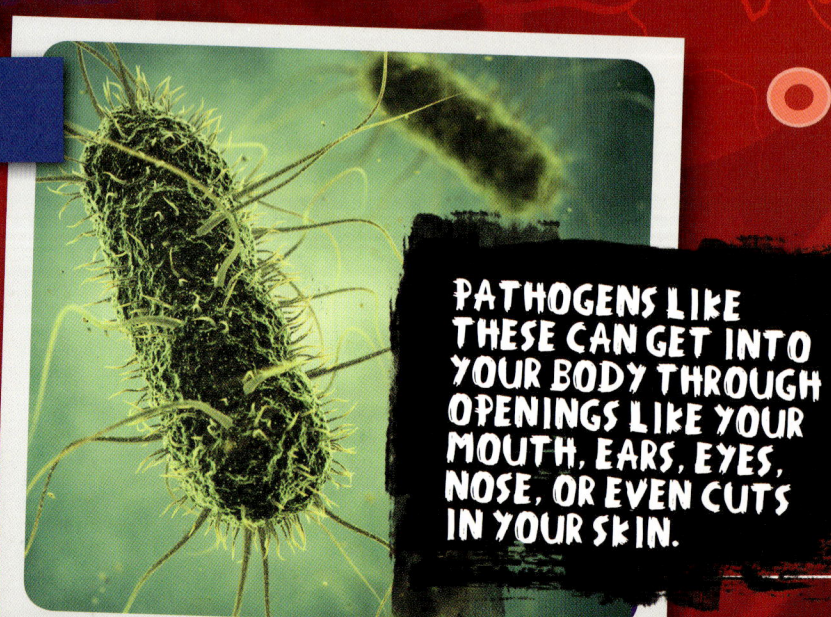

PATHOGENS LIKE THESE CAN GET INTO YOUR BODY THROUGH OPENINGS LIKE YOUR MOUTH, EARS, EYES, NOSE, OR EVEN CUTS IN YOUR SKIN.

THERE ARE MORE BACTERIA CELLS IN YOUR BODY THAN HUMAN CELLS. MOST OF THEM ARE GOOD FOR YOU, BUT SOME CAN BE BAD.

FIGHT!

The first white blood cells on the scene raise the alarm, and let the body know it's time to fight. The body then makes more and more cells, to fight the illness. White blood cells have lots of ways to fight. Some just gobble bacteria up. Many white blood cells can eat 5-20 bacteria in their lifetime, although some types can eat up to 100. Other white blood cells create antibodies. Antibodies attach to viruses and stop them making more of themselves. They also tag the viruses so the white blood cells know what to destroy!

Around a billion white blood cells are made in your bones every day, and each one of them is ready to kick butt.

IT IS IMPORTANT TO REST, DRINK WATER AND BE LOOKED AFTER WHEN YOU ARE ILL. YOUR BODY NEEDS A CHANCE TO FIGHT THE PATHOGENS.

FIGHTING DOESN'T FEEL GOOD

When pathogens get inside your body, it is called an infection. There are viral infections and bacterial infections. You have probably had these before – a common cold is a viral infection. Infections might make us cough, sneeze or have a runny nose. We might get a **fever**, which makes us feel very hot or cold. We might even get **diarrhoea** or be sick. These are all **effects** of the fight inside your body between white blood cells and pathogens.

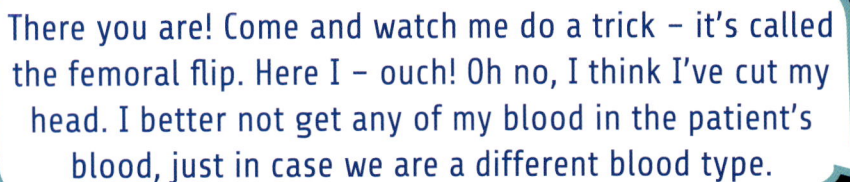

"There you are! Come and watch me do a trick – it's called the femoral flip. Here I – ouch! Oh no, I think I've cut my head. I better not get any of my blood in the patient's blood, just in case we are a different blood type."

LEFT AT THE LEGS

"You don't know what a blood type is? Well, I had a sneak peek at the next two pages, and luckily, they are all about blood types. Read on!"

GIVING BLOOD AT A HOSPITAL CAN HELP OTHER PEOPLE.

BLOOD TYPES

There are many blood types. The main ones are called A, B, O and AB. Each blood type can also be positive (+) or negative (-). For example, you might be A+, or maybe O-.

DO YOU KNOW YOUR BLOOD TYPE? YOUR PARENTS MIGHT KNOW, OR YOU MIGHT HAVE BEEN TOLD IF YOU'VE GIVEN OR RECEIVED BLOOD AT A HOSPITAL.

WHY DO BLOOD TYPES MATTER?

When people are injured or ill, they might lose a lot of blood. If they lose too much, doctors give them extra blood from other people. However, they can only give them the right type of blood. If they gave them the wrong type, some blood cells would clump together in what is called a clot. Clots are very dangerous because they can block blood vessels and **starve** body parts of oxygen.

BLOOD CLOT

ANTIGENS

The reason blood comes in different types is because of things called antigens. Antigens cover the outside of a red blood cell, like a coat. There are different types. Different blood types have different antigens covering the blood cells.

ATTACK!

If the body is injected with the wrong type of blood, it goes into attack mode. This is because the new blood has strange antigens that the body has never seen before. The body thinks that it must be bad and sends white blood cells to fight it. One of the ways it fights is by clumping blood cells together. This causes clots.

HOSPITAL BLOOD IS STORED IN BAGS LIKE THESE. THE BLOOD TYPE IS WRITTEN ON THE SIDE.

SOME BLOOD TYPES, LIKE O-, ARE LESS STRANGE TO OTHER BODIES, SO THE BODIES DON'T ATTACK IT.

WHO CAN GIVE TO WHO?

Most of the time, people are given more of the same blood. Someone with A+ blood would be given more A+ blood. However, some blood groups are special. People with AB can be given A, B, or more AB. People with O- blood are very special – they can give their blood to anyone with one of the main blood types. However, O- people can only take in more O- blood.

BACK UP THE BACK

VEINS IN THE HAND

The tubes that take your blood back to your heart are called veins and venules. Venules are much smaller and, just like arterioles, they are connected to the capillaries. Venules begin to join up into bigger blood vessels, called veins. Veins are big, like arteries, but they take blood back to the heart instead.

VEINS ARE CLOSER TO THE SURFACE OF THE SKIN THAN ARTERIES. YOU MIGHT BE ABLE TO SEE YOUR VEINS.

VEINS AND VENULES

The walls of veins and venules are much thinner than arteries and arterioles. This is because they are farther away from the beating left side of the heart, which means there is less blood pressure. A lower blood pressure means that the walls don't have to be as strong. On this side of the circulatory system, being thin is fine.

However, because there is less pressure pushing the blood along, veins and venules have valves. This is to stop any blood accidentally flowing backwards.

THE BLOOD THAT FLOWS THROUGH VEINS IS A MUCH DARKER SHADE OF RED. THIS IS BECAUSE THERE IS NO OXYGEN IN IT.

Ah, my clever little assistant, there you are. So, do you like the veins? I think it is time we made you even cleverer, and told you about two other things sloshing around us in the circulatory system: hormones and plasma!

HORMONES

Hormones are **chemicals** which send messages around the body. There are many types of hormones which send all sorts of messages. Different hormones are made in different glands, and they often use the circulatory system as a quick way to get around the body. Adrenaline is an example of a hormone – it is released into the bloodstream when we are angry, scared or excited. Its job is to tell the rest of the body to get ready for action.

ADRENALINE IS MADE IN THESE GLANDS, CALLED THE ADRENAL GLANDS.

ADRENALINE ON THE MOVE

Adrenaline goes to the lungs and tells the airways to get wider, so we can breathe more air.

Adrenaline goes to the heart and tells it to beat faster.

Adrenaline makes the blood vessels wider, so more blood can get through.

PLASMA

Plasma is the liquid which carries all the things in the circulatory system, such as red blood cells, white blood cells, hormones and **nutrients**. Just over half of our blood is made up of plasma.

ON ITS OWN, BLOOD PLASMA IS YELLOW.

LOOK, IT'S THE LIVER

If you look to your right, you will see the liver. Doesn't it look lovely? Well, it sort of does, if you squint your eyes. But it turns out that the liver is also very important to red blood cells. Let's find out why.

OLD CELLS

Red blood cells don't last as long as many other cells. At the end of their lifetime, they begin to break up. This can be a problem. For example, the iron inside the red blood cell can cause damage to organs, such as the kidneys, if enough of it builds up in the blood.

THE KIDNEYS ARE FOUND NEAR THE LOWER BACK.

MACROPHAGE

BIG EATERS

To deal with old or broken red blood cells, the body sends out special cells called macrophages (say: mak-row-fay-jez). These cells are mostly found in the liver, spleen and bone **marrow**, but they can travel anywhere in the body. They gobble up and destroy the old red blood cells, and then travel to the liver or spleen.

BLOOD GRAVEYARD

The liver is one of the main places in the body that cleans up old, dead red blood cells. For most red blood cells, this is the last stop they make around the circulatory system. The other main organ that does this is the spleen. The liver and spleen both filter out lots of old, broken red blood cells. The spleen has a kind of net that catches unhealthy blood cells, but lets the healthy ones through. Most macrophages also travel to these organs after eating.

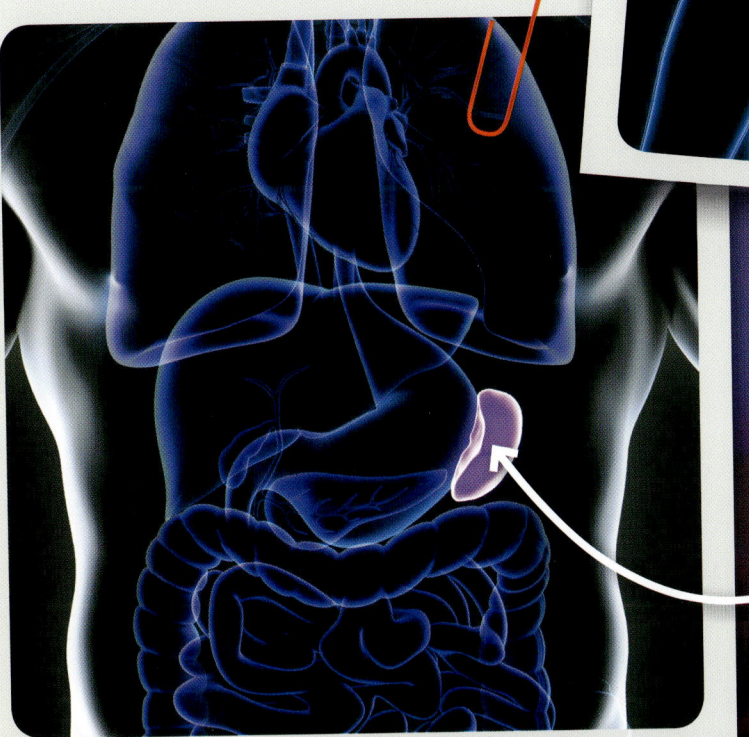

THE LIVER

THE SPLEEN

THE CIRCLE OF LIFE

The body tries not to waste things – if it can reuse anything, it will! Because of this, after the old red blood cells have been collected, their old parts are **recycled**. Some parts are sent to the bone marrow, so it can make new cells. The iron is usually sent to the liver, where it is stored until it is needed. Eventually it is used to make new red blood cells.

WHEN OLD RED BLOOD CELLS ARE BROKEN DOWN, THEY RELEASE A CHEMICAL. THIS IS THE CHEMICAL THAT MAKES YOUR WEE YELLOW AND YOUR POO BROWN.

ALL ABOARD THE ARMS

It... it can't be! There's a cut in the skin ahead of us! All the blood is leaking out of this blood vessel! We're doomed! We're dead! How are we going to survive this?

PLATELETS TO THE RESCUE

If something cuts you, the tiny blood vessels under the skin might become cut too. This would cause the blood to leak out, which is called bleeding. As you know, blood is very important, and the body can't afford to lose a lot of it. To stop the bleeding, platelets are sent to the cut. It's the job of platelets to stick together like glue. This causes the blood to clump up, which is also known as a clot. This blocks the exit, so the blood stops leaking out.

BLOOD CLOT

The skin around a cut or scab can become red and sore. This is because the blood vessels around the cut get bigger in order to allow more important cells in from the circulatory system.

THE BLOOD CLOT CREATES A HARD COVERING ON THE CUT, WHICH IS ALSO CALLED A SCAB.

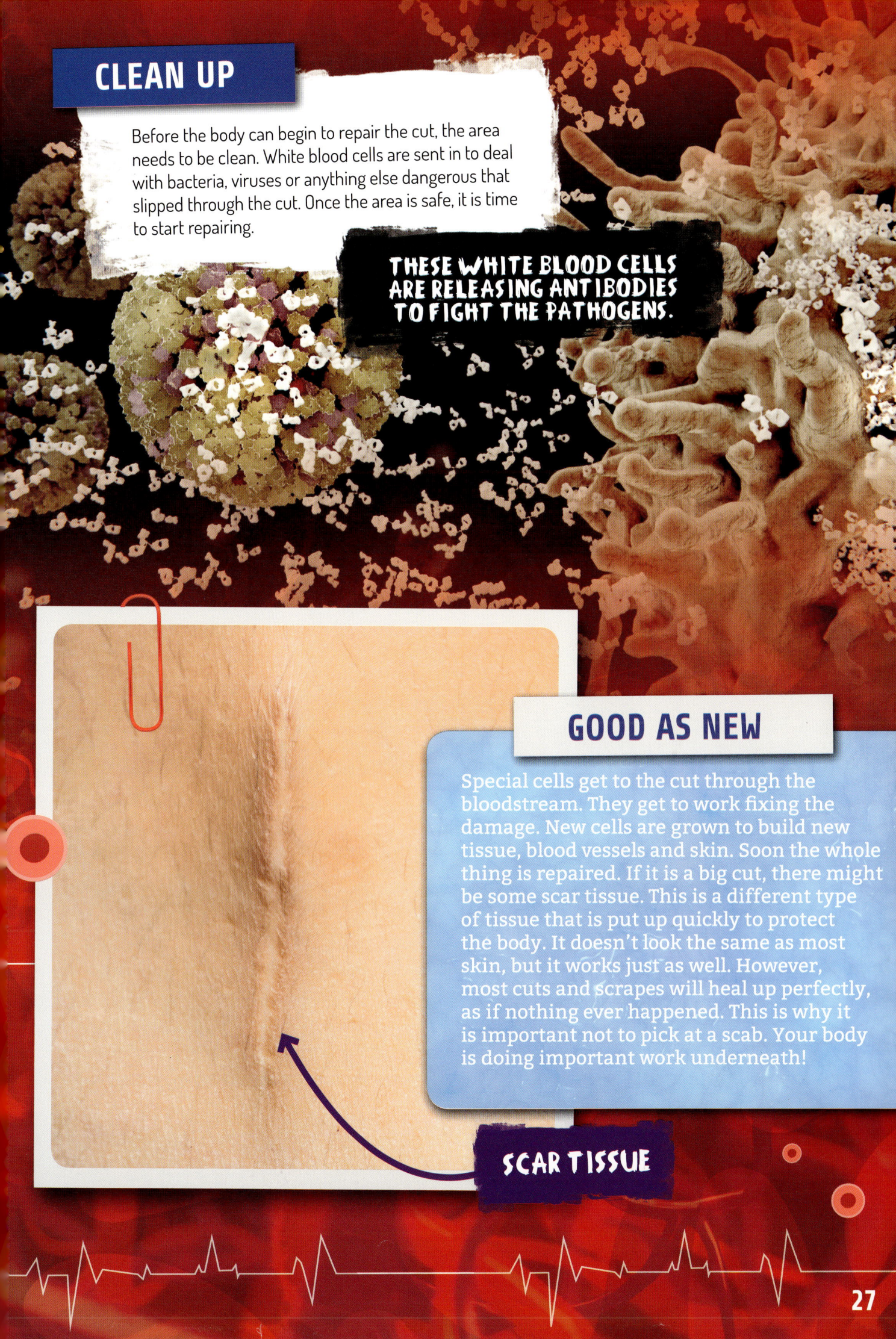

CLEAN UP

Before the body can begin to repair the cut, the area needs to be clean. White blood cells are sent in to deal with bacteria, viruses or anything else dangerous that slipped through the cut. Once the area is safe, it is time to start repairing.

THESE WHITE BLOOD CELLS ARE RELEASING ANTIBODIES TO FIGHT THE PATHOGENS.

GOOD AS NEW

Special cells get to the cut through the bloodstream. They get to work fixing the damage. New cells are grown to build new tissue, blood vessels and skin. Soon the whole thing is repaired. If it is a big cut, there might be some scar tissue. This is a different type of tissue that is put up quickly to protect the body. It doesn't look the same as most skin, but it works just as well. However, most cuts and scrapes will heal up perfectly, as if nothing ever happened. This is why it is important not to pick at a scab. Your body is doing important work underneath!

SCAR TISSUE

HEAD BACK TO THE HEART

The circulatory system doesn't always work perfectly. If the heart doesn't work properly, it is called heart disease. However, heart disease can mean all sorts of different problems.

MISSING THE BEAT

The heart is controlled by a bundle of nerves in one of the chambers. However, sometimes this bundle of nerves is interrupted. There can also be problems with the valves and walls of the heart. Problems like these can cause the heartbeat to be a little too fast or slow, or not in a steady rhythm. Most heart problems aren't too dangerous as long as you listen to your doctor's and your parents' advice. It is important for people with heart problems to be **responsible**.

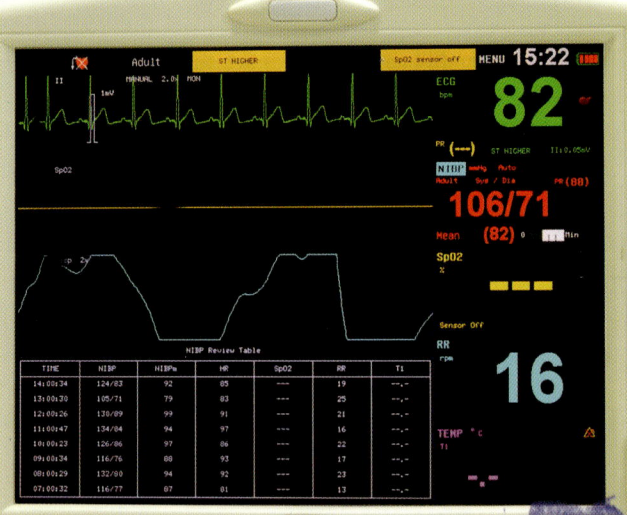

At the hospital, heart rates are **monitored** using machines. It tells the doctors information about the heart rate on the screen.

RAYNAUD'S DISEASE

People with Raynaud's disease have problems with blood getting around the body properly. When they are cold or stressed, some blood vessels go into spasm. This can block the blood getting to some parts of the circulatory system, usually in the fingers or toes. Raynaud's is not dangerous most of the time, although it can be annoying to live with.

THIS IS THE HAND OF SOMEONE WITH RAYNAUD'S DISEASE.

HEART ATTACKS

Some adults have a heart problem called coronary heart disease. This is where there is a build up of fat inside the blood vessels around the heart. The fat is called plaque. Plaque can stop blood and oxygen getting to the heart. If no blood can get through, the heart becomes damaged and stops working. This is called a heart attack, and it can be very dangerous. Heart attacks are much more likely to happen to older people and people who smoke or have very unhealthy diets.

PLAQUE

A BALANCED DIET

HOW TO STAY HEALTHY

There are lots of things you can do to keep your heart healthy.

Eat a healthy, balanced diet, with lots of fruit and vegetables. Try to eat less sugary or fatty foods.

Do some exercise every day. Sports and outdoor activities are great ways of exercising.

Yes, exercise is important! I try to do 10 minutes of blood-vessel skipping a day. I wonder... if I tie these blood vessels together, will it stop the patient's bleeding?

ALL BETTER

Ooops! Well that didn't work. I guess, come to think about it, I could have just given our patient a plaster... Oh well! This was much more fun and we learned a lot. I just hope she wasn't bleeding for long!

So now you know all about the circulatory system. Isn't it incredible? Here are some extra blood facts.

DIFFERENT BLOOD TYPES ARE MORE COMMON IN DIFFERENT COUNTRIES. IN THE US, O IS THE MOST COMMON. A IS COMMON IN PARTS OF EUROPE. B IS MOST COMMON IN CENTRAL ASIA.

IT TAKES A MINUTE (OR SOMETIMES LESS) FOR BLOOD TO BE PUMPED ALL THE WAY AROUND THE CIRCULATORY SYSTEM.

THERE IS A VERY, VERY SMALL AMOUNT OF GOLD IN YOUR BLOOD.

GLOSSARY

ARTERIES	tubes that carry blood away from the heart to the rest of the body
AUTOMATICALLY	without conscious thought or control
BILLIONS	one billion is one thousand million
BODY TISSUE	what organs and other body parts are made of
CELLS	the basic units that make up all living things
CHEMICALS	substances that materials are made from
DIARRHOEA	when the body produces runny poo, usually because of an illness
DISEASES	disorders that cause physical symptoms in a person and can make them very ill
EFFECTS	the results of an action or event
ELASTIC	stretchy and flexible
ENERGY	the power needed for something to work
FEVER	an unusually high body temperature
GAS	an air-like substance that expands freely to fill any space available
MARROW	the spongy tissue inside bones that makes red blood cells, white blood cells and platelets
MONITORED	recorded or kept track of
NUTRIENTS	natural substances that people need to grow and stay healthy
ORGANS	(self-contained) parts of a living thing that have a specific, important function
PRESSURE	a continuous physical force exerted on an object, which is caused by something pressing against it
RECYCLED	used again to make something else
RESPONSIBLE	to be trusted to do the right thing
STARVE	to die or be damaged because of a lack of something important, like food or oxygen
VEINS	tubes that carry blood back to the heart
VIRUS	a microscopic thing which causes illness and disease in living things

INDEX

ARTERIES 6, 9, 14–17, 22

BEATING 8–9, 15, 22–23, 28

BIG 4, 12, 15, 17, 22, 24, 26–27

BLOOD TYPES 20–21, 30

BONES 10, 15, 18–19

BRAIN 5, 15

CAPILLARIES 17, 22

CARBON DIOXIDE 17

CELLS
- **RED** 10–11, 20–21, 23–25
- **WHITE** 18–19, 21, 23, 27

CIRCUIT 6, 8, 10

CONTROL 12, 15–16, 28

CUTS 7, 18, 20, 26–27

DEAD 25

DISEASE 11, 18, 28–29

EATING 19, 25, 29

EXERCISE 8, 29

HEALTHY 4, 25, 29

HEART 6–10, 13–15, 22–23, 28–29

HORMONES 22–23

HOSPITALS 20–21, 28

LUNGS 6–7, 9–10, 12–13, 17, 23

MUSCLE 7–8, 12, 14, 16

NERVES 5, 28

ORGANS 12–13, 16, 24–25

OXYGEN 7–8, 10–11, 13–17, 20, 22, 29

PLASMA 22–23

PLATELETS 26

REPAIR 27

SMALL 5, 8, 12–13, 16–18, 22

VEINS 6, 9, 11, 22

WALLS 13–17, 22, 28

birds of prey

Based on characters created by
Ben Aaronovitch & Andrew Cartmel

James Middleditch

CANDY JAR BOOKS · CARDIFF
2023

The right of James Middleditch to be identified as the Author of the Work has been asserted by him in accordance with the Copyright, Designs and Patents Act 1988.

Birds of Prey © James Middleditch 2023

Characters from Remembrance of the Daleks
© Ben Aaronovitch 1988, 2023

Doctor Who is © British Broadcasting Corporation, 1963, 2023

Range Editor: Andy Frankham-Allen
Editor: Shaun Russell
Editorial: Philip Bates
Range Consultant: Andrew Cartmel

ISBN: 978-1-915439-85-7

Printed and bound in the UK by
4edge, 22 Eldon Way, Hockley, Essex, SS5 4AD

Published by
Candy Jar Books
Mackintosh House
136 Newport Road, Cardiff, CF24 1DJ
www.candyjarbooks.co.uk

All rights reserved.
No part of this publication may be reproduced, stored in a retrieval system, or transmitted at any time or by any means, electronic, mechanical, photocopying, recording or otherwise without the prior permission of the copyright holder. This book is sold subject to the condition that it shall not by way of trade or otherwise be circulated without the publisher's prior consent in any form of binding or cover other than that in which it is published.

For Neil and Boe

THE THAMES itself seemed to be ablaze. Flames crawled and crested in pulsing ripples against the side of Blackfriars Bridge. Apart from the sheer black of the shadow of that arcing structure, the expanse of water was shining with liquid fire.

A man watched from the centre of the bridge, and he raised an arm to protect his face from the heat. He rocked back as more explosions sent debris flying from within the factory through empty windows, through which he could now see hell itself. Holding himself still against the urge to retreat, torn between the need for cooler air and a horrified fascination with the inferno, he squinted to see into the light.

Shapes, strangely static amid the flames, loomed inside the factory's buckling walls. He could see giant cogs and wheels and pipes and containers, the iron organs of a brick-built body, the mechanisms of the biggest and most productive factory in the whole of London.

Towards the far end of the bridge and on the north bank of the Thames, the men and women who had toiled in that factory danced and cheered. The man turned to watch them, wondering how they would make their living now that the beast that fed them was dying. Were they dancing because they were free of their enslavement, or because they knew that in the morning, their problems would really begin? He looked at them, bathed in firelight, spinning and whooping at the end of their world.

When he turned again to face the factory, he was not alone. A woman stood before him, even closer to the source of the heat than he was, although she did not shrink back. She seemed to bask in its glow. Her cowl covered most of her face and hair, but her eyes shone brightly from the shadows.

'Is it done?' the man asked her.

She considered, staring into the flames as he had, as if hoping to pierce the blackening shell and see deeper into its burning heart. 'We think so. We could return once the flames are gone and check. We could salvage any remains when it finally cools.'

'If it ever does, the unearthly place,' he said in a growl. 'But you're right, and we must.' His deep voice echoed from within his bulky frame, cutting through the roar of the fire and the collapsing floors inside the building.

The image of the boy came to him, as unbidden and vivid as all his visions. Through the rags that barely covered him, the man could see tears and lesions in the boy's skin. The boy had told him such tales before his breath had thinned and failed. He could see those stories come to life, charcoal drawings against the scorching yellow and orange of the fire. Children, merging with the machines. Arms becoming pistons, and cogs clicking around to the pulse of the heart.

The man closed his eyes but continued to see the burning factory and the children that had suffered inside it. He felt himself slipping into the trance state in which the patterns of time and history unfolded backward and forward, and he could *almost understand everything...*

'We have to save them,' he said with utter certainty, the deep rumble of his voice pulling him back to the bridge and the woman and London itself. 'Not just now, but always. The factory burns but the machines will wait. They will find new children.'

The woman nodded with resolve. 'Then we will be here,' she told him. 'For the future.'

Just before his visions fled, he could see a line of people stretching along the curve of the river into the future, through all the wonders and horrors to come.

'For the *true* Albion,' he said, and the last standing structures of the factory collapsed inwards, throwing angry, burning embers into the sky to join the stars.

CHAPTER ONE

Wednesday – Islington, London. 5.45pm

KOFI BAMBERA stood firmly against the lashing rain. The white edifice of the London townhouse row offered no protection as the wind whipped the downpour down the funnel of the street.

'It's another one, sir.' The police sergeant, equally resilient in the squall, delivered the news in a grim declaration. 'They said to wait while they cover the worst of it, but I'm guessing you want in right away?'

Bambera nodded, grateful for the pragmatism. If the sergeant was fazed by the presence of the Minister for Defence, he wasn't showing it. He turned to check one end of the street, then the other. Both were fuzzy in the haze of rain, but he could make out the dark backs of officers, police and his own, facing outwards to protect the scene, unmoving pillars along the length of fluttering crime-scene tape. Lights from the neighbouring houses, left on amid their hurried evacuation, shone weakly into the twilight.

'Lead on, Sergeant,' Bambera commanded.

He followed the man up the steps to the threshold, an imposingly solid door now held open by a constable, any sense of defence or protection it had previously offered now acknowledged as having failed. Bambera shivered as he entered, suddenly feeling as vulnerable as the solemn house.

Blood appeared on the cream carpet of the hallway as a deceptively thin trail, a pathway to follow to the scene that awaited. It widened and wound around a corner into the front room, tracing an invitation as it disappeared through the doorway.

The sergeant entered first, ushering three forensic officers from the room. They passed Bambera without making eye contact. He took a deep breath to begin his report. 'Shot on the doorstep...'

'Then dragged back in here to the armchair,' Bambera concluded.

The sergeant nodded. 'Just like the others, so I hear.'

'And the symbol?'

'Over here.'

Bambera moved further into the room to take in the familiar layout for the type of house and occupant. On either side of the ornate fireplace, bookshelves striped the full height of the room, holding the collected tomes of a lifetime and probably many from before. He noticed the generic nature of the spines and titles, familiar from evenings with his fellow Ministers, at least those of them who had deigned to invite him into their homes. As ordinarily British upper class as the rotund, silver-haired man slumped dead in his armchair in the corner beneath the reading lamp.

Pushing the door closed to see the symbol he knew would be painted in blood on its back, Bambera still felt his breath catch. Its jagged lines, each one having dripped and coagulated into a shiny carapace raised on the white wood, formed the stylised shape of lightning.

'That's why we called it straight in to your department, sir, as per standing orders,' the sergeant explained to Bambera's vague focus, his eyes remaining fixed on the back of the door. 'I know of about a dozen others from across the Met just today. Roughly one an hour since midday, I reckon. Word's got around, sir.'

'And those words won't be spoken from the moment you clock off, Sergeant,' Bambera stated with a calmness that only emphasised the instruction's icy warning.

'Of course, sir,' came the obedient response. 'I just mention it because Wednesday's usually our quietest day. Furthest from the weekend, I suppose. Should we brace for more?'

Bambera moved to the window, focusing his eyes beyond his own reflection at the raindrops tracing through the darkness. 'Wednesday,' he said quietly. 'Woden's Day.'

'Sir?'

'I think we must presume there will be more, Sergeant. With luck they won't be on your patch, but I think this might be a storm that is just beginning.'

As if responding to Bambera's ominous forecast, the yellow light from the reading lamp over the body started to flicker, dipping into darkness for a second at a time before struggling back to life.

'Not this again too,' the sergeant murmured.

Bambera looked out of the window, sharing the sergeant's fears. The lights from the other houses on the street, the only trace of warmth and comfort amid the pouring rain and rippling puddles, were flickering and fading. Single seconds of darkness started coalescing into longer periods and, in those moments, Bambera, stretching his gaze, could see that it wasn't just this road.

Street by street, London itself fell into darkness.

Ian Gilmore looked up from his half-eaten dinner as the lights flickered again.

His eyes met Dillon's across the table, and within seconds he knew he had to counter his instinctive fear with an illusion of reassurance.

'Dad, it's happening again,' his son stated, rather unnecessarily to Gilmore's mind.

'I know, Dillon, I can see that. Or rather I can't, which is the point I suppose.' His knife and fork clattered clumsily from his plate to the table, only adding to the tension as the patches of darkness spread more widely across the ticking seconds.

'Do you think it's just us?' Dillon asked.

Gilmore chose not to reply immediately, thinking of a way to protect his son from the worries that had been growing since the flickers had started a week or so previously. 'You remember last winter, Dillon? We got used to it, didn't we?'

Pleased with his chosen line of reassurance, he felt his way to the kitchen drawer, feeling the muscle memory of those power cuts guide his hands to the candles still nestling there, now buried beneath receipts and sundry other bits and pieces he couldn't identify by touch alone.

'I must have a word with your mother about these drawers,'

he muttered.

'Are you sure you should?' Dillon asked with an implied insight that took Gilmore by surprise.

'Mmm, maybe you're right,' he agreed, grateful for an ally in his often-flawed efforts to keep the peace in the Gilmore household. 'You remember the drill. I've got the candles, you grab the radio. Get winding.' He took the chance to retrieve something else too, from the top of the higher cupboards, feeling his way to its cold metal and dismissing the instinct that they might need more than just light.

Despite the darkness and his fears about what it could mean, Gilmore smiled at the sound of Dillon retrieving and winding the radio. The rituals of the three-day week and the power cuts had already passed into the realm of nostalgia. He had come to associate those times with his family huddling together, enjoying the playing of games and telling of tales that were a marker of a childhood already evolving into something new.

'Quick, quick, beat the pips,' Gilmore chanted, illuminating his face with a blaze of a match and grinning at his son.

'Dad,' Dillon groaned, sounding embarrassed at the reminder of their old, shared routines.

A year is a long time at his age, Gilmore reflected.

The wind-up radio crackled into life as the lighting of the candles brought a dignified resilience to the kitchen.

'*...are coming in about extensive and unexpected power cuts...*'

The voice faded in and out again, leaving Gilmore and Dillon staring at each other in expectation. Gilmore kept his face level, counting the seconds of silence. Radio 4 had become the background sound of his life, filtering the tensions of the world into calmly packaged bulletins, rewriting the terrifying reality of the world into rational patterns that he preferred to believe in when his imagination would allow. He also knew of the implications of the station falling silent for too long. Out there in the ocean, listening posts would already be twitching awake, the stretching silence as loud as the most urgent alarm...

'*...We apologise for the dip in transmission. BBC broadcasting has now moved to back-up generator power. As we were reporting, the extent of the power loss is becoming clear as reports make their way to us...*'

Gratitude at the return of the voice softened Gilmore's face, but Dillon's remained fixed in intent listening, picking up on the concern that the announcer was attempting to channel professionally into his report, but failing to hide entirely.

'We're assured that we'll be able to report on the likely length of the break in power supply shortly. In the meantime...' A shuffle of paper, usually imperceptible on the station, could be heard. *'Returning to our earlier report of the spate of road closures in London, we are expecting an update from the Metropolitan Police this evening. Locals have been urged not to draw conclusions from the presence of specialist officers and suggest that routine checks are taking place in the light of recent IRA threats in the area...'*

The clatter of keys and the door opening from the hallway snapped the two listeners from their trance.

'Mum! The power cuts are back!' Dillon called.

'I can see that, Dillon,' Rachel's voice snapped back. 'Or rather I can't. Which I suppose is the point.'

Relieved beyond measure to hear her voice echoing his own earlier attempt at humour, Gilmore took his deepest breath since the lights had gone out.

Bambera strode into his secondary office, relieved to find the back-up generators working here too from within the web of underground support systems spread beneath London from the hub of Whitehall.

Although he thought of it as secondary, this was where the really important work was done. His primary office on the surface was part of that ordinary, sanitised world of politics so important to the electorate but only really a fraction of the reality he knew from his time beneath ground.

A short, grey-haired figure stood waiting for him, gazing over the desk as if it were her own. Minister for Universities Jacqueline Grove met his eyes with a knowing sneer.

'I'm surprised to find you here at a time like this,' Bambera said, purposefully leaving off the expected, respectful welcome. 'The Emergencies Committee will be meeting shortly. You know I'll be a bit busy.'

'We'll be overlapping, Bambera,' Grove said swiftly. 'The power cuts are a matter for the whole government. So right now, this is exactly where I need to be. The network has been updating me throughout the day and the patterns are clear. I'm therefore surprised that you're surprised.'

Bambera offered a seat to his counterpart, making sure he himself took the one behind the desk, reminding Grove where the power of this office lay. 'We don't know for sure.'

'Let's look at the evidence.' Grove pushed a manilla folder across the desk towards Bambera, who looked at each sheet, picking out the details that had been highlighted and circled. 'Seven bodies in just one day. All connected to our work ending the Woden operation. All marked by the same symbol we found at Walsingham's after his apparent... suicide.'

'Lightning,' Bambera acceded. 'A simplistic reference from a childish rabble.'

Grove tilted her head downwards, staring intently at Bambera. 'The Association has grown up. You know that. They are... evolving.'

Bambera remained silent, allowing the truth of the matter to settle and the implications to unfold in his tired mind.

'Their capacity to conduct these executions in daylight is one thing,' Grove continued, 'but to manage it before we could work out the connection between the targets and ensure protection, and *then* to co-ordinate with these new power cuts...' She blew through pursed lips and shook her head.

'That could be more suggestive of our own shortcomings rather than their abilities,' Bambera offered, aware that there was a fragile hope lacing his tone that Grove would quickly dismiss.

'Tell me, where were each of the bodies placed?'

Bambera checked the pages in the file, confirming that what he knew of the sites he had seen was true of the others. 'Armchairs.'

'More than that. Each one was under a lamp. Some even had a lamp moved into position, to make the message clear. Power exercised and power withheld.'

Bambera could only nod slowly as Grove stood ready to deliver the parting shots he knew would chase all hope of rest in the days to come.

'It's time our own group comes together,' she stated. 'This is our wake-up call. There's one man who hasn't made it into that folder, who is surely next. Extract him immediately, and his family. Bring them here. And then our real work begins.'

With no further word, Grove swept from the office to make her way to the surface and the work of dealing with the power cuts that needed to happen in public.

Bambera knew his time was short before he would have to do the same.

His mind worked quickly through potential difficulties and options before he settled on the ideal agent. He reached for his telephone to arrange extraction.

The lights came back on, but the three figures huddling on the sofa still didn't move. Instead, they stared around the room at the lamps and lightbulbs, willing them to stay on and for this not to be one of the disappointingly brief interludes that often preceded the full reconnection of supply.

After a few moments, Gilmore shifted and stood, feeling the ache that told him how tense he'd been during the two hours of darkness. His instincts were still heightened, so he allowed his muscles to return to the level of tension that he actually felt more comfortable with.

'Ian, relax.' Rachel reached out and held his hand, knowing as always when his worries had risen over the threshold that triggered her own concern. 'Dillon, go and use the bathroom now please,' she instructed.

'Mum,' he complained. 'I don't even need to go.'

Rachel stared at him with the glare that told him she knew he did, and that he'd been holding on in fear of the dark. 'Well, go and check the lights haven't blown like they used to. Remember the surges when it used to come back on?'

Racing off under cover of completing a useful task, Dillon shared a conspiratorial smile with his father. Gilmore watched him go, suddenly feeling the chill of the absence of their huddle.

As soon as he was out of sight, Rachel's face creased in concern. 'Come on, dear, it was only a bit of darkness. We got used to it last year, and we can do again if need be. God knows we've faced worse.'

Gilmore swallowed, reluctant to shatter her valiant efforts at restoring a sense of normality to the evening. 'I heard noises,' he said quietly.

Recognising the authenticity of his tone, Rachel turned her hand hold into a grasp of his arm. 'Where?'

He nodded in the direction of the hallway.

'Are you armed?' she asked calmly.

Again, he nodded. 'Have been since it went dark.'

Not willing to risk Dillon starting back down the stairs, she called up to him, 'Stay up there, son, I'm just coming up too.' Nodding her permission, she moved to the bottom of the stairs to form a barrier.

Gilmore stepped slowly towards the front door. The muffled sounds had stopped but there was a dark presence blotting out the newly restored streetlights. Deciding to put himself out of the suspense, he ran at the door and flung it open.

The figure in the doorway raised his hands immediately. 'Bambera!' the man stated swiftly. 'I'm here on behalf of Bambera. Look.' Bright eyes shone from an earnest expression on his dark face. He indicated the ground at the edge of the front garden, where two lumpen shapes lay completely still. 'They were coming for you. But I'm here instead.'

Gilmore kept his pistol trained directly on the man's chest, processing the Jamaican lilt in the man's voice and wondering why it sounded so familiar. 'Why should I trust you? It could be the other way around.'

'Hannah Gordon,' the man replied, fixing Gilmore with a defiant stare. 'Hannah Gordon is... was... my sister.'

Gilmore found his arm drifting downwards as the implications of the name flooded through him.

'You and your family must come with me,' the man said. 'You're in danger. All of you.'

CHAPTER TWO

Wednesday – Approaching Whitehall, London. 9.10pm

DILLON GRIPPED his lucky bullet tightly as he stared out of the car window at the unfamiliar sight of London at night. He could feel the heat of his nerves amplified by the metal and returned in a form of comfort he wouldn't be able to explain if asked.

'I wish you hadn't given him that damned bullet.' Dillon remembered his mother chastising his father in one of her loud whispers, when her attempt to prevent him from hearing was overridden by her irritation. 'What a morbid object.' He still wasn't entirely sure what *morbid* meant, but the tone of distaste and the heavy, leaden sound of it as he repeated it in his mind gave him a good idea of its sentiment.

'He can learn a lot from that single bullet.' The memory of his father's calm countering argument opened the door in his mind to their many discussions about its story and the men who were fated to meet it in one form or another. The pencil drawn and painted images of Great War soldiers from his history books flashed before him, lending him their bravery as they often did when he needed it.

His mother leaned forward from the back seat of the Volkswagen Golf in which they were weaving through the London traffic. 'We must be nearly there by now?'

Dillon saw his father look at the man at the wheel, who had turned up at their house as the power had come back on and turned their evening even more upside-down. Dillon couldn't make out his face from where he was nestled in the back. The man continued to stare ahead intently while tiny movements suggested he was checking the mirrors frequently. Dillon recognised the habit from his father.

His father leaned around to face them. 'If Bambera wants us, and it's serious, we'll be going underground.'

The driver nodded confirmation.

'You'll be seeing parts of London people don't usually get to see,' his father said with an attempt at cheeriness.

'We've already seen enough of London for my liking this evening,' his mother shot back.

Mentally, Dillon separated himself from the backseat 'we' his mother was suggesting. His mind was racing with his heart as he watched familiar landmarks shine in the orange sodium glow of the rain-soaked city. He was mesmerised. With his bullet and his conjured bravery, he was riding the thrill of the dislocation from their cosy routine at home.

'We'll get to the bottom of this,' his father called from the front. 'An overnight stay probably, sort it all out and home for school in the morning.' Dillon could tell the higher pitch in his voice was meant for him.

Slowing to allow the driver to show a pass-card at various points, the car was enveloped by tall official buildings. Dillon caught sight of the Cenotaph, still littered with the poppies and wreaths of the recent Remembrance ceremonies. In his imagination, his lucky bullet pulsed a little harder in sympathy with the monument, and it lent him the extra strength to stay brave as the car started to travel down a darkening slope. He felt his mother grip his free hand until they emerged, beneath the ground, into a new kind of light.

Gilmore led his family towards Bambera's office, noting with renewed awe the sturdy pillars that rose and flowered into vaulted ceilings, above which went on the public work of the Ministry of Defence.

He knew that it was here, in these depths, that even more serious threats to national security were faced. He felt a jarring confusion at the suddenness of their transport and arrival here, and a clash of identity knowing that Dillon was a few steps behind him being led along by Rachel's hand.

He increased his pace to fall into step alongside their rescuer. 'You didn't tell me your first name,' he said, knowing that the man might open up more out of earshot of the others.

'My apologies, Group Captain,' the man said, turning his bright eyes to meet his and offering his hand. 'It's just Trevor.'

'Just Trevor,' Gilmore repeated, starting a little at the mention of his old rank and shaking the proffered hand as they strode on. 'I hope that turns out as apt a description as it did for your sister. I really am so sorry for your loss.'

Trevor stared ahead again, friendliness suddenly shadowed by grief.

'If we get time, I'd like to explain—'

'I've been briefed,' Trevor interrupted. 'I know what you both went through to expose Whateley and Woden. I know what was at stake. Whole cities. Maybe more if the conflict had escalated.' He faced Gilmore again, his eyes shining with more than pride. 'I like to think that she saved the world.' The Jamaican curl infused the words, connecting him to his sister even more closely.

'She did,' Gilmore confirmed, nodding briskly. 'Without a doubt. She never mentioned that it was a family business.'

'She followed me in,' Trevor explained. 'Bambera spotted her talents from the family connection checks and recruited her.'

Gilmore sensed an unspoken guilt at having led his own sister to the job that ended her life, and he turned back to see Rachel and Dillon catch them up, ruminating on how hard it was to keep danger away when family connections were so tightly intwined.

A heavy, studded wooden door swung open and Minister for Defence Kofi Bambera appeared. Gilmore noticed that he too looked taken aback to see a child with wide eyes approach his office. The moment passed and the mask of professionalism returned.

'Come in, all of you. Welcome, Group Captain Gilmore. Professor Jensen.' He looked down, taking the trouble to smile kindly. 'Dillon,' he added.

'This is Mr Bambera,' Gilmore explained for the benefit of Dillon. 'I've told Dillon that you'll be the one letting us know how we can get things back to normal as soon as possible.' He stared pointedly at Bambera, hoping the man would recognise the urge to protect his son above all else.

Bambera nodded, leaning down to meet Dillon's eyes at his level. 'I have a daughter a little older than you. She finds all this a bit strange too, when she visits.' Gilmore sensed this was as much for his benefit as it was for Dillon's. Straightening himself up, his arm protectively covering his recent gunshot wound, he spoke slowly and directly. 'Trevor will take care of Dillon for a while, then you can explain to him in your own words what's happening.'

Gilmore braced himself for the look of panic he knew would flash through Dillon's eyes at the thought of being separated from his mother and father in this strange underground world. He took Rachel's hand, knowing she would be feeling the same. 'Trevor can be trusted, believe me,' he said to her in advance of any protest.

'Dad?' Dillon voice was plaintive, echoing gently around the ancient walls.

'Go on, son,' Gilmore urged, leaning down and ruffling his son's hair. 'There's a lot of history down here. I'm told a famous king kept his favourite drink in here in vast quantities.'

'Which king? What drink?'

Trevor swept in with enthusiasm to capitalise on the distraction. 'Let me reveal to you the secrets of kings and their drinking habits, young man,' he said, guiding Dillon with a hand on his back away from the others.

Gilmore felt Rachel's hand tighten around his own as she held down her anxiety at the separation. He squeezed it back in equal measure, turning away from Dillon and trying to control his own. Together, they followed Bambera into his office.

Without the protective artifice of the presence of a child, the atmosphere chilled.

'I've been addressed as group captain repeatedly tonight,' Gilmore announced as Bambera settled into his chair. 'When I received that call to say it was a permanent reinstatement, I rather hoped it would be for paperwork purposes only. Am I to presume this means we have a wider emergency than just power cuts and some thugs with a grudge?'

'Think of this as a continuation of your recall.' Bambera's voice had deepened. 'We can quibble about rank later, but for now, time is short.'

'Then tell us what on earth is going on,' Rachel hissed. 'You've dragged my family here with no explanation. After what we went through with Woden, I thought we had earned some rest.'

'Woden was just the start,' Bambera began. 'Their fall has triggered a new phase of a conflict that has been building for a long time. Today has seen the assassination of a number of figures who were key to their downfall. Assets of ours who helped provide the information we needed to infiltrate them, and people they saw as having failed them.'

Gilmore's mind raced ahead of Bambera's explanation. 'But if Woden is finished, who's been carrying out the assassinations?'

'Woden was only one arm of a wider network. A particularly muscular arm, but one we were able to... amputate nonetheless.'

'Please, Minister, spare us the biological metaphors,' Rachel muttered. Gilmore suppressed a smile. Her impatience may serve them well in finding out the truth of their situation.

'Very well,' Bambera conceded. He pulled a folder from a pile on his desk and opened it, letting photographs spill out. 'I'll let these speak for themselves.'

Gilmore felt his breath catch as he recognised the monochrome faces staring out from the past through the photographs. 'Sergeant Smith...' The name caught on his breath.

Rachel put a hand to her mouth. 'Mike.'

Gilmore knew the face on the photograph beneath, the coldly angry eyes full of self-righteousness burning in black and white amid lined features. 'Ratcliffe.'

'The Association,' Bambera confirmed. 'These two, and so many more, then and now.' He picked up the pile of photographs, adding more from other folders, and let them drift one by one down to the desk. They formed a precarious pile, starting to slip and fall from the desk as face fell upon face.

Gilmore felt his cheeks flush. 'Why didn't we realise this before? Whateley's anti-immigrant stance, the attitudes of his followers...'

'It was more than anti-immigrant,' Rachel clarified, her voice wavering with barely suppressed rage. 'Downright racism, most of it. Unfortunately, it's so prevalent that we wouldn't have attributed it to a particular group. I thought they'd folded after Ratcliffe's death anyway.'

'The Association was always a fragile set-up,' Bambera explained, leafing through some of the documents buried beneath the photographs, pushing more of them to the floor. 'A loose alliance of extreme right-wingers. Nazi sympathisers, ex-National Front, Mosley acolytes. Ratcliffe held them together but only just, and only while he could promise real power.'

Gilmore looked at Rachel, recognising in her eyes the horror of the memories of Shoreditch and their recent reunion with its legacy.

'They have become emboldened again,' Bambera continued. 'Faces like mine are rising through the ranks, joining government, joining the Lords, making decisions. It's been a rallying call for action from those old frustrated guardians of white supremacy, as well as a new wave of young malcontents. Powell gave them renewed fuel, and now they're focusing around a new leader and a new promise of power.'

'If that promise is anything like the last one...' Rachel whispered. Gilmore ached to see her sternly beautiful features crumple in concern.

'You allude to the Child, Professor Jensen,' Bambera said, directing a piercing gaze straight at her. 'And you're right to.'

'Is Judith safe?'

'She is, and she must remain so. As must you both, and your own child.'

Gilmore grasped for Rachel's hand again, feeling new depths of chill penetrating him.

'All of you are at risk. We've plotted the Association's movement through the layers of betrayal they seek revenge for, and you're next.' Bambera stood, as if to confer some honour upon them. 'You've been called here not only for your own protection, but to work with a group that has been standing against the Association for as long as it's been in existence. When they rise, so do we. For every action—'

'We?' Gilmore echoed. 'You're part of this group?'

Bambera smiled grimly. 'You know that as a politician it would be inappropriate to confirm my affiliations. But rest assured, you're among friends. Some you know already. Some will surprise you. Some you're about to make. We can keep you safe, but you will need to play your part.'

Gilmore looked from Bambera to Rachel, but she was staring into the distance, her eyes already steely with resolve. He swallowed. 'Tell us what you need us to do.'

*

'So, they buried this whole place, rather than knock it down?' Dillon looked up in wonder at the arcing patterns on the ceilings and stroked the white walls of the cellar room.

'Pretty much,' Trevor replied casually.

'Wow.'

There was so much to learn, and Dillon could feel more questions lining up to be asked. But exhaustion was crowding them out now, and he couldn't find the words.

'You must be tired, little guy,' Trevor said, crouching down so their faces were level.

He had a kind face and a wide smile, but Dillon could see the frown-lines he saw in his parents' faces when they spoke in hushed tones so he couldn't hear, or when they drifted into their memories.

'I haven't been up this late for ages,' Dillon said, yawning as the floodgates to his fatigue opened. 'Not since Auntie Sarah let me stay up when they were away last time. I had a bad feeling and couldn't sleep.'

'Well, they're not far away,' Trevor reassured him. 'If you want a kip, curl up in the corner. You can use my jacket as a pillow or a cover. And if you can't kip, just rest your eyes.'

Dillon took the advice, folding Trevor's woollen coat in three and using it for his head. He took his own jacket off and pulled it over himself. He stared at the ceiling and tried to imagine the people that had used this room over the centuries. He turned his lucky bullet over in his hand, conjuring the ghosts of soldiers to sing him to sleep.

He hummed quietly to himself, reconstructing the lyrics of a song he'd learned for school.

> *They'll all march back with the Union Jack*
> *In history they'll gain fame.*
> *Just give them a cheer and banish the tear,*
> *For they'll return again.*

He sang the same verse to himself over and over, silently in his mind. Anything to keep the bad feeling at bay.

CHAPTER THREE

Wednesday – Beneath Whitehall, London. 11.50pm

'ARE YOU serious?' Rachel allowed the one question to express the extent of the frustration she felt.

Gilmore and Bambera continued to exchange pithy clues as to their existing and potential involvement in this anti-Association collective. She noticed, with more than a little irritation, that the corners of Gilmore's mouth were being tugged into an impressed smile. Bambera was pushing all his buttons, awakening the lightly sleeping soldier inside.

'Ian, can we stop and think about this before embarking on yet another life-threatening escapade?' Rachel asked.

Gilmore visibly calmed his enthusiasm, clearly preparing to deploy the tactics she knew he hoped would sooth her mood. As usual, that only made her temper boil all the more.

Bambera leaned in between them. 'Of course, you need to discuss this. Especially where the boy's concerned.'

'His name is Dillon,' Rachel interjected.

'Before I leave you to decide, there are two more things you need to know. I want you to make a fully informed decision.'

Rachel fixed him with a glare. 'Go on,' she prompted.

'The assassinations, timed to coincide with the biggest power cuts they've managed yet, are a declaration. If the Woden plan had worked, this would have been the next phase of the takeover of a broken country. We're not broken, but their plan is one that genuinely threatens the safety and stability of the realm, so they're going ahead regardless. They have developed systems that can disrupt energy supplies on a national scale.

Their next target is the back-up generator system that keeps essential services going when the main supply is lost.'

Bambera paused, allowing Rachel's mind to unfold the implications. 'Hospitals?'

'Hospitals, law enforcement, national and international defence systems. The transport network. The entire economy.'

Rachel glanced at Gilmore and saw her own fear reflected in his eyes.

'Last winter's power cuts were their training ground. They've seen what a little darkness can do, and are weaponising it.'

'But what can we do?' Gilmore asked, sounding to Rachel as if his earlier hope had drained away.

'By staying safe with us, you can also help us track down the systems they are bringing together to achieve their power grab. We know they're awaiting final components, and we have leads that will take us to them. If we can get hold of the technology before them, we can stop them completing their work, or at least allow us to develop counter systems.'

'Countermeasures,' Rachel said with irony.

'It's either that or a safehouse,' Bambera continued. 'You'd be completely secure. It's an option, if you'd rather.'

'You know full well he'd be climbing the walls in an hour,' Rachel said, unable to stop her expression softening as she recognised the inevitability of her acceptance of the plan.

'I'd be through the windows in less than half that, dear, let's be honest,' Gilmore added.

'You said there were two things we needed to know,' Rachel prompted.

Bambera's face clouded. Rachel could see the politician in him, composing the words to deliver a difficult truth. 'You mentioned the Child,' he said.

Rachel felt her heart thump harder. In her mind's eye she could see the tattered remains of the girl... no, the woman... who had been so intertwined with technology that her humanity had almost entirely fled in horror. The body left behind had been used, first by creatures beyond their world and their understanding, and then, even more troublingly, by her own kind. The urge to keep her alive had blended with a recognition of her extraordinary potential. The conflicting ethics chased themselves around in Rachel's head and haunted her sleep along with the memory of sharing a mental space with her for just a short time to avert the Woden disaster.

'Her name is Judith,' Rachel said quietly, wondering if every child was nameless to Bambera.

'The technology they're using to connect to the power grid is connected to it... to her. What they're searching for could assist you in your own efforts to make her... more comfortable.'

'You know about that?' Rachel cursed her own surprise. He was the Minister for Defence after all. She had become used to the stranger world she had known since Shoreditch being beyond the awareness of politicians like him. There was something different about Bambera though.

'I'd like to say this will be the final surprise of the night,' he said, indicating the door behind her, 'but I fear that would be optimistic. Someone was just behind you on your journey from Cambridge. I hope his presence will convince you that what I'm going to ask you to do is the right thing.'

Rachel turned to see her friend and fellow Professor, Albert Markson, crossing the floor towards them, his arms outstretched, a bright scarf flapping beneath his rosy features.

'Rachel,' he said, appeasement in his voice. 'I know you're surprised. Imagine mine when two strapping young gentlemen came to collect me at such an hour. Although it was a shame that the lights had come back on by then. And I know you might be angry. There are things I haven't told you. Forgive your old friend.'

His usual flamboyance and the welcome familiarity of an old and trusted ally disarmed Rachel completely, and she accepted his embrace.

Bambera took deep breaths of night air as he reached the surface and emerged amid the pale fronts of the Whitehall offices.

Rain was still pelting down, and he felt the relief of its coldness on his face after the artificial dryness of the underground complex.

He knew he had fed Gilmore and Jensen enough to guarantee their co-operation. A strategic withdrawal to leave the revelations to settle into acceptance was needed. He lit a cigarette and enjoyed a moment of peace.

Even as one of his aides rounded the corner, he knew the

moment was all he was going to get. 'What is it, Ramsay?' he asked, not bothering to disguise his tiredness.

'Come out of the rain, Minister,' the aide said, ushering Bambera back into the discreet entrance to the underground offices. Bambera felt a new rush of concern at the man's tone.

Once they were shadowed in the doorway, Ramsay took a last look outside before turning to Bambera. 'They're on the move, and they're angry. Possibly because we robbed them of Gilmore. They've skipped a few of the potential targets faster than we predicted.'

Bambera barely noticed the cigarette drop from his fingers. 'Have they come for me? My family?'

'They're safe, but yes,' Ramsay confirmed, taking another look beyond the doorway into the night. 'Your house has been ransacked. Your wife and daughter have been taken into protective custody. The attackers left a warning.'

Bambera took a hastily taken Polaroid with a shaking hand. He recognised the ornaments from the sideboards and shelves of his study, the reminders of his heritage, the awards he had collected on his way into government. They had been swept into a chaotic pile beneath a brightly coloured lightning flash inscribed onto the wall.

'They used her crayons,' Ramsay explained. 'For the graffiti.'

'Was she there when they did this?'

'They were hiding upstairs. We'd assigned agents to cover the area. There are a few of you on the risk list so we tried to cover as many as we could. It didn't take too long to get there, and we prevented anything worse. I saw them when we delivered them to the safehouse. She's a brave kid.'

Bambera let the Polaroid drop to the floor next to the wet cigarette. 'Her name is Winifred,' he said.

'You've got some explaining to do, Albert.' Rachel looked at him sternly, her hands on her hips.

Gilmore stepped between them, took the man's hand, and shook it briskly. 'I've heard a lot about you, Professor Markson. If you'll excuse me, I'd like to check on Dillon. I'll let you two catch up.' Rachel noticed him look between her and the new arrival as if wishing him luck at being left with her. 'I won't be long, dear,' he said, as casually as if he were popping upstairs to check on Dillon sleeping in his own bed in their own house.'

Rachel nodded, and he took that as permission to hurry away.

'He's even more handsome in three dimensions,' Markson said admiringly, staring at Gilmore's departing figure. 'The photographs in your office don't do him justice.'

Rachel rolled her eyes at the obvious delaying tactic. 'Albert,' she warned, and he held his hands up in admittance.

'Would you believe that this is all the result of the most extraordinary coincidence?' he said, sitting in the chair vacated by Gilmore and settling down into it with a smile as if appreciating its warmth.

'Go on,' she prompted, indulging him.

'As you know, my work in nuclear medicine has attracted some attention. I'm quite the desired one among a number of countries these days. Some of which are friendly, some less so. But the offers...' He waved his hands as if conjuring a number of exotic possibilities. 'Let's just say, if I'd been a younger man, I'd have been sorely tempted.'

'But what's this got to do with Bambera and all this?'

'When I refused some of the offers, there was the potential for things to get a little... heated. Ablaze, you could say. Bambera sorted out protection while things... cooled down.'

'Your skills are valued by the country. You know that.'

A shadow passed over Markson's face and he turned away from her. 'Yes, it must be that,' he said, as if unsure and trying to persuade himself. 'Yes...'

'You never told me. I could have helped.'

'We all have our secrets, Rachel.' He was more serious than she had perhaps ever heard him. 'Bambera's aide contacted me tonight and said you would need my help. On the way here I've been studying the files on this... Child.'

Rachel held his gaze, even though she felt like turning her head away in shame.

'Bambera wants us to return to Cambridge. He believes I can help stabilise her, make her comfortable.'

'He means useful,' she hissed. 'I've heard it all before. "It's in her best interests, at least she's alive." He'll want to use her for something, just like all the others. Besides, I can't leave Dillon.' She sighed and put her head in her hands. 'What a mess.

I'm tired. I hoped we'd earned some peace.'

She felt Albert place a hand on her shoulder. Had it been anyone else at that point, she would have shrugged it away.

'Peace is only ever temporary for people like us,' he whispered.

Bambera stalked the corridors through the underground complex, more determined than ever to initiate the plan.

With each step of his right leg, the twinge spread through his side to the point at which he'd been shot a few weeks previously. Turning the pain into fuel, he pressed on.

He found Gilmore watching over the boy, talking with Trevor. They stopped as they realised he was approaching. From their expressions, Gilmore was talking about the death of the man's sister. They turned to look at him, putting aside their shared moment.

'Is everything all right, sir?' Trevor asked, obviously noticing the change in him.

'Have you made your decision?' Bambera asked Gilmore, ignoring the concern.

'We need to talk about Dillon,' Gilmore replied, equally ignoring the demand. 'I can't drag a ten-year-old boy around with us while we search for this technology. Especially if we're being hunted at the same time. He could stay with Rachel's sister, like last time.'

'And can you guarantee that she would be able to keep him safe?'

Gilmore was silent, looking at the sleeping form of his son.

'Who do you trust most of all to keep him safe?'

Still, he said nothing.

'Then that's where he should be.'

Gilmore gave the tiniest nod of acquiescence.

'A father should do anything to protect his child,' Bambera said.

'Will yours be joining us?' Gilmore asked, his voice innocent but his eyes fixed upon him in challenge.

Bambera said nothing, but strode off back towards the office where the final agreement needed to be made. He could hear footsteps behind him, sullen but accepting.

*

Rachel stood as Bambera swept into the office, Ian trailing behind him. She knew that he had already agreed, and that she would not be able to stop him.

They gathered in the centre of the room, facing each other.

'Ian, you do know they want me to go back to Cambridge with the Child?' she said. 'I'm not invited on this mission of yours.'

Gilmore turned to Bambera. 'You expect Dillon to stay with me, while my wife goes back out there into danger?'

'Professors Jensen and Markson will be working with the Child in a bunker beneath Shire Hall,' Bambera explained. 'It's one of the nuclear protection shelters, designed to keep our best minds safe in extreme circumstances. I'd say it was the perfect place and the perfect time.'

'You're very well prepared,' Rachel observed, unable to keep the accusatory tone out of her voice. 'How long have you been getting ready for this?'

'Like I said, we mirror the Association. As they plan and grow, so do we. For every action...'

'Yes, you said that before. We provide the equal and opposite reaction.'

'A scientific principle I'm sure you can appreciate.'

'Don't patronise me, Bambera.' Rachel took a deep breath, aiming for a calm that would allow this to be over as painlessly as possible. 'What about Dillon?'

'He stays with me.' The certainty in Gilmore's voice left her speechless. 'Do you trust me?'

'You know I do.'

'I will do everything I can to keep him safe.'

'He could come with me to the bunker,' she said, knowing already that the decision had been made.

'I don't want him near the Child,' Gilmore said, more gently than he could have done. 'You need to do what you can with her without distraction. From what Trevor has told me, I'll mostly be working through military hardware and archives. Bambera's forces will be our shield. Dillon and I will be at the dry end of it all. You know how he loves history. We can treat it like an education.'

Rachel shook her head. 'You always were a ridiculous optimist.' She grasped his hand, not in affection, but in the sealing of a pact. 'You keep my son safe,' she demanded. 'If not, I'll come and retrieve him myself.'

He held her hand with equal pressure. 'Agreed. And I promise.'

Seconds passed and she was dimly aware of Bambera and Markson looking away from the moment between them. The pressure with which they gripped their hands together softened. She couldn't tell who had started to release first.

Rachel closed her eyes, not caring who was watching or not, and kissed him.

They parted and stepped back away from each other.

'We do this to achieve the peace we deserve,' said Bambera gently, 'to keep our children safe. All of them.'

CHAPTER FOUR

Thursday – Shoreditch, London. 8.00am

RATCLIFFE SMILED as he watched the children skitter and dance around the windswept playground. Puddles shattered and reformed as they jumped into them. They laughed with delight at the sudden chaos that calmed around them, before being fractured again by their kicking and splashing.

Wrapped in their duffel coats and balaclavas, they seemed oblivious to the biting cold. Their apparent invincibility belied the fragile lives they led, awareness of which was the burden of their parents, not them. For now, they could run and jump, land and splash, and the puddles would always reform around them exactly as before.

Ratcliffe knew, like their parents, that things could break for good. The power to impart that knowledge, the thrill of doing so, ran through him in an unseen shiver.

His eyes settled on a pair of boys crouching together in a corner of the playground. The mothers of the pair were deep in conversation, likely about the power cut of the previous evening, grateful for the time before school when they could stand and chat with someone like themselves.

Except this pair weren't like each other. Ratcliffe's mouth curled into a cruel smile as he noted the dark skin of one of the boys and that of his mother. He felt his breath quicken with irritation at the easy chat between the mothers. It was obviously too late for them.

Passing the mothers, he beamed his most charming grin, rubbing his hands together and sharing a comment on the cold that would melt any concerns they might have about him. *People were so easy to manipulate when you could see them from a height.* The thought was so familiar to him, he barely registered it in words, but the certainty of it lent him an impressive credibility.

'Any problems now the power's back, blown fuses and the like, you just let me know, ladies. My men'll sort you out.' He flicked a business card at each of them like a magician, and they giggled as they caught them and at the hint of flirtation and innuendo in the patter. 'Lads playing marbles? I might have some ball bearings going spare if they want them?'

The mothers smiled even more, indulging what they thought was more business-touting charm. The white one casually indicated that he had their permission to join the boys.

Careless, thought Ratcliffe. *Is it any wonder that fragile things get broken so easily?*

'All right, lads?'

The boys looked up from their marbles with wide eyes, instinctively straightening themselves and puffing out their chests. They shot quick looks at their mothers, half-remembering warnings about approaches by adults but almost immediately putting them to one side as they nodded their assent and returned to their own talk.

'Who's winning?'

'Caleb's got one more than me,' the pale boy said, not unhappily.

'And what's your name?' Ratcliffe asked.

'John.'

'Ah, good English name, my man.'

John looked pleased, his cheeks flushing rosier at the sudden elevation to adulthood. Caleb bent down to collect his winnings.

'I've got these,' Ratcliffe said, crouching to their level and holding out a hand to show them four gleaming ball bearings. In comparison to the brightly coloured glass marbles, they looked industrial and exotic. 'Want them?'

The boys looked at each other, uncertain. 'Two each?' John asked expectantly.

'You decide,' Ratcliffe said, fixing John with a look of challenge.

John looked at Caleb, who watched impassively.

'One, two, three, or four. Entirely your choice, young man.' Ratcliffe held them out closer to the boy. 'Your little friend gets whatever's left.'

John reached out and rolled one over and into his hand, and then a second. His hand hovered near a third. A battle between fairness and equity or outright triumph played over his brow, which creased as he mulled his choice. Ratcliffe watched him look at Caleb, saw a conspiratorial smile flick between them, and he closed his fist around his two prizes.

Ratcliffe's smile became a sneer, and he didn't stop it. Giving Caleb the remaining two ball bearings, he said, 'Your mate still wins then, he's still got one more than you.'

Caleb fixed him with a stare that seemed older than his seven or so years, as if he knew the game that was being played out and had seen it many times before.

'That's all right, I can win them back later,' John said, pleased enough with his small haul of winnings. 'Thanks, mister.' Gathering the rest of their marbles, they made to run back to their mothers.

'How about this then?' Ratcliffe said, a little louder than he meant. He put his hand dramatically inside the inner pocket of his long woollen coat and pulled out what looked like a silver wand. Ratcliffe wielded it expertly, flicking it between his fingers and from hand to hand until with a final flourish he illuminated the tip with a push of a switch. 'Pocket torch. You never know when you might need it, especially with these blackouts.' He shot a look at Caleb at the final word.

The boys, uncertain but impressed by the object, paused between the safety of their mothers and the thrill of a new possession.

'So, John, you want to share this as well?'

John, confused, stared up at Ratcliffe. 'How?'

'Well, if you want half each, you'll have to snap it.'

Ratcliffe could feel the moment, and watched the tiny changes on the boys' faces.

'But then it won't work,' Caleb said.

'Exactly. No light for anyone. So, John. Who gets the torch? You, your mate, neither, or both?'

The second choice between four options played across his face, aging him visibly.

'Keep yourself safe in the dark,' Ratcliffe added quietly. 'Don't feel bad. Your mate will understand, won't you?'

Caleb kept his face level, but Ratcliffe could see the disappointment at the old preferential treatment rising.

John reached out and slowly took the torch. He tested the switch a few times, staring at his newfound power to create light, and to snuff it out. The smile he gave Ratcliffe was one of gratitude and alliance. He didn't look at Caleb as he put the torch into his pocket, away from eyes that might covet it.

'Good choice,' Ratcliffe said, turning away from them, sending a cheery wave to the mothers, who smiled and waved back.

At the entrance to the playground, he stopped one last time and looked at the group. He fixed Caleb with a stare, drawing in the new sadness that had fallen over the boy's features, a sullen acceptance at having won a game of marbles but somehow lost a friend.

As pleased with the work of that morning as he was of the day before, Ratcliffe grinned and walked away.

Gilmore checked his watch.

Rachel would be safely back in Cambridge by now. His back ached where he had sat in the hall near Dillon with his back against the white stone wall, dozing through the early hours of the morning, waking with a start several times, uncertain as to where he was.

Dillon stretched loudly, having slept well, wrapped tightly in Trevor's overcoat.

'Where's Mum?' he asked, bringing the inevitable explanation and reassurances.

'Trevor's going to keep a close eye on you, so if I'm busy and anything worries you, you let him know, all right?' Gilmore had concluded the pep talk.

Gilmore noticed that Trevor had already taken on a subtle frown of concern when he looked at the boy, as if they shared a need to protect him as well as the memory of his lost sister. Perhaps the two were really the same thing, Gilmore pondered. Either way, he was grateful.

'I'm going to work in my sketch book while you do the boring stuff,' Dillon told him, pulling the book from his hastily packed rucksack, and delving in to retrieve his pencils.

'The boring stuff?' Gilmore asked.

'All the talking,' Dillon clarified. 'Let me know when you're done and when we're ready to go.'

Sharing a look of amusement with Trevor, Gilmore shook his head at his son's new confidence. The sleep had done him good, and he seemed buoyed by the sense of adventure rather than troubled by the dislocation. *Long may it continue*, Gilmore thought.

He found Bambera in the main office, hunched over more piles of paper. He could make out more grainy photographs but not what was on them, along with maps and diagrams. Bambera had changed from his formal suit into an outfit more like combat fatigues, darker and more practical.

'My son is keen to get going,' Gilmore announced.

'I can guess where he gets that from. We're almost ready to go.'

'So where do we start?'

Bambera reordered some of the papers to bring to the top a map. Gilmore recognised the curve of the Thames at the bottom and some of the faint lines that crossed it and spread away northwards. Darker than these bridges and roads were other lines, which he guessed indicated tunnels. Bambera traced a line with his finger that took them eastwards from their present location, beneath the Strand, past Waterloo Bridge and the grids of Covent Garden.

'Here,' he announced. 'Kingsway Telephone Exchange.'

Gilmore searched his memory for information on the place. It seemed vaguely familiar.

'It's a deep-level shelter, now home to some of the most sensitive communications equipment in the country.'

'Covered by D-notice?' Gilmore asked, nodding in anticipation of confirmation.

'Most definitely. As well as being key to our communication with the US, there are experimental systems there laying the foundation for our future mobile telecommunications. If it were to go down in a power outage, we'd be on our own, literally. An island nation in the worst sense. We need to shore it up, but while we're there, we might be able to get our hands on something useful for the Child.'

Gilmore shuddered at the use of the word, still unused to such a symbol of innocence being used as a shield for the horrors Rachel had described. 'And what would that be?'

Bambera took a deep breath. Gilmore guessed that he wasn't used to sharing information this sensitive. 'Something from the last war. Just before it ended, the enemy were on the verge of developing an even more advanced form of code. It could have rendered the Enigma work irrelevant. Details are sketchy, but we know the extra layers of encryption were created using a kind of interface, filtering the heavily coded messages through one more extraordinary scrambling system.'

'Go on,' Gilmore urged as Bambera paused, guessing at some of the possibilities given the connection to the Child.

'Imagination. The messages were to be passed through the sleeping minds of teenagers, emerging garbled beyond recognition.'

'I'm sure they were.' Gilmore couldn't help but smirk. 'I dread to think what my teenage mind would have done to them.'

Bambera ignored that. 'The plan was to decode using the same process. As our scientists prepared to try to crack the new method, they developed an interface to be worn by another teenager, which would translate the subconscious codings into recognisable words and images. Feeding it into them subliminally while they slept would unlock the messages.'

'Good God,' Gilmore breathed, beyond smirking now and genuinely both amazed and appalled at what he was hearing.

'The work was advanced, but never used. Turing's work on the Enigma code turned out to be enough, just. But if things had gone on much longer...'

'So, this interface could help us communicate with the Child more effectively?' Gilmore remembered Rachel's attempts at explaining what she had seen when melded with the creature... the woman... at the end of the Woden business. He could see the value in avoiding a direct mental connection in order to communicate with her.

'Ticks both of the boxes,' Bambera replied. 'If she can let us know her needs more clearly, we can perhaps ease any suffering she still experiences.'

'While we can let her know what we need from her, when the time comes.'

Bambera nodded, and Gilmore realised in the silence that followed exactly why Rachel had been sent away; the stern judgements and ethical arguments were on hold, for now.

The warehouse was even colder than the open air.

Ratcliffe rubbed his hands together and blew into them. He stalked through the outer edge where the illusion of a building business grew from propped up fencing panels and piles of pristine bricks.

Behind these visual and physical barriers, the real work continued. The large space was separated into smaller portions, each containing an element of the operation. His workers milled about within their own regions, never daring to venture into each other's. They'd seen what had happened to the idiot who in his friendliness had strayed into a neighbour's compartment to try to muster interest in a five-a-side team.

Only Ratcliffe had the ability to move between all areas. He did so imperiously, noting from the corners of his vision the envious and curious glances his workers risked. He didn't mind them looking when he could sense the awe and envy in their faces and the deference with which they turned away when his gaze swept near them.

They knew that if they looked too hard, they lost their eyes.

By the time he reached the centre, the air temperature had risen, a result of the power being generated by the various processes and experiments. He allowed the warmth to thaw his tense limbs, and he looked around at the equipment appreciatively.

'Boss,' a respectful voice came from behind a bank of electrical wiring.

Dr Daniel Hareward, his best engineer and one of those trusted to work in the centre, poked his head around the edge of the mesh of coloured strands. His unkempt hair lent him an air of bafflement that Ratcliffe knew from long association was an affectation to prevent his intelligence seeming like a challenge.

'Hareward, how's it going?' Ratcliffe undid his coat and prepared to receive the report.

'It took them longer to bring it back up this time,' Hareward explained, removing his insulating gloves and slapping them down on a desk with satisfaction. 'We're getting there.'

'You think we're ready to move to the back-ups?'

'I've found a way into St Thomas'. We could try there if you want. We'll still be reliant on the physical transfer of the block, but at least it'll show them what's coming.'

Ratcliffe nodded, envisioning the chaos that would ensue at the failure of the hospital back-up generators. He worked through the likely sequence of events, focusing his imagination on the panicked faces as equipment failed and went dark. A thought occurred to him. 'Can we give it a while between the localised power cut and then the block on the back-ups?'

'We could, although we'll risk the power being reinstated. Was there a reason you wanted to delay?'

'I want the back-ups to go just when they feel confident that they're holding on. Pride in their systems, before the fall.'

Hareward nodded obediently. Ratcliffe knew the man was more of a pragmatist than a sadist, and that the emotion of the moment was less important than the technicalities.

'Did you want to do the whole hospital, or just one bit?'

Ratcliffe met his eyes, careful to show that he was unashamed of what he was about to suggest. 'The children's ward,' he said calmly.

Hareward swallowed. Ratcliffe narrowed his eyes. Hareward nodded again. 'If you're sure,' he muttered.

'They're the future, right?' Ratcliffe said, smiling, remembering the boys from his journey to the warehouse. 'Which ones will they decide to save, if it comes down to it? Two sick children, but only enough space for one. Simple maths. A matter of resources. There just isn't enough for everyone.'

Hareward turned away, returning to his switches and wires. Ratcliffe could sense the man wasn't in the mood for talk. That was fine, as long as he got on with the job.

'One more thing,' Ratcliffe turned back on the threshold of the central workspace. 'Talking of children, how's my boy doing?'

Hareward paused. 'We're going to need those materials if he's going to be any use to us,' he explained. Ratcliffe could almost smell his nerves at coming close to admitting failure. 'That's if they even exist.'

'I'm expecting news on that soon,' Ratcliffe reassured him.

Hareward returned to his work once again.

Ratcliffe left him, passing back through the men who were

too afraid to greet him. Ideas and images swam through his mind as he strode on, but it always came back to the forthcoming panic of the doctors and nurses. That noble profession, plunged into darkness and forced to make the choices they had shied away from for too long. Who would they save, when they could only save some? Who would come with them back out into the light? Their own children, or those of the invaders? They would need help to be brave enough to make the right decisions.

He would be the one to help them.

CHAPTER FIVE

Thursday – Beneath Holborn, London. 9.00am

'WHAT DO you know about these allies of ours?' Gilmore asked as Dillon ran ahead into the open stretch of tunnel, giving them a moment alone.

Trevor replied while his eyes continued to dart around, alert for danger. 'I've been told that you already know one of them, and the others are an arm of Bambera's anti-Association coalition. Super clever apparently, some kind of special academic branch of the operation.'

Gilmore groaned. 'Just what I need in my life. More academics.'

Trevor flashed one of his genuine smiles, relaxing his vigilance and looking between Dillon and Gilmore. 'Missing her?'

Gilmore smiled sadly back and cleared his throat. 'We're used to various missions and projects pulling us in different directions. If I had to pick an academic to spend time with though, it would be her. We can trust these new ones I presume?'

'I believe so. I wouldn't be leading you to them if I didn't.'

'Fair point. Dillon, come back alongside please!' Gilmore called, pleased to see his son obeying without the questions that sometimes accompanied such instructions on their rambles out and about... on the surface in more ordinary circumstances.

They approached an iron door studded with bolts and locking mechanisms, mostly circular to fill the shape of the tunnel, with a flattened top and bottom to match the floor and ceiling. The pale light of the bulbs that seemed to be shining only reluctantly on this deserted route below The Strand left the mechanisms of the barrier shadowed, until Trevor used his torch to illuminate it. Gilmore felt for his own in the rucksack, as grateful for its reassuring bulk as he was usually felt with a weapon. His discomfort at the narrow spaces sat in his chest, the old echo of claustrophobia, and he took another deep breath to steady himself.

'Save yours, just in case,' Trevor warned. 'If the Association do manage to step up their attacks on the power systems, these torches will be our lifeline down here.'

The torch is at least as mighty as the sword, Gilmore thought in a twisted but appropriate realisation.

'The rendezvous point is beyond this door,' Trevor announced. 'Let's see who's waiting for us.'

Gilmore noted with admiration that he was keeping his tone balanced in the presence of Dillon, lending it just enough warning to bring them to alertness but not anxiety. He felt the boy grasp his hand while Trevor followed the instructions for the locking mechanism. A series of clicks deep within the metal coalesced eventually into a satisfying *thunk*, at which the door began to open with a pull.

As their eyes adjusted to a new level of gloom and their noses wrinkled at the staler air of this new portion of the tunnel system, all three tilted their heads to listen to a repeat of the unlocking sounds, coming from the other side of the space. Gilmore found himself tensing in anticipation.

'It'll be them,' Trevor whispered. 'The codes for this section are only known by Bambera's team.'

'I hope you're right,' Gilmore said, subtly manoeuvring Dillon into a position behind them.

An arc of pale light appeared like a crescent moon, illuminating the bunker space in between the doors. It grew as the heavy barrier swung back, revealing three silhouettes standing hesitantly in the new threshold.

'Ian?' A soft female voice echoed around the space from the far end, and the figure in the centre stepped forward.

Gilmore recognised the voice immediately, matching it to the shape and the suspicions he'd had since the start of this journey. *Who else would it be?*

'Allison.'

*

Candles flickered gently in the darkness of the storage space between the heavy doors. The group positioned themselves in a rough circle around them.

They had divided naturally into the two sets of three they had arrived as, and Gilmore found himself looking at Allison from across the makeshift light source, her serious face illuminated by the flames.

To her left and right sat her academic companions. One was a heavy-set man with dark hair and beard, who Gilmore guessed must be in his mid-forties. His size seemed to be muscular rather than the result of the indulgences clearly enjoyed by Rachel's friend Markson. He defied the stereotype of a man who had let strength of the mind take priority over the strength of the body.

'This is Dr Percy Saunders,' Allison introduced. 'He's our historical and archaeological specialist, and our guide through the tunnels.'

The other was more difficult to make out. Their thin, lined face was wrapped in a dark headscarf and Gilmore found it impossible to tell whether they were male or female. 'And this is Bes,' Allison continued. The following silence only emphasised the lack of prefix or suffix to the name.

'Just Bes?' Gilmore asked, carefully repeating the precise sound of the name and remembering how that little joke had broken the ice with Trevor and hoping he might repeat the trick.

'Bes,' came the reply from Bes themself in a voice equally poised between male and female. 'Voice of the Order of Albion.'

'The what of the who?' Gilmore asked, his frustration already piquing amid the need for clarity among his mission companions rather than a candlelit mystery.

It was Allison who took over the explanation, while Bes continued to stare at Gilmore with a steadiness he found unnerving.

'The Order of Albion, Ian. A highly respected group with unmatched understanding of the type of history and technology we're dealing with here.'

'Well forgive my ignorance,' Gilmore said, his voice still stern, 'I haven't heard of you.'

'Likewise,' Dr Saunders shot back, breaking his silence. 'Anyway, that's how we like it. Secret society, you could say. But I presume, as Bambera has recruited you too, that we share the same goals. That's enough for me to believe it's a pleasure to meet you. All three of you.' He gave a welcoming smile to Trevor and Dillon, his face transforming from earnest to warm within seconds.

'Bambera has taken care in preparing the different branches of the group for this moment,' Allison continued.

'I wasn't aware that I was even part of a group,' Gilmore protested. He clamped his mouth shut tightly, holding on to the wave of uncertainty he was trying to ride out. He'd been stripped of his role in the Air Force, and even the identity afforded him by the Counter Measures Group had eroded and deserted him over recent years. Seeing Allison reminded him of that, and he remembered Rachel's refusal to discuss her in recent weeks following their difference of opinion in relation to the Child.

'If it's any consolation, we're all the same,' Allison explained, leaning forwards so her face was illuminated. New, dark worry lines revealed themselves around her mouth and eyes that took Gilmore by surprise. 'My role at Devesham with the Child was preparation for this, although I didn't know it at the time. Yours in the Woden Operation, the same. And the Order has been ready for this for a very long time. We're defending against the rise of a power that could tear our country apart. Bambera has played a clever game, but it's the *right* one. We have to trust him and each other if we're going to find what we need to beat them.' She sighed and sat back, even more shadowed than before.

'Hello, Allison,' came a small voice from Gilmore's side. Dillon had leaned forward in concern.

Allison looked at the boy, her face softening as Saunders' had. Gilmore felt a lift of pride at the impact his son's presence was having on the group, or most of them.

'Dillon,' she said, her voice almost catching. 'It's been too long. Perhaps we can catch up on the trek along to the next stop.'

'We're relying on you for that,' said Trevor, breaking his own silence. 'Trevor Gordon, by the way. Bodyguard, on this occasion. And our instructions ran out with the opening of that door. Bambera told me you were in charge from here.'

Gilmore noted that Allison had looked at him as if waiting for permission to fulfil that promised function. He nodded, keeping his face level so as to hide the return of his discomfort and a general feeling that things were beyond his control. He glanced again at Bes, who was still staring, either at Dillon or into the flames between them; there was no way of telling which.

Allison led the way, Saunders and Bes flanking her.

Gilmore mentally adjusted to this new hierarchy in which knowledge trumped the different type of expertise offered by Trevor and himself. Dillon stayed between the two men and slightly ahead of them, enclosed by the group as a precious cargo.

'We're heading for the Turing Archive,' Saunders explained from ahead of them.

'My wife worked with Turing,' Gilmore said. 'That can't be a coincidence.'

'Luckily it's hidden away from the main telephone exchange and the workers down here. Once we've got what we need, we'll leave them with this, and be on our way to the next target.' Saunders indicated a second rucksack he'd been carrying. 'Extra defences. We think Association agents are aware of the importance of this place, even if they don't know exactly why. An attack could come during or after our visit.'

'Attack?' Dillon's worried voice piped up from between them.

'Hey, man,' Trevor said, his voice full of confident ease. 'You'd better be tracking our progress along that map. We'll be needing that later.'

'I'm marking off the junctions as we pass them,' Dillon explained, showing Trevor the map he was marking with a red pencil.

'Good lad.' Trevor smiled down at him and Dillon returned to his task with renewed intent.

'We're nearly there,' Saunders reassured them.

As the tunnel narrowed, it started to lose the concrete struts of the main construction. Running parallel to the main exchange, this area had clearly been used to store documents and equipment no longer immediately useful, but potentially under restriction orders, or awaiting more formal archival. Plain doors with dusty black handles striped the corridor. Jumbles of letters and numbers acted as codes to the contents on plastic signs on each door, meaningless to Gilmore but apparently read with ease by Allison, who was looking for a particular combination.

'This is the one,' she announced.

The group spread out around the door, watching as Allison prepared to enter a code into the locking mechanism.

'Wait,' Gilmore urged suddenly, his gaze bouncing from the door to the corridor ahead, which stretched into darkness as the bulbs gave up the weak glow they had been providing up to that point. 'Why aren't those bulbs ahead working?' he whispered.

'These tunnels are hardly ever used now,' Allison replied, 'especially further along. The supports and the archive rooms run out. It's just for maintenance and an escape route if the main channel was compromised.' She turned back to the door, but Gilmore stepped in front of it.

'Dillon, pass your map,' he instructed. 'You've definitely been marking this correctly?'

Dillon nodded earnestly. 'Yes, Dad.'

Gilmore held it up to show Allison, and the others peered towards it to see what he was worried about. 'There are many more rooms still ahead. The defunct section doesn't begin for another hundred metres or so. We're not as far along as you thought.' He felt for his pistol.

Before he had the chance to hold it, Saunders and Bes pushed past him, facing the dark end of the corridor. To his surprise, they adopted the stance of hand-fighters.

'Get inside,' Saunders instructed without turning.

Allison clicked the tiny metal numbers on the code box, her hands shaking. 'Damn,' she said, clearing the code and starting again.

The bulbs furthest down the corridor from them, already pale and wan, flickered and dimmed. Those now taking their place as the furthest, closer to them by several metres, then did the same. Darkness was engulfing the corridor, one set of bulbs at a time, like a slow tide of spreading tar.

'Allison, hurry,' Saunders hissed. 'They won't fire until you've unlocked it, but when you do, we're all fair game.'

Allison continued inputting the code, until, with a 'Yes!' of relief, she pushed the door open and Gilmore pushed Dillon inside, Trevor close behind him.

Ignoring the racks and shelves that stretched off perpendicular to the tunnel they'd escaped and leaving Allison to start her hunt there, Gilmore returned to the doorway, desperate to see if his suspicion that they had already been hunted down was correct.

An echoing explosion of a gunshot, followed by another and then the swift ricocheting echoes around the tunnel walls, confirmed his fears.

'Get him further inside,' Gilmore urged Trevor, seeing the man decide swiftly to do so despite a clear urge to protect the threshold with Gilmore.

Hearing a strangely muffled follow-up to the gunshots, he inched his head around the doorway to peer into the darkness. Amid the faint glow from the last of the bulbs to light the way further down the corridor, he could make out a striking movement of arcing bodies, calmly stretching arms, the supple crouch and kick of expert fighters. To his amazement they were dressed in the blue cagoules of Saunders and Bes. The academics completed their expert motions, overpowering the two black clad attackers and leaving them prone on the floor, disarmed and unconscious.

Rising to their full height and content that their enemies had been vanquished, the pair stretched out the effort they had made, dusted themselves down and turned in unison back towards Gilmore and the archive room.

Bes remained impassive as they passed, no hint of expended effort or breathlessness. Saunders, however, caught Gilmore's look of amazement, and gave one of amusement in return.

'Well, I wasn't expecting that,' Gilmore admitted.

'You've heard of warrior monks?' Saunders asked casually. 'Warrior academics doesn't have quite the same ring, but you get the gist.'

'I'm beginning to. They're Association?'

Saunders nodded. 'They won't be waking up for a while. We'll get the Exchange security to hold on to them as soon as we're finished here. Bambera will want to interrogate them. If they knew we were coming, we need to find out how much else they know and if we're going to find them at our next location too.'

'How did they do that with the lights?'

Saunders held up a wire-strewn construction that melded together a metal box with a small metal dish. The dual spike of an angry-looking protuberance emerged from the centre of the parabolic metal, like a forked tongue tasting the air. 'Portable power drain,' he explained. 'Very bad news. Their capacity to attack back-up systems as well as the main network is increasing. A stronger one of these in the wrong place could cause chaos. Imagine what it could do in an airport or a hospital.'

Allison returned to Gilmore's side. 'There's good news and bad news,' she said, holding a metal strongbox before her. The top face was a complete jumble of lines and dots, divided into tiles like a sliding puzzle. 'I've found what we're looking for. Only trouble is, it's locked, and the puzzle lock is virtually impossible to complete, especially down here in this gloom. I dread to think what happens if you try to force it or get it wrong.'

'Given what's inside, that's probably for the best,' Saunders reassured her. 'We can study it back at the base.'

'The base? Whose base is this now?' Gilmore said, desperate to claw back a sense of direction and purpose.

'The Order's base,' Saunders explained. 'Let's get the Exchange onto maximum alert, get those out there to Bambera, and regroup.'

'But where is this base?'

'Somewhere useful for a forgotten bunch of academics whose time has now come,' said Bes with no trace of humour. 'Under the British Library.'

CHAPTER SIX

Thursday – Beneath Cambridge. 11.00am

RACHEL WATCHED the final preparations for the arrival of the Child.

She sipped another coffee, consciously focusing the caffeine hit into mentally preparing the work she would need to do and nudging it away from the irritation and anxiety she knew it could fuel.

Some of the team Bambera had assembled for the transfer of the Child were familiar to her from Devesham. Rachel noticed how they kept an eye on her, suspicious at her stillness on the mezzanine that overlooked the bunker's central space. She sensed their wariness, as if they expected her to spring and snap at short notice. She had been known as one of the 'Gorgons' at Devesham, and her stern glances and clipped instructions had earned her a reputation that may have justified that. Unhappy at the thought that she might be predictable, she resisted any urges to behave like that, and simply watched.

When it came to the Child, her manner was a mask. She kept it in place to hold down the flood of compassion and sorrow that, if left unchecked, could overwhelm them both.

She felt a presence by her side, instinctively reassuring. 'Albert,' she greeted without turning.

'They're almost here,' he said gently.

They watched together as the curved cradle was completed. Its masses of wires, cables, tubes and pumps rested in ornate swirls around the empty space, as if waiting too.

'How much of my life has been leading to this?' Rachel asked quietly.

Markson took a deep breath. 'I'd take it as flattery. From what I know of Bambera and his plans, you and your husband are absolutely key. So, whatever you've been doing, it's earned you his highest respect.'

Rachel stifled an ironic laugh. 'But even you, Albert,' she said, turning to face him directly. 'You knew this was coming, and you didn't tell me.'

Markson had the good sense to lower his eyes in apology. 'I wanted to,' he said, and she could hear the earnest belief in his voice. 'But matters of national security... You know how it is. It was made clear to me what I had to do, and what the consequences might be if I didn't.'

When he didn't raise his eyes back to her, Rachel lowered her own gaze to try to meet his. 'Albert, what is it?' she urged, keeping her tone level so as not to frighten away whatever was reaching tentatively for the surface.

'It wasn't just my work that had attracted attention. There were other concerns about my possible involvement with foreign powers, and the potential that I could be... coerced... into doing so.'

Rachel could see the shame and embarrassment clouding his downturned features and recognised the pattern. 'Like Alan,' she said, taking hold of his arm.

Markson gathered himself, shaking his head and looking at her finally. 'We're decades on from Alan, but the fears are the same,' he explained in an urgent whisper, even though no one was near. 'My... preferences... make me an ideal target for blackmail by powers who would like to use my mind even as they condemned my soul. "Turing's Shadow", we call it. The lingering fear that people like us are automatically a danger to national security.'

Rachel gripped his arm more tightly, as much for herself as for him. 'You know, I entered science for a life of rationality and stability. If I'd known it would contain this much sadness, I might not have bothered. I'm sure there are easier lives.'

Markson placed his hand warmly over hers. 'You know that some of Alan's work has been harnessed in our adaptations for... the Child?'

Rachel was glad to see that he hesitated with the name. He

didn't want to dehumanize Judith... But Rachel knew they had no choice, in order to achieve their goal. She looked down at the berth into which the Child would nestle.

'Alan's dreams of a future harmony with machines and computers look a bit far away, currently.'

'They could be closer than you think.'

Rachel turned to question him, but stopped when one of the workers approached tentatively, caught between reluctance to interrupt and a need to make an announcement. 'Well, what is it?' she asked.

'Our arrival,' he replied carefully. 'She's here.'

The dampness in the air had hardened into a fog that refused to lift. It hung over the Thames and curled coldly around the bridges and banks. Buildings poked only their very tops out of the low cloud as if trying to peer beyond it, the lights below shining weakly and blurring amid tiny, floating droplets.

Ratcliffe watched his breath join the fog as he stood on Westminster Bridge, his eyes sweeping across the river and its two banks, the Houses of Parliament on one side, St Thomas' Hospital on the other. He took a few paces to his left, aligning himself equidistant between them, smiling at the symmetry.

With a nod, he acknowledged a new arrival to his right. The man was puffing from where he had hurried, his thin face red and drawn within a dark hood.

'This side, Professor Atkinson,' Ratcliffe told him, indicating that he should stand on the side nearer the hospital, keen to maintain his own position at the exact centre of the bridge.

'Mr Ratcliffe. Sorry I'm late.'

'You're just in time, Professor. We've timed the test to coincide with the bongs, for extra impact. Nothing like a good toll, eh?' Choosing to tell the time from the just-visible clock on the Elizabeth Tower rather than his Rolex Explorer II watch, he saw that there were just a few minutes remaining until midday.

'Aren't we a bit obvious, if we're found here watching?' Atkinson asked nervously.

'An eagle doesn't hide before it swoops down to feed, Professor, it basks in the open.'

'How confident are they that it'll work?'

'Very.'

The two men stared across the grey to the bulk of the hospital, its regimented windows glinting at intervals across its concrete structure.

'Any more news from Cambridge?' Ratcliffe asked, keen to use the remaining minutes wisely.

'Jensen's gone underground, as expected.'

'She must have an ally. Someone who can lead us to her.'

'I have my suspicions. Let me do some checking when I'm back there.'

Ratcliffe shifted his focus from the hospital to his companion. 'How does it feel, being back here?'

Atkinson greyed visibly as he thought of how to answer, hoping perhaps that the chimes of Big Ben would save him from having to. 'Bad memories,' he offered.

Ratcliffe nodded, knowing the thoughts he had triggered would lead him closer to acceptance and compliance. 'This is for your wife, then,' he said, watching the impact of each word on his face and in his eyes. 'Foreign doctors treating foreign patients, here of all places, while allowing her to suffer and die.' He glanced smoothly at his watch, seeing the second hand start its climb towards the midday moment, timing his words impeccably. 'We can't allow that to continue. Let's see them choose who they save when they can only save a few. And if they make the wrong choice...'

In the space of what he left unspoken, where he knew Atkinson's nightmares lurked, the bells began to chime.

Rachel stepped towards the Child, slowly. Markson remained behind.

The area was empty of all others where the workers had been asked to withdraw, their preparations complete.

She looked much as she had when Rachel had last seen her in Devesham. Her blank eyes stared ahead, beneath the last remaining strands of lank blonde hair. Her skin was grey, and her shrunken body sank down into the casing that held her in place and regulated her biological functions. Wires and cables draped around her shoulders and across the cream-coloured covering that preserved what little dignity remained.

Rachel moved closer and tried to align her eyes to the Child's. Even though they were unmoving, their focus seemed to slide away from all her attempts.

'Hello again, Judith,' she whispered.

Any hint of a lingering connection was absent. Her chest rose and fell calmly, untroubled by the reunion. Occasionally she would blink slowly, but Rachel knew that this was timed to the pulse of a tiny electric prompt to prevent her eyes from drying out completely. Her thoughts, Rachel guessed, were submerged within the depths of the numbers being fed directly into her brain, in patterns, sequences, and recursive formulas designed to keep her occupied and calm, buoyant in a steady stream of stimuli.

Markson stepped closer too, and Rachel could see in her peripheral vision his attempts to keep his face steady as the details of the Child's hybridity became clear. Rachel could tell his eyes were fixing on the places where the machine parts made their entry into the Child's body, which still seemed clumsy and roughly done. Some of the skin around the implants was reddening, and Rachel remembered how Allison had administered the soothing creams and balms to those parts, so gently. She made a mental note to find the creams and repeat the process.

'She seems to have accepted her new home well enough,' Markson whispered.

'We have a day or so before any new materials arrive from London,' Rachel told him. 'That gives us time to observe just how stable she is, which will give us a good control level. Any changes triggered by the new systems will be trackable from the base levels.'

'That's assuming nothing else interferes with the... experiment.'

Rachel nodded, looking around at the concrete walls of the bunker and suddenly wishing for some daylight. 'I guess that's why they've sealed us in here.'

'We've got the telephone, and the radio,' Markson reminded her.

'Which have been suspiciously quiet so far.'

'The Association had a busy day yesterday. Maybe they're all having a lay-in.'

Rachel smiled at him, allowing her eyes to leave the Child, forcing herself to adjust to the presence without having to focus entirely on it. 'We can but hope.'

Ratcliffe put a hand firmly on Atkinson's arm and squeezed. 'Stay calm,' he hissed.

Sirens wailed as police cars raced over the bridge towards the hospital. Their blue lights illuminated the area around the hospital in overlapping flashes, lighting the fog-laden air and smothering the South Bank in an aura of urgency.

At the centre of the strobing blue, St Thomas' Hospital sat stricken, a dark gash sliced through it where the power refused to return.

'That's not my wife's ward,' Atkinson growled. 'What have you done?'

'I told you to stay calm,' Ratcliffe urged, dialling up the threat in his voice. He rarely did this, so he knew it would shock the man into obeyance. Once he felt Atkinson's muscles harden into control, he spoke again in a return to the calm with which he liked to conduct himself. 'It's the children's ward.' Atkinson's arm twitched in response, then stilled again. 'We might as well get them to make the really tough choices.'

Atkinson stilled even further, his breath slowing as he took in the sight before him and the one imagined behind the walls. 'How will we know? It's probably chaos in there.'

'My men will report back. Porters can watch it all and no one even notices. Without their machines, they will have to move some of the children to the adult wards. There's little room as it is. Who gets the bed? Who gets the last remaining equipment?'

'You don't mean *who*. You mean *what colour*.' The accusation was level, without judgement or disdain.

Ratcliffe nodded. 'All the time there's enough to go around, we can't know what people really think. They don't even know themselves. They've had it easy for too long. Time for people to decide.'

'And if they make the wrong choice?' Ratcliffe could hear the temptation in Atkinson's voice.

'Well then, your favourite project comes into play.'

Atkinson licked his lips. 'Jensen shut me down. Without the funding I asked for, I haven't been able to refine the process.'

'That won't be a problem. We've got enough of our own

research from our contacts abroad. Carstairs has been co-ordinating it.'

Ratcliffe let Atkinson's arm go at last, and the man smoothed down the arm of his coat. 'You've done well,' he said.

Ratcliffe, admiring the man's bravery in making the judgement, positive though it was, flashed his easy smile. 'Things have moved on since my father's days. We've got a little more sophisticated.'

He watched Atkinson nod in acceptance, seeing the impact of the dreams dangling in front of him. He looked toward the hospital just in time to see the lights flicker and return where the darkness had been, and the whole hospital shift back to full power as the main supply returned. He checked his watch.

'Not bad. This experiment is over. Time to collate the results. But don't worry, Professor, there are plenty more experiments to come.'

Atkinson faced him, the blue lights of the emergency vehicles giving him a pulsing outline. 'I'll go back to Cambridge and await your instructions,' he said, before moving off towards the South Bank.

Taking in the view from the bridge one last time, Ratcliffe too moved away and disappeared into the fog.

'I think we spoke too soon,' Markson announced, placing the portable radio on the desk next to where Rachel sat applying cream into the puckered skin of the Child.

Rachel jumped at the noise, and marvelled at the stillness of her companion in contrast.

The voice on the radio continued its report. '*...what seems to be a further power cut even as investigations into the cause of yesterday's continue. This more localised event has affected St Thomas' Hospital in London. Reports are coming in that not only was the supply to the whole hospital affected, but a failure of the back-up system meant a total loss of power for part of the hospital. We are awaiting confirmation of which areas were affected by this total blackout. Witnesses are reporting chaotic scenes as patients were moved to areas with power...*'

'It's them, isn't it?' Rachel said, realising only afterwards that she was addressing the question to the Child, who of course did not respond.

A new urgency in the voice and the stumbling non-fluency of a troubled presenter drew them back to listening. '*...unconfirmed reports that it was the children's ward most badly affected by the loss of power. I stress that currently... yes... currently these reports are unconfirmed by officials. Likewise, we are yet to hear of any casualties... any patients adversely affected by the power cut to, as we're reporting, London's St Thomas' Hospital on the South Bank...*'

'Should we contact Bambera?' Markson asked.

Rachel shook her head. 'He'll have enough to be dealing with. They'll be in touch soon enough I'm sure.'

Markson nodded and returned to his own work, familiarising himself with the Child's support equipment, while Rachel focused on the task of soothing the painful looking connections between skin and metal.

The radio continued its urgent, unfolding tale. Rachel drifted in and out, remembering the noise of the radio quietly in the bedroom she shared with Ian when he couldn't sleep, when its familiar drone soothed him out of his nightmarish remembrances, and further back to her work on the radios in the war that still haunted them both. Human voice, filtered through microphone, radiowave, and speaker, the hiss of static infusing it, merging it with the sound of machine...

Coming back into awareness suddenly, Rachel looked up from the Child's wrist, where she was rubbing the cream into a cannular connection. Eyes stared down, directly focused upon her, as if in recognition.

CHAPTER SEVEN

Thursday – Beneath St Pancras, London. 2.15pm

GILMORE MADE sure his formation with Trevor and Dillon held as they trudged through the last portion of tunnel before their promised destination beneath the British Library.

The initial rush of adrenaline from the retrieval of the first artefact had faded into a focused disquiet; he was tired, but not able to drop his guard. He wanted Allison and this Order of Albion ahead where he could see them.

Of course, he needed them to lead the way too, although he pushed that more practical reason to the back of his mind. He hated feeling beholden to strangers. Only his past connection to Allison kept him from refusing to play ball at all. How strong that connection was given the passing of time and circumstance, even he did not know.

'I feel a bit redundant,' Trevor said quietly through one side of his mouth, leaning in so the others couldn't hear and making it obvious to Gilmore that he was feeling something similar. 'They seem pretty adept at looking after themselves.'

'Don't you even think about pulling out,' Gilmore whispered back, emulating the conspiratorial stance. 'You're not leaving us here with this lot.'

He was slightly startled by his sense of trust in a man he didn't even know existed a day ago. He expressed so many mannerisms and vocal inflections that reminded him of Hannah, and he had already come to appreciate Trevor's instinctive protection of Dillon and easy way with him; he envied that even. Hannah had been there for him, and now Trevor was there for his son. He already owed the Gordons so much. He would have to find a way to repay them.

The tunnel continued to slope downwards in its final approach. Gilmore noticed the dissipation of the modern wartime struts and ribs that characterised the tunnels under Holborn. Somewhere along their journey they had merged into tunnels that looked and smelled abandoned and neglected, and, as he felt the pull of gravity dragging his footsteps in a sloping trajectory, he felt as if they were entering a much older world.

Allison took the role of the keeper of the codes, although this time the locking mechanism had been grafted on to a gnarled wooden door that seemed blacker than even the lack of light explained, as if it had been scorched.

'Most of this place is built from the remains of the Albion Mills,' Bes explained, having stepped back alongside Gilmore without him noticing and making him jump. 'Including the door.'

'Is that where you got your name?' Trevor asked.

'Not just our name. Our entire purpose comes from that place.'

Before Trevor or Gilmore could ask any more, Allison pushed the heavy door open, revealing the chamber beyond. Low levels of electric light illuminated the circular space, coming from lamps and light fittings from all across the century, as if each new visitor had brought their own from whichever decade they were living in. Around the walls, blackened beams of wood arced upwards to the stone ceiling while huge cogs and wheels were studded across the walls. Gilmore reached out to the nearest wall and touched one of the towering poles and the metal struts that splayed out from it like ribs from a spine.

'Dad, what is all that?' Dillon asked, his face alight with curiosity and awe.

'If it's from an old mill, I think it's what they used to grind the flour.'

'But what happened to it? Why is it here?'

'Hopefully we'll find out.' He ruffled his son's hair, and smiled as the sketchbook and pencils were retrieved from deep within the now-battered rucksack and, without any need for comfort, Dillon sat in the dust and started recording what he could see. Gilmore continued to take in the relics and artefacts that decorated all available surfaces. Masks and helmets lurked amid the remnants of the Mills, impassive faces with blank eyes staring down at them. And were those limbs, disembodied and hanging like trophies?

Allison drew alongside Gilmore while Trevor was shown deeper into the base by Saunders and Bes. She gave him a sad smile containing the traces of that old connection. 'Our countermeasure work continues, it seems, Group Captain,' she said with the dry humour and gentle mocking he knew of old.

'Allison, are you sure about these people? This place?'

Allison guided him to a pair of old armchairs, dusty and heavily patterned. They took one each. He felt the soft invite of the comfort clashing with his rigid alertness.

'I do trust them, Ian,' she said. 'Bambera has brought together the most extraordinary minds and resources for this fight.'

'Bambera,' Gilmore breathed. 'Quite the chess master. I've never quite trusted those who can spin that many plates while looking so spick and span for the crowds. So why this lot? Why here? What's all this Albion business?'

He watched her carefully preparing an answer, wondering whether she thought of herself as one of them.

'The Order was set up a long time ago to keep track of human endeavours to... make changes... to our basic nature. To guard against adaptations that could distort us out of shape and put us all in danger.'

The spectre of the Child rose up in Gilmore's mind. He guessed Allison was alluding to it, and he remembered the unresolved ethical debates about it between her and Rachel and its use in the Devesham rocket mission.

'What danger exactly? You were all for those adaptations when they served a purpose.'

'The Order will always seek to monitor the balance between advantage and threat to the things most important to our nature. Our use of the Child had noble intent, and still does. To preserve something inside her worth saving. The very thing she was chosen for. The technology we're seeking now must not fall into the hands of people who would use it with no concern for the humanity of the subject, or those who would suffer if they unleashed its full potential.'

Gilmore felt his heart quicken at Allison's wavering words.

'Are you saying they are trying to make another Child?'

Allison visibly swallowed down her fears. 'That's why we have to trust the Order, Ian. They know that technology must advance, but they want to protect what makes us human above all else.'

'And what is that exactly?' Gilmore asked testily.

Bes had again drifted close, and stood between them. The hood was down revealing short white hair framing the lined, intense face. Gilmore still had no clearer idea of her exact age, race... Although he realised he had settled on thinking of her as a woman. Her eyes remained fixed, as before, not on Gilmore, but on Dillon, who continued to sketch obliviously on the ground nearby.

'Imagination, Group Captain Gilmore,' she said. 'Imagination.'

Ratcliffe enjoyed walking against the tide of cold, worried-looking people who hurried in the opposite direction without even noticing him.

Some of them brushed against him accidentally in their urgency, but he let them go, this time. Only when a young Pakistani mother struggling to keep hold of two small children bumped into him did he stop. He stared her down into a frightened apology, allowing his bright smile to darken into a threatening smirk. No one else noticed, or challenged him, or helped her.

He could almost hear the clamour racing through the air on radio waves to be broadcast on emergency updates. The tension in the air was thick, making the cold feel sticky and penetrating. He had done that.

News of the hospital blackout was spreading, and with it the hyper-stimulated imagination of what might come next, and where this could lead.

It was already late afternoon, and the darkness of a winter night was not far away. Tonight, he would leave that natural darkness to do his work. Let them watch for the slightest flicker of their lamps and huddle in the warmth he lent them. Let them realise how fragile they really are. No more spectacle was needed for now. Their own nightmares, waking and sleeping, would do the rest.

The Shoreditch warehouse was alive with activity. The fear of the outside world sharpened into excitement and confidence among the men. Word of their attack on the hospital had spread there too, and each man linked to the network felt personally proud even though they had contributed nothing to it. It was a collective power they felt, guilt and triumph by Association, they might say.

Ratcliffe found Hareward at his monitor bank and grasped his hand tightly.

'It worked, my friend,' he said proudly. 'And for longer than we thought it would.'

Hareward allowed himself a brief smile. 'The dampeners are definitely improving.'

'You say that like they're doing it themselves. Take the credit, man.'

'Boss, there's something you should know about today's other mission.' Hareward's voice lowered and deepened. Ratcliffe could tell he was nervous, keen to bask briefly in the success but worried what failure might bring.

'The Archive? Did the dampeners not work there too?'

'It wasn't the tech that was the problem, it was the men.'

'They were three of our best.'

Hareward took a deep breath. 'They weren't good enough, Boss. Two of them haven't returned, and our sources say Bambera has them.'

Ratcliffe felt his fists clench. 'They'll follow orders. They knew the risks. They'll find a way out.'

'Of the Ministry?'

'Of life.' Ratcliffe shook his head in disdain, mentally rehearsing the punishment he would exact on the men's families if they didn't go through with their instructions to self-terminate on capture. He hoped the description of it he had left them with would spur them on to do the right thing.

'It means we haven't been able to enhance the boy as we'd hoped. We'll still be reliant on the physical dampeners until we do.'

Ratcliffe allowed the failure to sit along the day's earlier success and find equilibrium. Uncomfortable at the emptiness of balance, he probed further. 'What about the next artefact? Any more progress on that?'

'There's better news there. The third man stayed back. Luckily he's the one we put there a while ago, so he's had plenty of time to dig around. He's befriended some of the older women who worked down there in the War.'

'I don't want to know about his proclivities,' Ratcliffe said without humour. 'Just what he's found.'

'I'll show you. It's all noted down. It looks like we'll be heading into Jewish territory.'

Ratcliffe smiled ironically. 'First, let me see him.'

Hareward's features became shadowed as they always did when faced with their creation. Ratcliffe followed him to the deepest part of the warehouse, through locked doors and into a sealed chamber at its heart.

There, in a cradle of cables and thick, pulsing tubes, sat within a throne-like construction of dark metal studded with silver bolts, was a little boy. His arms gripped the side panels in the pose of a king, but his face stared as blankly as a fool's. A few strands of greasy hair fell from under a dark helmet, within which Ratcliffe knew wires and tendrils were reaching inside his brain.

'There's our boy,' Ratcliffe whispered in admiration. 'There's our Child.'

Dr Saunders pulled two battered wooden chairs over for himself and Trevor, joining Gilmore and Allison while Bes remained standing.

'Bes, the group captain deserves something a bit more tangible as an explanation. He's been dragged down here with his son, and he needs to know he can trust us.'

Bes nodded in assent and Gilmore could read a mutual understanding in their partnership.

'Are there many more in your Order?' Trevor asked.

Saunders smiled at Bes, who did not smile back. 'It's just us here now,' he replied. 'There are others around the country and some abroad too, but the network has diffused somewhat since the War.'

'And why here?' Gilmore had questions lined up. He glanced over to Dillon, grateful that the boy was instinctively averse to people sitting around and talking. He had shifted position and was clearly now sketching the chamber from a new perspective, counting the teeth on a giant cog and transferring the detail to his drawings.

'Easy access to the Libraries is helpful,' Saunders started.

'Libraries plural?' Gilmore noted the small doors at intervals around the chamber, wondering if each led to a different one.

'There's the biggest and best on our doorstep of course,' Saunders continued. 'The British Library's tunnel network not only acts as the biggest archive of published material in the West, but a hub through which the other hidden parts of the city can be accessed. Then there's the Library of Saint John the Beheaded, and others.'

Gilmore saw Bes start a little at the name of the other location, as if they were unused to sharing such information. Saunders had noticed too and carried on regardless, keen to make good his promise to explain properly.

'But I thought it was technology you were after,' Gilmore said, 'not history. I can't imagine poor Beheaded Saint John having much in stock to help with that?'

'Humanity evolves in cycles, Group Captain,' Bes interjected. 'We've been here before and will be again, around and around. There's an urge that seems to have existed as long as we have, an instinct to meld with the machines we make. Sometimes it's our own inventions that lead us there. Sometimes we make use of things left behind from more advanced... visitors who have got there before us.'

It was Gilmore's turn to start, and he found himself instinctively looking around for Rachel, even though he knew she wasn't there. Instead, he found Allison, her eyes locking on to his and taking him back eleven years to another cold November...

'The Order tries to understand this urge and where it has risen up through our history,' Saunders continued. 'Our founder saw first-hand the efforts of one particularly precarious moment, when we came close to losing ourselves completely. He taught us that the imagination must be protected at all costs, that if we lose it to the machine, humanity as we know it ends.'

Gilmore remembered, amid the smoke and unnatural fire of that November, talk of the alien technology that had spread its destruction. He visualised the Child, the spider at the centre of a web held in place by the men of Ratcliffe's gangs. He remembered Rachel explaining that the technology was using the girl specifically for her imagination, harnessing its uniquely playful and inventive quality to solve problems its own limited logical pathways couldn't.

'But what has this got to do with the Association?' Trevor took the chance to ask his own question.

'In the original Child, the imagination was slaved to the machine, the Battle Computer. That imagination remains active, salvageable...'

'Useful,' Gilmore interrupted bitterly.

Saunders ignored him. 'The Association have remnants of that original technology, but none of the intellect of the aliens. We know they are working on the creation of a new Child with similar capacities, hoping it will be able to reach out and control the power systems of the whole country. They will have little care for the imagination of that new Child, they will only care for the vast processing powers of the human brain. And then there's what they'll choose to do with that power, the people they'll remove or destroy. Imagination feeds on new experiences, on diversity and difference. Wipe that out, and our collective imagination dies a slow death, starved of stimulus and bound in an ever-narrowing tunnel of conformity.'

In his own imagination, Gilmore could see one of the creatures he had fought through that chill air all those years ago. It rolled calmly over the cobbles of a London street, through the rubble of the last War and that new one. He stood before it, holding firm as it came closer and closer. He stared at his own reflection in the tight circle of its eye.

'They wouldn't need to invade,' he said. 'We'd already be like them.'

CHAPTER EIGHT

Thursday – Beneath St Pancras, London. 7.35pm

DILLON ARRANGED the last of the contents of his rucksack in the den he had constructed with the help of Trevor. An ornately patterned cloth, draped over salvaged metal poles that had been propped in one of the corners, formed the walls of his space.

He knew his dad had given him the task of den-building to keep him busy and calm, but he was grateful too. It felt safe when he entered it, an old battery-powered lantern by a tatty old pillow, his sketchbook and pencils carefully laid to the side of an equally ragged sleeping bag, and his lucky bullet placed exactly where he could grasp it should he need to if he woke in the night.

His looked over at his dad, still in one of the armchairs, talking intently with Allison and staring at the box they had retrieved from the Archive. He had offered to join Dillon in the den for their 'kip' as he called it, but Dillon had felt the urge to take control of at least one part of the experience and keep the space to himself. *Had his face fallen at that?* Dillon wondered, looking back. And had his response been more clipped than usual when he had asked Trevor to help him build the den? *Parents are hard work*, he decided.

Yawning, but not yet tired enough to sleep, Dillon plucked up courage to circle gradually towards Bes. She was seated, cross-legged on the ground, face peaceful, not asleep but resting somehow. Curious to see if he could work out how old she was, he looked from the corner of his eyes as he passed, first one way that the next, trying to see if the shape of the shoulders or the number of lines on her face would reveal something definitive. He was sure he was being discreet.

'Can I help you, young man?' Bes asked, eyes remaining unopened.

Dillon paused his investigative rotation, attempting to divert his attention swiftly to one of the strange metal helmets hanging in one of the storage units. 'I was just trying to work out... what this is,' he explained, pointing at the helmet and certain that he had successfully covered himself.

'You were staring at me,' Bes countered.

Dillon felt his cheeks redden, imagining them shining his true intentions like a beacon through the gloom of the chamber. 'I'm... sorry... I was just curious.'

Bes opened her eyes and raised gracefully to a standing position. 'Curiosity is the fuel of the soul. Never apologise for it.'

Dillon thought he could see a smile twinkling in her eyes, even if it wasn't appearing on her lips. He relaxed. 'What were you doing?' he asked, selecting the question diplomatically from the many he wanted answers to.

'Reflecting on what's been, preparing for what's to come. Useful, in these moments of calm, for we never know how long they will last.'

Dillon replied with a 'hmmm', unable to find words he felt would do the job of a reply, feeling, as he often did when listening to his parents, as if the meaning of things was just beyond his reach. It reminded him of the jump from wall to wall in the back garden, a gulf he would manage one day, but not yet.

'You must have something you do, when you're worried about something?'

Dillon thought about this, grateful that Bes had adjusted her words and tone to something he could grasp on to. 'I have a bullet,' he replied, deciding that if he revealed that, perhaps Bes would explain more about herself in reply, an exchange of truths.

'Well, I wasn't expecting that,' Bes said amid a chuckle. 'Show me.'

Dillon raced to his den, a new energy animating his tired limbs, retrieved the bullet, jogged back and held it out to Bes with pride.

'Do you know where this comes from?'

'Dad got it for me. It's from the First World War. From France.'

Bes nodded sadly. 'And how does it help?'

'I hold it. It makes me feel safe. Like Dad is protecting me.'

'Do you know about the War this comes from? What those men went through?'

'Some of it. Me and Dad, we talk about the battles and the uniforms and the weapons. Mum tells him off for being too gruesome sometimes. Then he stops, like there's stuff he doesn't want to say, and tells me we'll talk about it later.'

'And you know what the bullet was meant to do?'

Dillon nodded.

'It doesn't trouble you?'

He looked at the bullet, gleaming gold in the flickering lights of the chamber, feeling its warmth against his skin. 'No,' he said with a certainty that took him by surprise. 'I know what it *was*, but it's something different now.'

Bes stared at him, her eyes shining as if the light from the bullet was reflecting in them. 'Transformation,' she said. 'From war to peace.'

Dillon said nothing. In the shared silence as they both looked upon the bullet in his outstretched hand, there again was that thing, that *something*, on the edge of understanding but just out of reach. He remembered the last time he had tried that jump from wall to wall, the thrill of not knowing if he would make it but wanting to try it anyway. Standing on the edge, arms out for balance, poised.

Gilmore scanned the chamber, wondering what Dillon was talking about with Bes. He shot a look over at Trevor, who was also watching the pair from the corner in which he was talking with Saunders. Trevor nodded in reply, clearly sensing the concern, and to Gilmore's relief he went to join them. He felt himself relax whenever he knew Trevor was overseeing the boy, and with that distraction resolved, he turned his attention back to Allison and the box.

She picked it up and tilted it into the light. 'I'm just concerned that if we try and open it without having arranged the pieces correctly, we may lose what's inside.'

'You think Rachel might know the answer?'

'She worked with the man, so there's a good chance.'

Gilmore remembered his wife's face whenever the memory of Turing came up, either in their shared recollections or if she saw or heard some mention of him on television or radio. A sadness would fill her eyes every time.

'Well, she'll be expecting a call anyway. She insisted on speaking to Dillon before he sleeps.'

Allison nodded, looking hopeful.

'Do you want to speak to her?' Gilmore asked as he rose to cross the chamber. 'I'm sure she'll be happy to know you're back on board.'

'Maybe next time,' Allison replied with diplomatic politeness. 'Let's get this mystery solved first.'

Gilmore nodded, accepting that he would never really understand the tension between the women and the debates they'd had about the care and fate of the Child. Still, he hoped one day they would return to the easier relationship they had once shared.

As he reached the corner where Dr Saunders was waiting, it seemed the man had anticipated his needs. 'We're fully connected down here,' he explained, pushing an old beige Bakelite telephone towards him. 'I'll leave you to it.'

Gilmore dialled the number Bambera had given him for the bunker, presuming that the line and both ends were safe from tapping. After a number of flat dialling sounds, just as disappointment was starting to settle, he heard the line click and a familiar voice say sternly, 'Yes?'

'Well, that's a welcoming telephone manner,' Gilmore said, unable to stop the smile from spreading across his face and into his words. 'What a way to greet your husband.'

'Ian!' Rachel's voice betrayed her genuine relief.

'That's better,' he said, wanting so much to be able to hold her at that moment. 'I'm here.'

'Are you well? And Dillon? Where are you?'

'We're both safe and well,' he said, conscious still of the possibilities that someone could be listening despite Bambera's efforts. 'You know how things are, perhaps best not to be too precise. But we're all right.'

'Thank goodness. Have you heard about the hospital?'

'We have.' Saunders had reported the news late that

afternoon, which remained confused and panicked. 'Any updates?'

'Well, there haven't been any more cuts yet tonight, but it's all the radio's been talking about. People are terrified.'

'Casualties?' he asked, echoing the dreaded question he had been forced to ask so many times in a past he had hoped had been left behind.

'They're not saying. I think they want to contain the panic. Albert thinks there must have been some though. The hospitals are so dependent on power now, especially with some of the newer machinery. We've become too reliant, Ian, it's not a good situation to have allowed to happen.'

'It's a bit late for that now, dear.' Gilmore suppressed a shudder, remembering the nature of the Order and their warnings about the instinct to depend on technology. It was one thing hearing them talk about it in their semi-mystical tones, another to think of the fallout unfolding for real in the streets and buildings of London. 'Let's focus on something we can influence. We found the first artefact, and from what Bambera told us, it's something that could be useful if you're to communicate with the Child.'

The line went silent for a moment. Then Rachel said, 'I think I already have been.'

'What do you mean?'

'It's nothing really. Just the occasional hint that something is there, inside her, reaching out.'

Gilmore shivered again. 'The thing is, it's locked away. In a box. With a pattern on the top that looks like a kind of key. A puzzle. Allison's worried that if we try to open it without the correct sequence achieved, the contents might be compromised.'

'Allison's there?' Gilmore noticed the hardness return to her voice. 'I should have guessed Bambera would involve her too.'

'The box, love. What do you think?'

'It's from the Turing Archive, I believe? Albert's filled me in on the basics. Describe the pattern.'

Filled with a new confidence at the sound of her voice and a certainty he hoped would yield access, Gilmore pulled the box towards him. 'It's somewhere between stripes and spots. It's all a jumble though.'

'It won't be once you've moved some of the panels around.

It's a Turing Pattern,' she said as if he'd missed something obvious. 'A reaction-diffusion form of morphogenesis.'

'For the simpleton in the room, please, dear.'

'It looks random, but like a zebra's stripes, it's guided by a mathematical formula. In six moves you should be able to make the pattern complete, so that every stripe lines up around the spots.'

'Why six?'

'Six states generate a Turing Pattern. Don't over-think it, dear, just clear your mind and move the pieces, making sure you only match up the stripes rather than the dots. If you only do that, you'll release the mechanism in six moves.'

'And if I get it wrong?'

'Whatever's inside is drenched in acid and rendered useless.'

'Oh.' Gilmore turned and to his relief saw Allison watching him nervously. He waved her over frantically. When she was near, he mouthed the words 'Turing Pattern!' urgently to her.

'Ian?' came Rachel's voice from the telephone.

'Yes, dear, sorry, I'm just doing it.'

Allison's face was still creased in confusion. Gilmore repeated his exaggerated mouthing of the phrase, and was rewarded by an eventual recognition. She opened her palms and mouthed back, 'Of course!' Nodding, she set to work.

'Is someone there with you, Ian?'

'Hold on, dear, just a few more moves.'

Checking with Allison as each piece of the puzzle slid into position, spurred on by her nodding, and cautious when she held her hand up to correct him, he took a deep breath and completed the sequence. The pattern revealed was beautiful in its simplicity, as if it had always been there, just out of sight, waiting for them to know it. A satisfying click of springs being released greeted them, and the top of the box opened.

'Ian, did it work?' Rachel's voice was becoming insistent. 'God this is frustrating. I should be there. That's Alan's work...'

'It's worked,' Gilmore announced.

'Tell me what's inside.'

'It looks like a mesh of some kind,' he described, watching as Allison lifted the contents carefully from the darkness of the cavity inside the box. 'Yes, like it would go over the crown of a head. Fine wires, clustering above the ears as if that's where—'

'They enter the brain,' Rachel completed.

'Do you think it'll help the Child?'

'If Bambera and Albert are right about its potential, yes. It could translate the jumble of her thoughts to allow us to communicate clearly. Rather than inputting code for war, we can just use words. We could be giving her a voice again.'

'How do we get it to you?'

'Bambera is due a visit, first to you and then to us.'

'I see. His movements are becoming as mysterious as a well-known deity.'

'Is there anything else in the box? Some clue as to what's next? Alan would often leave a credit to the source of his inspiration, like a thank you. Maybe a note, a name perhaps, or someone who helped develop it?'

Gilmore felt around into the corners of the box. Something soft was laying on the bottom. His fingers traced its outline as he pulled it out, half-recognising the shape as he revealed it to the light.

'Ian?'

'It's a star, Rachel,' he said carefully.

She was silent for a moment before asking, 'Yellow?'

Gilmore nodded, even though he knew she couldn't see. 'Yes,' he confirmed.

'Anything else on it? Check the back.'

He turned the cloth over. 'Black stitching. Letters. ECZ.'

Rachel was silent again.

'Initials?' he suggested.

'Could the Z be the number two?' she asked finally.

He looked more closely, feeling the stitches. 'Yes! There's a slight curve at the top. EC2.'

'First Turing, now this,' she said, a darkness in her voice. 'Maybe that's why Bambera really chose us.'

'What do you mean, darling?' Gilmore asked, concerned.

'It's a postal code, Ian. The Old Jewry is there, where my people first settled in London. Alan must be attributing his work to someone from the Jewish community. Or something from the Holocaust.'

Dillon pulled the sleeping bag over himself, wrapping enough of it together into a bulk he could cuddle in place of his absent teddy bear.

He also held on to the sound of his mum's voice, tense and swift though it had been when he had taken the phone receiver, hot from his dad's grip, and spoken to her.

His dad, and then Trevor, had reassured him that sleep was the best option for the rest of the night, and that nothing else would happen. He had nodded a goodnight to Bes, who had nodded, almost as low as a bow, in return.

Just as he was drifting off to the soothing pattern of cogs and wheels that turned behind his closed eyes, he caught his name being spoken. Returning to alertness, the voices of his dad and Allison became just about audible, as if he had turned up the radio a little louder to turn faint babble into distinct words.

'She doesn't want him knowing about it,' his dad said, completing whatever he had started that had mentioned Dillon.

'It's his heritage,' Allison replied. The word was only just familiar to him. 'But I can understand why it might be too painful for her.'

'She says she wants him unburdened by that part of his family history. I try to understand, but she finds it difficult to talk about.'

Dillon leaned closer to the overlapping flaps of cloth that formed the doorway to his den, listening even more carefully.

'Did she say what she thinks Turing got hold of?' Allison asked. 'Presumably something that enabled him to create the coding interface.'

His dad did not reply at first, and for a moment Dillon held his breath, wondering if his eavesdropping had somehow become known. His dad did have an uncanny ability to know when he was up to mischief.

'She's heard rumours of experiments, from the Holocaust.'

That word, wreathed in shadow, had lurked at the edges of his awareness for years.

'We'll need to get in touch with members of the community,' Dad continued. 'She's given us some leads. I'll have to leave Dillon here for this one. Rachel made me promise.'

'What were the experiments?' Allison asked.

Dillon continued to listen. They spoke of things he had never conceived of before. The word and all it contained started to unfold, skeletal figures peering from its darkness, faces contorted in pain or just staring blankly at the horror of the things they had seen. His father and Allison spoke of those horrors, and he listened, his breath quickening, his fists clenching, feeling moment by moment as if he were changing into something from which he would never turn back.

CHAPTER NINE

Friday – Beneath Farringdon, London. 8.15am

THE TUNNELS started to change again as Gilmore and his two companions neared their objective.

As they drew closer to the City itself, their surroundings became more natural, the manmade struts and pale electric lights dissolving into plain rock and darkness.

'Keep your eye out for Roman finds,' Saunders told him.

'Could they be useful?' Gilmore asked swiftly in reply. 'Surely the Romans weren't into all this human-machine fusion business too?'

'No, Ian,' Allison clarified in her gently teasing way. 'He just means we're around some of the oldest colonised parts of London. They discovered a temple to Mithras not far away.'

Saunders reached out and let his hand drift gently over the smoothed rock of the tunnel wall. 'Bes says this area has always attracted worship and mystery.'

'She would,' Gilmore muttered. He was already anxious about Dillon, who hadn't been himself in the brief moments they spent together before he had to leave. He remembered gently opening the cloth of the boy's makeshift tent, expecting to see that peaceful face, which would usually light up with tired welcome as he woke. Instead, Dillon's eyes had already been open, staring upwards from shadowed eye-sockets. The boy looked as if he had aged since that last teatime they had shared together not even two days before.

He's just tired, he heard Rachel reassure him in his mind. That was her answer whenever their generally happy boy was in a grumpy mood. He hoped it was only that. He had remained sullen and uncommunicative, only expressing any of his usual affection in the tightness of the hug he gave Gilmore before he left. Trevor would look after Dillon, he was confident in that. Maybe he was getting to the stage where he would want to chat with someone other than his father if he was worried.

Conscious that neither Saunders nor Allison had expanded on Bes' odd nature and resigned to having to worry about Dillon later, Gilmore shook his head to clear his mind and focus on the task in hand.

'Tell me more about our contact,' Allison said, drawing alongside. 'What else did Rachel say about her?'

'Old family friend, apparently. Her father was Rabbi Goldsmith. Rachel still talks of her time with him from when she was observant. He taught her much.'

'She's a woman of faith as well as science, then?' Saunders asked.

Bristling a little at the attempt to define her in such simple terms, Gilmore nevertheless found himself smiling, wondering how best to describe her. 'She's a woman like no other,' he settled on.

'And this Rhoda,' Allison probed, 'how can she help?'

'Rachel said she's the keeper of the community's archives. When Rachel's family and the others arrived before the War, or afterwards, they sometimes brought family heirlooms, records, connections to the homes they'd left. They were entrusted to the Rabbi, and his family would act as custodians. They were often hidden below ground for protection.'

Allison and Saunders were listening thoughtfully. 'Imagine what the Association would do if they knew of these stashes,' Saunders pondered.

'I'm sure they suspect. Rachel said there are frequent raids on the synagogues, masked as mindless vandalism but seeming to be seeking things out.'

'Could they have the same lead as us do you think?' Allison asked. 'Could the Association be heading in the same direction?'

Gilmore noticed how Saunders tensed in preparation at the prospect. He had confidence in the man's fighting ability and sheer strength. Nonetheless, he patted his Browning for comfort too.

They said no more until they reached their destination.

When Rhoda approached them through the gloom of the tunnels, it was as though she knew exactly what to expect and was not surprised at all.

The welcome was not warm, but professional. She looked each of them up and down in turn, nodding in confirmation. She was a stout woman, a little older than Rachel, Gilmore observed, but her hair still dark and pulled back neatly.

'Rachel told you we were coming?' Gilmore asked as she swept away back down the tunnel as if expecting them to follow without being told.

'Oh, we've been waiting for you for a long time,' she replied without turning back. 'You, or someone like you. One side, or the other, or both.'

'What do you mean?' Allison jogged to try to come alongside the swiftly marching woman.

Gilmore increased his own pace and shared a confused look with Saunders as he did the same.

'You think we don't know what we possess?' Rhoda stopped abruptly, forcing the three followers to do the same. 'You think we are simple hoarders of treasures of which we are ignorant?'

'Not at all,' Gilmore said placatingly. 'It's us who could do with a bit more to go on.'

She strode on again, leading them further down into the depths of the stone tunnels, past gently flickering bulbs that continued to become further spaced out as they went, allowing the darkness in the spaces in between to seem bolder.

Rhoda stopped them at a junction. At last, she turned and addressed them directly. 'My apologies,' she said, her voice kinder but still strained. 'Now the time has come, I feel... the significance of the moment... more than I thought I would.'

'What can you tell us about the artefact?' Allison asked.

'It has been my family's duty to preserve much. The box in question is not old, not compared to much that we guard, but its journey has been a particularly troubling one. Only one person has been allowed access to it since it arrived in our care almost thirty years ago.'

'Turing?' Gilmore asked.

Rhoda nodded. 'We trusted him, as your knowledge of him

and his work means we must trust you. And Rachel... We remember Rachel fondly.' She looked intently at Gilmore for a moment, and he felt a silent accusation at having perhaps stolen her away from her origins. 'Our promise to Alan dictated that we would only open the box for those who could read his patterns and follow his signs. He warned us that many others would come looking. I've kept his secret from my own community, my own family even, in case those within it might want it for the wrong reasons.' Her face seemed clouded.

Saunders reached out a hand and gently supported Rhoda's arm. Gilmore watched in admiration of the easy compassion, seemingly at odds with his bearing, but all the more powerful for it. 'You can trust us,' he said, his deep voice sincere and concerned.

Rhoda met his eyes and spoke as if to him alone. 'I know. Others of your Order have contacted us over the decades to warn about the darkness that gathers again. It follows us from country to country, it seems.'

Gilmore rallied himself, cursing his impatience even as he spoke, knowing he might disrupt the pace at which she wanted to reveal what they needed. 'Rachel told us its likely origins. Experiments from the... concentration camps. Some kind of technology, an attempt to merge machine parts to the body?'

'Yet more Nazi evil,' Allison breathed.

Rhoda gave a mirthless laugh and turned her attention to Allison. 'As usual, the presumption of victimhood,' she said with weighty judgement.

'Then tell us,' Gilmore urged.

'The artefact is not something that was done *to* us, but done *by* us. It was a painkiller. An... implant... for here.' She indicated the top of her head, jabbing fingers through her thick grey hair. 'Our doctors designed it in secret, in the camps, to help us survive the torments. It was meant to work with something else, which could even have saved us from the worst of those places. Something from much earlier back—'

'Mother,' came a warning voice from the darkness of the tunnel.

Gilmore and the others swung around to face the direction of the voice, and he took a defensive stance, his Browning swiftly poised.

'Jacob!' she said in genuine surprise. 'What are you doing here?'

'Stopping you from betraying us all.' A tall young man stepped forward into the light, flanked by two others. He held aloft a wooden box, inscribed with intricate patterns. His two companions had an arm raised each, aiming small handguns at the group.

'Don't be ridiculous, son,' Rhoda said in fury. 'How many times have I told you? When the time comes, we have to release it.'

'It's already too late for that, Mother,' Jacob said with confidence, and he held the box out to her. A key was sticking out of the lock.

Rhoda blinked in realisation. 'I was only to retrieve the key when I was sure about them, which I am.'

'I've saved you the trouble. You checked it last night after your phone call. I followed you.'

'Look here, now,' Gilmore said, stepping forward and letting the three arrivals know he too was armed. 'Perhaps we can talk about this. Negotiate.'

Jacob shook his head. 'We're handing the artefact over to our associates.' Gilmore's eyes narrowed at the word. 'They've promised to use it for what it was intended. Our defence. No one will be able to hurt us again.'

'How long have you been planning this?' Rhoda asked, sounding beaten.

'Not long. We were approached a little while ago and told to expect interest from outsiders.' Jacob sounded sorrowful in his explanation.

Allison stepped forward to join Gilmore. 'The people you're dealing with, they're just a new iteration of the ones who persecuted you before. They're using you and will turn on you as soon as they have what you can give them.'

Jacob looked guiltily at Allison, his eyes flicking to his mother and away again as if in shame. 'This time we're not the target,' he said. 'You think we don't know what they want? You think we haven't checked? We know they're going for the blacks. We get protection if we help.'

The tunnel fell into an eerie silence as Jacob's words sank in.

A blur of motion broke the frozen moment. Saunders had used the focus to prepare himself, and now he was rushing towards Jacob, dodging around him and behind, turning in an almost balletic arc and crouching to kick his two bodyguards' legs from under them. Jacob turned in confusion.

Gilmore raised his pistol. 'Hand over the artefact, young man,' he instructed.

'Use the device!' Jacob shouted angrily, not in reply to Gilmore but as instruction to his friend.

Quicker than even Saunders could stop him, one of the men brandished a black box. In the frantic seconds before the device did its work, Gilmore recognised it from the Kingsway tunnels. He had just enough time to shout, 'Down!' before total darkness fell.

By the time the light returned, all trace of the three young men was gone.

Saunders was disembowelling the dampener device angrily. As its baleful influence faded, the electric lights flickered back on shakily, recovering from the assault on their circuits. Allison was crouching next to Rhoda, who had fallen to her knees and now looked utterly bereft.

'I'm... so sorry...' she uttered, her words dissolving into a whispered sob. 'My own son...'

'Ian, the box.' Allison pointed to the ground near Saunders, where the wooden box was laying on its side, its lid half open and some remaining contents pushing their way out of the gap.

He lifted it up and felt inside with a fragile hope that faded quickly. His fears confirmed, he shook his head. There was nothing electronic inside; the artefact had indeed been taken. He thought of the potential it offered Rachel's work with the Child, the possibility of an end to her pain. Then he realised the advantage it would give their enemies, the dark reflection of what it had been intended for.

'What else is in there?' Allison asked.

'Take it, for all it's worth,' Rhoda said, sounding broken. 'Take the box and go.'

'You could come with us?' Gilmore offered.

She shook her head. Allison took her by the arm and helped her to her feet. 'I have to prepare the community,' she said.

Gilmore looked at Allison, who returned his concern. Neither of them wanted to ask her to explain, fearful of what she might say.

'They'll come, soon enough,' she said in reply to their silent question. 'It's all starting again. History repeats.'

CHAPTER TEN

Friday – Beneath Cambridge. 2.00pm

THE ATMOSPHERE in the bunker noticeably changed when Bambera entered.

Rachel noticed that his impressive physique was less formally enrobed than usual. A khaki-coloured jumper and dark green coat lent him the quality of a guerrilla fighter rather than a politician. The slight imbalance in his gait, a legacy of his last campaign against the forces ranging against them, only enhanced the aura of someone waging a war.

'Mufti day?' she asked, puncturing any pretention he might be aiming to engender.

'Great look,' Markson added quietly, making it difficult to hide a smile.

'Professor Jensen,' Bambera greeted her, ignoring the comments. 'Professor Markson. I bring equipment, and news.'

'Are they all safe? Ian and Dillon?' Even now, knowing the stakes, Rachel's concern was first and foremost with her family. She could apply her skills to the task in hand, but needed that firm foundation established first.

'Both safe and back at base.'

Relief swept through her, and her mind switched swiftly to her next priority. 'Have you brought the artefacts? The one from Old Jewry, the handover went well?'

'I have good news and bad news, it has to be said.' Bambera took a seat at the main desk and indicated that they should do the same. 'I have the first artefact for you. It should allow a level of translation between us and it... her. How's she been in her new surroundings?'

Rachel found herself mentally filtering her recent interactions with Judith. They had remained at the instinctive level, a sense of recognition in the eye contact, an intangible flow of familiarity between them, taking Rachel back to their telepathic communication. 'She remains stable, which is an achievement given the move.' She stopped there, fearing that any more information may give away more than she wanted to at this stage. 'What happened to the second artefact? Did my contact come good?'

'Betrayal within the community it seems. The Association have been dripping their poison there. Once the artefact was compromised in preparation for handover, they took their chance. It's gone.' Bambera brought a clenched fist down on the desk. 'Each step we take, they match us.'

'Equal and opposite works both ways, it seems,' Rachel pronounced, trying not to sound too smug at the puncturing of his confidence.

'What advantage would the second artefact have given us?' Markson asked. 'We've been speculating, moving back from Turing's coding work, but we can't find a clear path of development.'

'We weren't sure either,' Bambera admitted. 'Thankfully it seems that the advantage would have only been a compassionate one.'

Rachel winced. 'Only?'

'It was some kind of numbing device, removing the discomfort of the implants.'

'There's nothing "only" about that, Mr Bambera,' Rachel said, exasperated. 'Pain relief isn't just compassion. Pain is one of the greatest limiting factors in any human endeavour. You should know that.' She noticed with satisfaction that recall of his gunshot wound made him physically flinch. 'Whichever Child has the second artefact could be several orders more efficient than the other.'

Bambera looked downcast at her rebuke, and the room was silent for a moment. Rachel glanced over at Judith, wondering whether she was listening to them, whether she knew that she had come close to relief from the constant levels of discomfort that her life support systems simply couldn't chase away. The human body was just not designed to be contorted into such a form. Her face remained blank, eyes staring ahead but not seeing.

'I do have some other news that might be of interest,' Bambera said eventually, as if wanting to offer something to break the silence but finding only a new concern to distract them with.

'Go on,' Rachel said, bracing herself and resigned to a new disappointment.

'We've gathered more intelligence on the attack on the hospital. The area around Westminster has been under extra surveillance since the power cuts, in case anyone takes advantage and tries to compromise Parliament. We think they chose St Thomas' because of its proximity, like a warning shot. But, as two of them couldn't resist coming out to watch in person, they might have given themselves away.'

'A bad case of over-confidence, it sounds like,' Markson said judgementally. 'Flaunting it never ends well.'

Bambera seemed to supress a roll of his eyes. 'I have two names for you. The first we've known about for some time. The Association's new guiding force, responsible for their new level of organisation and influence. The second may surprise you.'

'Put us out of our misery, Minister,' Markson urged.

'Number one, Ratcliffe.'

Rachel could only nod in unsurprised resignation. 'Son of, I presume.'

Bambera nodded. 'Thomas, yes. And, number two, Atkinson.'

'Neville Atkinson?' Markson asked in disbelief.

Rachel remembered her last encounter with the professor, when she had led the funding panel to reject his research proposition on the grounds that it moved unethically close to biological weapons that could target people based on racial origin. Her instincts then had taken her back to her roots, the horrors her parents had escaped from and their legacy. The lines of the pattern connected in her mind into the form of a spider's web, a trap she had been walking into since before she had even been born.

Ratcliffe felt the familiar sensation of rage swelling in the cavity of his chest. It spread through his blood and into his limbs, somehow managing to combine both pleasure and pain.

'You're sure this is correct?' he asked through clenched teeth.

Jack Ashton admirably held his tremors in check. 'Yes, Boss,' he said evenly. 'The children they moved included blacks and Asians. One of the porters was there when the Ethics Committee confirmed the criteria for movement. Order of sickness.'

'So, they left some of ours there in the dark?'

'While taking the dark out into the light.'

Ratcliffe could see Ashton watching him carefully to see how his attempt at humour was being received. It was crass, but as his mouth curled in distaste, he found it continuing into a smile.

'Indeed,' Ratcliffe said, to Ashton's visible relief. 'Ethics Committee. Right.' He made a mental note to seek them out particularly. They would make a useful example. 'Get me their names.'

Ashton nodded briskly and exited the office, clearly glad to have something to do elsewhere.

Ratcliffe sat alone and lit a cigarette. He probed his feelings as the rush of nicotine calmed his immediate need to smash something. Was he disappointed? Surprised? Relieved? He had expected at least some innate, righteous prejudice to rear its head in the hospital, some recognition of the need to prioritise the white children. Without that, there was little hope for a more peaceful transition into the future he would make for his country. A more aggressive purge would be needed. In the silence of that lonely moment, he allowed himself to recognise that he felt more pleased than annoyed. He had been validated. Permission for war had been implicitly given.

Even now, he could feel the urge of those outside to feel as if the danger had passed. It had been a day since the last power cut. Like a scab forming over a cut, they congratulated themselves at their resilience and basked in the relief that the problem had been solved. Some would still be watching the lights nervously as Friday night fell early, but many would already be thinking ahead to whatever lazy pleasures the weekend offered.

A knock at the office door brought him out of his contemptuous imaginings.

'What?' he called.

One of his lackies, nervous as usual, poked his head around the door, ensuring a smaller target than a whole body. 'Visitor,

Boss,' he said apologetically. 'Not someone we'd usually let in, but he used the code.'

'Which one?'

'Cable Street.'

Ratcliffe felt a thrill even more satisfying than the rage, or the cigarette, had provided. 'Let him in,' he ordered, sitting up straight in anticipation.

The tall figure of Jacob entered. His dark suit was grubby, and his hair fell in uncharacteristically messy strands across his grimly set face.

'Tell me you have it,' Ratcliffe ordered, unable to keep the enthusiasm from his voice. It was a sign of weakness he knew, but there wouldn't be time for advantage to be taken.

'I have it.' Jacob held a leather bag out, but as Ratcliffe reached eagerly for it, he pulled it back out of his reach. 'I've given up my family, my home, to bring you this.'

Ratcliffe left his hands where they were, ready to receive the bag. 'You've saved them,' he lied. 'I had to fight with my associates to keep you out of the purge to come. But our new alliance against the rest of them will give you greater security here in Britain than you've ever managed to find anywhere else. You're on the winning side this time, my friend.'

The words melted Jacob's resolve as Ratcliffe knew they would. His body softened and the bag came closer.

Ratcliffe took it, looking inside and seeing the artefact glinting with promise from the darkness. 'Go and get some rest,' he told Jacob. 'In a while, I'll show you what we'll be using this for. You'll have no doubts. Your mother, your family, your whole community, they will thank you. You've made your people welcome here. Let it sink in.'

The enormity of the moment made Jacob's face crumple into relief as if decades or even centuries of pain was about to be undone. His eyes gleamed and Ratcliffe saw a tear escape before he turned away.

Ratcliffe felt moved by something he couldn't explain. He had a decision to make, in the moment that followed the turn, and he cycled through the three options within seconds. Let Jacob go, let realisation of his error dawn gradually as the shop fronts shattered once more and the trains returned to take the occupants away? Tell him now, so Ratcliffe could see the moment of realisation, the moment of horror, before his very eyes? Or let the man's last moments remain filled with the relief that he had saved his people after all? Let him die victorious, at the apex of hope.

Ratcliffe chose the latter, fired his pistol at the back of Jacob's head, and watched the body fall.

Surprised at the mercy he was capable of, wondering where his cruelty had gone, he lowered the gun and lit another cigarette.

Rachel passed the delicately woven wires of the first artefact to Markson, who took it with reverence.

'Before we try it on her, I need to know where this thing is going.' She gave Bambera a stare that lanced through any pomp he might feel his government position afforded him. 'I need to know what you're really planning. You won't get any collaboration from me until I do. I will keep her comfortable for the duration of whatever's going on, but I won't turn her into a weapon.'

Bambera finally looked at her with the respect she had been waiting for. 'You're right,' he said, and his voice betrayed the same acceptance. 'I'll tell you what you deserve to know. Then if you still feel it's in Judith's interests to continue, we can move to the next stage.'

Rachel nodded, sat opposite him, and listened.

'We talked before of there being an equal and opposite reaction against the rise of the Association. I, and others, have been building this for some time. Those of us in the government who have their origins in other countries, whose skin colour marks us out, have been aware of a much deeper and more threatening form of the casual racism we'd become used to in the '60s. The Association and its activities used to be just rabble. Ratcliffe Senior knew it and he kept their ambitions simple until the alien technology fell into his hands. Even when he got hold of the technology, George's ambitions were still limited by two things,' Bambera continued. 'His own petty obsession with how he'd been treated, and the quality of the men he had surrounded himself with. Tommy, as Ratcliffe Junior prefers, seems to have overcome both of those shortcomings. He was always an intelligent boy, doing well at school, showing a genuine aptitude for business and organisation. He chose his friends carefully, those who have risen in society but who maintained a baser, crueller interest in racial purity and white superiority.'

'I don't like you equating intelligence with those views, Minister,' Rachel cut in. 'Surely the latter precludes the former.'

'This is the most frightening thing about it,' Bambera conceded. 'And something I don't want to acknowledge any more than you do. We feel safer by attributing those views to stupid people, but I think you know they are not exclusively theirs. Perhaps intelligence is the wrong word. But we have to accept that some of the Association, the most vigorous in their beliefs, have acquired talents and abilities that are supremely dangerous in their hands.'

'And your group. Does it have a name?'

'Naebbetold,' Bambera said grandly, sounding each syllable carefully.

Rachel gave him a purposefully blank look, unwilling to give him the satisfaction of asking for an explanation.

'It's a bit obscure, I know,' he said, back down to earth again. 'It wasn't my idea, believe me. It refers to the old Scandinavian ritual of clipping the beaks of birds of prey. Men would be obliged to hunt them and show their beaks as evidence of a kill.'

'Sounds grisly. Are we at that stage then?'

'Well, we need to clip some wings, that's for sure. But if need be, beaks too. The predators need to become the hunted, and the prey need to lead the fight back.'

Rachel narrowed her eyes in reluctant acknowledgement of agreement. 'And how will this help Judith?'

'If they take control, they will come for her. They're preparing their own Child, but having two of them, plus all the artefacts, will give them more power than we can ever allow. If we don't use her as a weapon first, they will.'

Rachel looked at Markson, who had listened intently while studying the coding implant. She hoped he might say something cutting to burst Bambera's certainty.

'It won't just be her they come for, Rachel,' he said instead. 'It'll be us too. All of us. Anyone who doesn't fit their narrow vision of acceptable human.'

Rachel looked at him sadly and nodded. 'We'd better get started then,' she said, taking the implant device from him. 'Let's see what this thing can do.'

Ratcliffe swept into the chamber containing his Child.

Hereward was squeezing a drip-bag, encouraging its contents through the tubes and into the boy's body.

'What's his status?' Ratcliffe asked.

'Look at him,' Hereward instructed daringly. 'The pain's increasing. It'll soon render him useless. We can't get the painkillers into him quickly enough, and the side effects are becoming as damaging as the implants themselves. We'll lose him if we're not careful.'

Ratcliffe could see muscles in the boy's face tensing. The overriding blankness was holding, but there was an autonomic struggle going on that threatened to break the calm surface.

'Good job we have this, then.' He held the silver device aloft.

Four flat, round panels were connected together with thin wires. Needles jutted from the centre of each.

Hereward took it eagerly. 'Looks like they match up with the pain centres,' he said, inspecting it with care.

'We're moving to the next phases.'

'Plural?'

Ratcliffe nodded, grateful to be able to share the burden of his ambition with someone for a moment. 'You work on the Child. Pain-free, it should be able to tackle the scale of the next attack, agreed?'

Hereward nodded.

'I'll contact Atkinson and tell him we'll need his input after all.'

'We're really going that far?'

'If the hospital experiment is anything to go by, we'll need to. They're further gone than we thought. We'll issue the ultimatum, but have the weapon ready in case they make the wrong decision and put up a fight.'

Hereward took a deep breath. 'We'd better get started then.'

Ratcliffe looked at the little boy who sat twitching very slightly between them. 'Let's see what this thing can do.'

CHAPTER ELEVEN

Friday – Beneath the City, London. 2.00pm

GILMORE WAS content to watch Saunders perform his calming charms on Rhoda.

Since her son's betrayal and disappearance, she had manifested an apocalyptic zeal, gathering herself to send out carefully prepared messages and codes into her community. She had barely registered the lingering, forlorn presence of Gilmore and his so-called team.

Not knowing what to do next, they had watched in admiration as she activated long-ready preparations for what might come next. Members of her family had come, gathered and gone, and she had issued orders to them like a general. It had taken the gentle firmness of Saunders to get her to even pause and sit down. When she did, she was shaking.

Now he spoke to her in a way that Gilmore could only dream of being able to, his persuasive tone gradually drawing her attention to their mission.

'So, you see, you could be more use to your community by helping us track the artefacts back to their origin,' Saunders concluded, ending on a silence in which he allowed his logic to work.

'They will be preparing for flight,' she said heavily. 'What if we're separated, or I am left behind?'

'The Order is sworn to protect you and the system that has brought you to us to settle,' Saunders explained, making Gilmore feel edgy at a transparency he wasn't used to. 'Our country is fighting its own worst instincts, but the climax to that battle will be decided over the next few days. At least help us translate the other documents in the box, then you can decide what you want to do.'

Rhoda looked at her watch nervously, then met Saunders' eyes. After a silent interrogation of them, she took her watch off, pocketed it, and instructed, 'Bring the box to me.'

Grateful for something practical to do, Gilmore retrieved the box from where Allison had been looking after it. The sheafs of thin paper, scrawled upon in a language he could not identify, sat inside, free of the implant that had been stored with them for almost thirty years.

Rhoda studied the sheets, handling them with reverence. Saunders hovered by her shoulder, expertly prompting her onwards without crowding her.

'It's a confession,' she said eventually.

'Will you read it to us?' Saunders asked. 'Anything might help.'

Rhoda tilted the sheet to the weak light from the nearest bulb, and read:

The price for our salvation was collaboration. I sincerely hope this will be understood by whichever generation uncovers this testament. I wonder how many years will have elapsed until it is, and whether the danger will have passed, or whether new dangers will beset you, for which my crime might still prove useful. If it is, perhaps my sins will be wiped clean by my legacy, and I will rest peacefully.

The device, if woven into the scalp, will protect against pain itself. It is the soothing sister to another device, and this is where my collaboration became necessary. Dr Johan Keisel of the camp knew of this older device. It could save lives, but the price in pain was too high, until together, we developed the implantation device contained in this box.

Dr Keisel's initial progress required the use of the bodies or our brothers and sisters, our sons and daughters. He knows that these and his other crimes will be accounted for, in this life or the next. He has sworn to me that if the regime falls, he will ensure the devices are given over to the triumphant powers, as small compensation.

My own efforts, under his protection in the camp, cannot

continue much longer. The commandant becomes suspicious, and we have no idea whether our devices can be replicated on the scale we need. We hope that if even one child is saved, they may, through their own actions, spread some kind of good in the place of the evil that has reigned for so long.

I appeal for understanding. Both Keisel and I have walked the blurred pathway between right and wrong in this world where it seems impossible now to stay simply on one side or the other.

Forgive us.

Rhoda let the paper drop and sat back, exhausted, as if the voice from across the years speaking through her had drained her. Gilmore imagined that she was drifting in the patterns of the decades. Rachel took on the same look when she reminisced about her family and her heritage. What he couldn't imagine was how Rhoda was coping with the betrayal of her own son. He thought of Dillon, suddenly desperate to be back with him, to bridge the strange, new gulf that had separated them that morning.

Saunders had taken the sheet from her and looked determined. 'Keisel,' he said. 'That's our lead. Let's get ready to go.'

'But where?' Allison asked, voicing Gilmore's own confusion.

'Back to base, with a stop on the way.' Saunders looked almost gleeful, containing his enthusiasm out of respect for Rhoda, but the glint in his eyes gave him away. 'This is what the Order was made for. We collect the Nuremberg records from the archive under Chancery Lane. That's halfway between here and the Library. We get everything we can on Keisel and hope that he kept his promise that his work would find its way into Allied hands.'

'The right Allies, hopefully,' Gilmore warned. 'Bit of a coincidence that these records happen to be on our way back?'

'London's like that,' Saunders said, almost admiringly. 'There is order to the chaos. Must be meant to be. *Maktub*.' He smiled at Gilmore's quizzical frown. 'Arabic. *It is written*.'

Gilmore returned the paper to the box, wondering what else might be in there on the other sheets. 'Let's hope so,' he said, feeling caught between hope and doubt. 'Let's hope so.'

Dillon allowed the footsteps of his dad to approach, but kept his eyes closed.

He fought against the instinct to clamp them shut with a screwed-up frown, instead following Bes' instruction to let them sit closed as if it was as natural a state as when they were open.

Only when he was ready, and in answer to his dad's concerned and confused repeating of his name, did he open his eyes.

'Dad,' he said, unable to prevent the relief from sweeping through his body and his voice at the sight of Dad's face close to his.

'What on earth were you doing? I thought you'd phased out or something.'

'I was meditating. Bes taught me.'

'Oh, I see,' Dad replied, clearly not seeing at all, and not hiding his discomfort at the prospect either. 'Well, you seem a bit better than earlier.'

Dillon pondered that judgement, and allowed himself to nod in reassurance, even though he could still feel the weight of the past day sitting inside himself like a heavy fog. 'A bit,' he conceded.

'You've been drawing too?' Dad asked, and Dillon realised that his sketchbook was open on the page he had left it. The stick-thin limbs and bulging eyes on the page disappeared as Dillon snapped it shut.

'He is... processing,' came a voice from behind them both, the voice he had come to rely on throughout the day, which seemed to Dillon as if it had lasted much longer than it had. Whatever Bes was going to tell his dad, Dillon trusted it would be the right thing, so he let the conversation happen around him, allowing for his dad's expected testiness.

'And what does that mean, exactly? Don't think that your codes and prophecies apply where my son is concerned. Speak plainly.'

'He overheard you last night,' Bes explained with just a hint of disapproval. 'He got quite the history lesson. Perhaps a little later than might have been sensible, in more ways than one.'

Dillon didn't need to look at his dad to sense him seething.

'His mum has always cautioned against going into too much detail about... what went on. You're welcome to take that up with her. Just remind me to stand well clear when you do.'

Bes gave a small tilt of the head, as if accepting a challenge. Dillon made a mental note to stand clear too.

'Anyway,' Dad continued, gruffly covering over the simmering disagreement, 'we have work to do. Saunders wants your help with the Nuremberg records we've brought.'

Dillon watched Bes calmly take in the instruction and its implications. His dad took the lead back to the main desk, where Saunders, Trevor, Allison, and a woman he didn't recognise were gathered around a box, pulling out papers and dividing them up.

'Stay there, Dillon,' came the thrown-back instruction as he started to follow.

Bes placed a hand on his dad's arm, stopping him and speaking to him in a low voice, close to his ear. Dillon couldn't hear, but he recognised it enough to know it was adult talk, in the language of urgency that always excluded him from understanding.

Annoyed at both of them for a moment, he stood still, controlling his breathing as best he could.

Then, to his surprise, his dad turned, and although his face remained set in reluctance, he offered a hand for Dillon to take. 'Come on then,' he said, a little sadly, as if in reaction to the change in his son, he was changing too. 'Maybe you're ready after all.'

Dillon wasn't sure that he was, but the outstretched hand was enough to make him brave enough to try, and he took it.

It took them nearly an hour to locate the section they needed.

Bambera's authorisation had enabled them to quickly retrieve the general collection of documents relating to Dr Keisel, but as always it was far more complex to locate the exact information they needed. The records from the Nuremberg Trials were as detailed and fastidious as those that had been kept by the people they were holding to account.

Having heard fragments of the story of the capture of the camp, the rounding up of Keisel, and his work and the liberation of some of his subjects, it was Trevor who exclaimed, somewhat cautiously, 'I think I've got it.'

The group looked to him as one. Gilmore noticed Dillon's keen eyes settle on his new best friend. He had been listening to the tales intently, tilting his head and nodding slowly as he pieced together the climax of the story he had heard the terrible middle of unintentionally the previous night. If there was a voice he trusted to share what they needed to know next, it was Trevor's.

He read:

Testimony of Dr Johan Keisel, freely given upon initial hearing.

I would like it put on record that my work at the camp included the development of a device that was intended to relieve the suffering of the occupants by numbing the pain centres of the brain and allowing further adaptations to enable survival beyond the natural point, especially given the tortures and terminal processes employed there. This was in collaboration with a small team of Jewish scientists, since deceased, whose intellect and dedication to their people humbled me beyond words.

The eventual goal of our work was to resurrect and continue the work of a prior process, developed during the earlier conflict by the British, but acquired by my people just before its end. This involved a smaller and more portable equivalent to what has become known as the "iron lung". Rather than enabling breath after severe respiratory damage, the device was intended to allow soldiers to survive the increasingly frequent gas attacks of the Western Front, without the impeding dangers of the gas mask. Implants in the neck and around the chest would allow a secondary airway to function, if connected to a supply of oxygen.

The original experiments had ended for two reasons. Firstly, the amount of pain caused to the human body was outweighing the quality of continued life to the point at which survival meant permanent agony. Secondly, the end of the conflict deferred its need. The work of my Jewish colleagues has solved the first problem. The work of my own countrymen has made the second sadly defunct.

Compromise of the pure state of humanity of the subjects has been discussed, and a balance between ethics and need was assessed. There has been speculation of further evolution of the process, given not only the continued use of gas as a weapon but the on-going and increasing pollution of the atmosphere as a result of the Industrial Revolution and its consequences. We determined therefore that rather than allow these mechanised forces to be used purely for life's end, we may adapt them to allow life to continue.

The group was silent for a moment as they pondered the implications of the testimony. Gilmore's eyes were drawn to some of the silver body parts adorning the walls, salvaged, according to Saunders, from the sewers beneath the city. Some of them seemed to emulate, blockily, the torso of a person, with tubes that could be windpipes leading into the space above where a head might have been.

How far had humanity got with its efforts to transcend the need for natural breath? He stared into the blank eyes of one of the silver masks. How far had others, from further out? Was this urge towards the machine not just human but universal?

'There's something else,' Trevor said, his lilting accent bringing Gilmore back to the moment gently. 'Additional comments, presumably by those assessing his claims. A cross reference to a catalogue system.'

At the mention of an archival reference, Saunders and Bes leaned forward. They looked at each other and nodded.

'Well?' Gilmore prompted.

'We're going full circle. The World War One Archives beneath Whitehall. The reference tells us where we can find the third artefact.'

'But what use will it be?' Allison asked, as if puzzling it out as she did so. 'Artificial lungs? I can't see how it would enhance the Child.'

'Maybe Rachel and Markson will have worked that out by the time we get it,' Gilmore offered hopefully. 'I suggest we get moving. We don't know how far this puts us ahead of the Association, and we can't risk them getting hold of—'

The lights dipped, before returning to full strength.

The group looked around at each other and moved instinctively a little closer together. Gilmore felt for Dillon's hand and took it firmly. They stood, waiting, hardly breathing.

Then, just as his hope was about to triumph over his fear with the belief that the dip didn't signify an attack on their power, the lights faded, slowly, into nothing.

Gilmore blinked, but as he recognised the silence that descended as the subtle hum of electricity flow faded too, he realised that it no longer mattered whether his eyes were open or shut; all was darkness either way.

CHAPTER TWELVE

Friday – Saint Pancras, London. 5.05pm

THE SMELL of incense led the group, one-by-one, into a candle-lit sanctuary.

Gilmore pulled Dillon gently onwards, warning him to step carefully through an old wooden door that connected the tunnels below the British Library to catacombs serving St Pancras Old Church. Ahead of him, Bes looked appreciatively around at their new surroundings, breathing the fragrant smoke so deeply it was as if she were drawing in the candlelight and the history of the place too.

Although the candles in the stone chamber had been lit, there was no sign of any church officials or congregation. Gilmore switched off his torch. While allowing some basic navigation, the torches had not alleviated the instinctive claustrophobia of the stiflingly narrow spaces.

'One of the oldest sacred sites in London,' Bes told Dillon, who to Gilmore's concern seemed to be emulating the strange academic more and more.

He felt the boy let go of his hand and join Bes in a deep-breathing appreciation of their escape from the pitch darkness of the tunnels. Rolling his eyes, Gilmore counted the others out as they joined them.

'Our tour guide seems to think we're on a jolly,' he said to Trevor, grateful for someone to be able to share the sarcasm with. He knew it was fuelled by frayed nerves, and he missed Rachel even more; she was always one to share a scathing cut-down when it was needed.

Trevor smiled indulgently and with clear relief at having made it safely out. Allison followed behind him, still grasping his hand and continuing to do so while she too looked around in awe. Gilmore noticed that Trevor didn't complain, and it was only when Rhoda and then Saunders emerged too, pushing them onwards into the light, that they broke away from each other.

'Where are we?' Rhoda asked.

'Oh, I'm sure our resident guru will tell us all about it,' Gilmore replied, regretting his snide tone as he noticed the look of disapproval she gave him in return.

'We're not far from the Library,' Saunders explained. 'Most of the tunnels in London connect to church sites, especially the older ones. From here we'll have to go overground to the War Records. We'll make it under an hour if we don't stop.'

Trevor moved to a door on the other side of the antechamber. He opened it to reveal a stone staircase that presumably led to the main worship area. 'If the power cut extends across the city, we should expect some trouble,' he warned. 'This could be their biggest attack on the supply yet. People are going to be terrified.'

Gilmore joined him to lead the group upwards. They went slowly and carefully, unused to the surface world after the intense hours underground, and uncertain as to what the power-starved city might look like.

When he emerged into the main space, Gilmore felt awed into silence. Every pew was filled, row upon row of people huddling together. Men and women of all ages and races, children nestled between them, sat in eerily stillness. Each one gripped a small white candle, their flames creating a golden glow around the arched interior. No one spoke aloud; there was only the gentle whisper of muttered prayer.

As the rest of the group emerged and saw the spectacle, only a few of the near congregation gave them a glance, as if their arrival was not unusual in this strange, darkened world they had found themselves in. Having felt the ancient urge to gather together around flame and appeal to some higher power to bring back the light they craved, the congregation went on with their prayers, oblivious to the people tasked with saving them.

Ratcliffe stood alone at the top of an iron staircase which formed the fire escape from the top-level offices of the Shoreditch warehouse.

He looked across the city south-westwards, where only the very faintest vestiges of sunset still streaked, trying but failing to hold on to the night sky. Out of sight but clear in his mind's eye was Parliament itself, where the idiots of the government would be scrabbling desperately for their torches and wondering how far the power cut had spread this time and why some, but not all, of the back-up generators were also starting to fail.

He heard footsteps on the metal behind him but did not turn. Instead, he allowed Hereward to join him and revel quietly in the darkness for a while. Occasionally a building would flicker back to life, or streetlights would splutter back on, as the cat-and-mouse chase for energy supply continued. These minor triumphs only enhanced the desperation, little moments of hope soon snuffed out. Each one added to his happiness.

'He's doing very well, our boy,' Ratcliffe purred.

'The pain relief has freed him to expand further through the network,' Hereward responded. 'He can keep up with their efforts to divert the power and remotely dampen the back-ups at a rate we've never seen before.'

'How long can he maintain this level of impact?'

'Another few hours, I'd say. He's still subject to the need for brain-sleep. He's had a big day, what with the operation.'

Ratcliffe felt the need to stretch building within him, perhaps an autonomic reaction to the mention of sleep. He wondered if he would manage any. The hours had been scant these last few weeks in the build-up.

'Speaking of which,' Hereward continued, 'are we aiming to increase his capacity further? The cut is limited to London this time. Without further improvements, it might well stay that way. There must be more artefacts out there, and if the others are searching for them, we'll need to be ready to defend against their own Child if they end up with the advantage.'

Ratcliffe pondered this. Looking again westwards, he wondered where his enemies were. They had likely been flushed out from their underground hibernation. If they had a plan, there were now new ways of stopping them.

'They'll probably be heading back home to Bambera,' he surmised. 'I'll step up our presence in the area.'

Hereward nodded and turned, clearly eager to return to his main concern, the Child. Sometimes Ratcliffe wondered how much the scientist cared about their core objective, the cleansing of Great Britain, and how much he just wanted to test his own powers through the boy.

'Oh, and we'll activate the Bolts too,' he added, noticing how Hereward paused at the mention of the codeword. He enjoyed the reclaiming of his power by giving the announcement, having had to seek permission from another link in the Association chain, the mysteriously distorted voice he spoke to but did not know. 'By the end of this night, I want things to be a bit clearer for them all. Crystal clear, you might say.'

By the time they reached Russell Square, it became clear to Gilmore that something else was wrong with the city.

Trekking through a thick drizzle, they wove their way through the frantic crowds as people combined their Friday commute with a new urgency to find out what was happening and when the power would be back.

He could tell that the behaviour of the masses was starting to divide into groups who followed the driving force of the herd they most aligned to. There were those heading to the churches and temples to pray, like those they'd seen before. A synagogue they passed, already open for the start of the Sabbath prayers, was offering sanctuary to anyone who seemed troubled. Then there were the drinkers, whose Friday night relaxation had become a more heightened and tense affair, the free alcohol being offered by reckless landlords fuelling an undertone of simmering tension and increasing noise.

Shops were starting to close their doors despite the banging of people on the verge of panic-buying, and it was these that caught Gilmore's attention. He spotted similarly-aged and dressed youths at each of the shops along one street. They had an air of performance about their demands that the shops open, as though spouting lines rehearsed or read from a script. Their attention was drawn too by the sight of Trevor and Rhoda as they passed, their eyes latching on to them with ominous intent.

Something was building within the mist. As they waited for confused traffic to pause to let them cross a junction on the corner of the Square, the streetlights flickered on, then off again, casting strobing glows over the seething mass of frightened people. It made those who seemed without fear, those with an organised confidence and a look of intent in their eyes, show up even more obviously.

'You've spotted it too?' Trevor asked as he pushed alongside Gilmore, taking Dillon's free hand so the boy was safely enclosed between them.

'A while back. What do you think?'

'I have a nasty feeling... I've known those particular looks all my life. In this context, they worry me.'

Rhoda joined them, hearing Trevor's warning and nodding in agreement. 'I recognise this too,' she said. 'If I'm right, I'll need to get to safety, to my family.'

Gilmore felt shame burning in his chest. He was in his own capital city and yet it was starting to feel alien to him.

'Dad, why are they drawing lightning on that wall?' Dillon looked up with wide eyes at his dad.

When the sound of glass came scything through the air all around them, they ducked along with everyone else. The sound echoed, merging with the shouting and cheers of triumph and the crunching of broken glass underfoot.

Gilmore locked eyes with Rhoda, seeing the terror there.

'*Kristallnacht*,' she whispered. She grasped his hand in a final gesture of good luck, and, before he could stop her, she turned, ducked and moved away. Still rippling from the noise of the smashing windows, the crowd surged around her and she was lost to his sight.

Reports of the attacks continued to arrive, and Ratcliffe marked each one with a pin on his wall map of central London. When the reports slowed and he looked at the spread of the pins, each red ball like a drop of blood, he felt content.

The Bolts had been primed well. Prepared by a network of Association members, they had been kept away from their main activities and inveigled themselves into community positions such as youth workers, sports coaches, and the like. The boys had been loaded with pent up frustrations and prejudices. Ratcliffe had learned this technique from his father. He had seen it enough times and had absorbed the invigorating poison just by proximity.

All the Bolts awaited was the order to release that stored up energy upon those they now blamed for their own poverty. *What better night to unleash the lightning than one of complete darkness,* he thought, smiling to himself. All the better to illuminate it with. Even the most stubbornly and sickeningly hopeful and liberal of them out there could not fail to see the symbolism.

Fuelled by the chaos, sleep seemed further away to him than ever. Now the glass had been smashed, something had been unleashed, something that would not stop until it had burned its way through the city and the people and cleansed it fully. The steps beyond this point unfolded in his mind as his eyes danced around the map.

While the horrors of the past were resurrecting in its streets, he needed to turn his attention to the future. While everyone was looking backward and around them, he would be the one to look forward, eyes like a hawk on the final goal.

Picking up the office telephone, he felt the power that still allowed it to work make his hand tingle. It came directly from the Child, energy drained from out there and redirected to him alone.

'Atkinson?' he asked when the voice answered the call.

'What's happening there?' the professor asked. 'It sounds like chaos.'

'Oh it is. We're on our way to where we want to be. But I will need your extra help after all, Professor.'

'There's a bit more to do, but the formula is almost complete. The test subjects provided by your men have been worth more than Cambridge University funding would ever have given me.'

'It's not just about that. We need to protect our Child from theirs. You need to find Jensen. Use that other freak to get to her if you need to.' The line went quiet and Ratcliffe allowed the man a moment to respond.

'Very well,' he said eventually. 'Do you need them alive?'

Ratcliffe pondered this. 'What we need can be taken from their dead bodies,' he said. 'A shame to lose their intellect, but there's no room for people like them in our new future, Professor. Although... it might be fun to make them truly understand how badly they've lost. They've elbowed enough decency out already. Including your wife.'

'I don't need reminding.' The voice was cold and emboldened. Exactly what Ratcliffe needed. 'Leave it with me.'

The crowd thickened as it came up against a cordon of police officers in full riot gear protecting the Houses of Parliament, Buckingham Palace, Downing Street, and Whitehall. The line held firm around Admiralty Arch and the edge of Trafalgar Square, the impassive faces of the officers looking on as the confusion settled into jostling, singing and shouting. Half protest, half party, the melee seemed finely poised on the edge of aggression.

Gilmore felt finely attuned to any particularly raised voices or aggressive shoves, aware that the collective force of the crowd could quickly swell into a full-blown surge.

He led the others to the barrier and spoke to the officer, using the correct command words and poise to convince them, reluctantly, to let his group through.

Released from the crush of bodies, he breathed deeply and watched the others do the same as one by one they passed the barrier and emerged into the empty space beyond.

Lights continued to flicker on occasionally, illuminating the thick drizzle and reflecting off the drenched surfaces. The Whitehall concourse was empty before them, and Gilmore led their walk along it, feeling as if he were trapped in a strange dream, the flickering lights causing long shadows to appear and jump around them as they moved on.

The Cenotaph rose in pale stone in front of them, and together they paused in front of it, a strange parody of the ceremony that had only occurred a fortnight before. The etchings of soldiers and the words chosen to commemorate them jumped into sharp relief with each flicker of light.

Remembering his son's recurring obsessions with the conflict, the soldiers, their songs and stories, Gilmore looked down at Dillon. He was staring at the edifice, his wet hair plastered to his scalp, its boyish sandy waves now dark and severe.

'Is it true about the Unknown Warrior?' Dillon asked in a quiet, reverential voice.

Still wanting to learn amid all this, Gilmore thought with a surge of affection for his son.

'Is what true, Dillon?'

'They really don't know who he is?'

'That's right. It means anyone who lost someone who couldn't be found can believe that the body might be theirs. Nothing to say it isn't.'

He watched Dillon nod slowly. 'Dad?'

'Yes, son.'

'What was it all for?'

Gilmore looked again at the memorial. He could still hear the sound of the crowd from the Square, no words distinct, just a collective babble of noise, of confusion, of pent up fear devoid of direction; an energy, waiting to be earthed.

He found no words for an answer.

CHAPTER THIRTEEN

Friday – Beneath Cambridge. 8.00pm

THE SILENCE emanating from the radio seemed to have physical presence, chilling the air with solid waves of absence. Markson bit his lip and waited for someone to speak.

'For goodness' sake, turn it off,' Rachel snapped eventually. 'It's not like we'll be missing anything.'

Markson obeyed, relieved to replace the eerie nothingness with a more natural silence.

Bambera stepped back into the bunker. 'I managed to get through to the emergency line, just for a few moments,' he announced. 'There are small bursts of power from the back-ups, but from what we can tell London is down.'

'What did they say when you got through?' Rachel asked.

Bambera clamped his lips shut and looked away from the scientists towards the Child.

'Minister,' Rachel said, slowly and threateningly. Markson watched Bambera's reaction keenly. He had always been intrigued by the interactions between opposing forces and immovable objects.

Bambera relented. 'It was a code on repeat, reserved for severe emergency, recalling all ministers and forces to London. Anything on the radio?'

'A deafening silence,' Markson replied.

Bambera nodded. 'That confirms it. The regional centres can take over the bandwidth. But to broadcast silence... It's a call to arms.'

Rachel moved towards the Child, keeping her eyes on

Bambera, who seemed fixed upon her too. She had the bearing of a protective parent. 'You'll be off then?' she asked him brusquely.

Bambera blinked, slowly, as if weighing a great decision. Markson was proud of his ability to read body language, of men in particular, an essential skill for determining possibilities where words were forbidden. If he were to guess, Bambera was about to make a big decision, to commit to a path from which there may be no return. He had seen that stillness before, a pendulum suspended at the apex of its swing, held there, before release.

'I've just resigned,' he said through a strange smile of both relief and sadness.

Rachel's mouth dropped open and Markson enjoyed a moment of seeing her genuinely shocked, although he didn't let that show. 'What?' was all she could manage to ask.

'Refusing to return under these circumstances is a sackable offence anyway. Leaving the government without its Minister for Defence while in a state of emergency...' He seemed on the verge of a hysterical laugh as his decision sank in. 'Well, temporarily. Letters have been prepared, my replacement lined up already. I haven't left them without what they need. It was always going to come to this at some point. Looks like it's today.'

'Is that why you've dressed for the occasion?' Markson asked, unable to prevent a hint of flirtation from lightening his tone. He noticed Rachel shake her head. It did explain the army fatigues.

'They now have deniability,' Bambera announced, growing in confidence as he visibly relaxed into his new status. 'The things I need to be able to do can't be done in the name of the British Government. I've been preparing this for years, but always within certain restraints. I'm free of that now.'

'Do they know about this already?' Markson asked, impressed but not surprised at the levels of planning and counter-planning that must have been taking place in response to the threat of the Association's rise.

Bambera shook his head. 'You don't need to concern yourself with them now. You work for me. Our previous agreements transfer to me alone, so you are also authorised to act beyond the usual restraints.'

'And Ian too?' Rachel asked. 'And those others he's with?'
Bambera nodded.

'I'm not sure he'll like that.'

A movement caught their attention and they all looked over at the Child at the same time. It had only been a tiny movement, but her usual stillness made any twitch or response stand out. She had tilted her head and now stared with purpose. A line of drool, imbalanced by the angle, dripped slowly from her mouth. The coding device, newly added to her scalp, glinted like a crown.

'Is it the new implant?' Markson asked, rushing over to her. He had been so careful while fitting it, so frightened of hurting her even though he knew from her brain scans that she was permanently existing at a base level of pain.

'Or the power cuts?' countered Rachel. 'Or both?'

Bambera examined the cables running from her body into the machinery around her throne. 'Is she still connected to the systems I gave you access to?'

'Yes,' Rachel confirmed. 'Her readings seemed to settle when we connected her. Since she lost the connection to the Cerberus network, whole areas of her brain had been redundant. We've had to feed her data constantly to keep her going, but she had started to spot the patterns in the cycle and reject it.'

'She was bored,' Markson breathed, translating for her without realising.

She twitched. Was that a flicker of recognition towards him when he had said it? Her eyes were starting to dart around the room.

'Whatever it is, she likes it,' Rachel told Bambera. 'What is it?'

'Computer-controlled power supplies,' he explained. 'A whole system beyond the conventional cables and back-ups, only for use in cases of energy terrorism like this.'

'I had no idea,' Markson admitted, impressed again.

'Obviously. And as a government minister I was sworn to secrecy at a level beyond even the Official Secrets Act.'

Rachel smiled in understanding. 'Good job you resigned then.'

Bambera nodded. 'She needs a command. Something simple, to activate the systems and restore the power to London. I'll bet they've achieved this with their own Child, so it's time she defended us.'

'Well, the coding implant should help us with that, but we haven't tested it yet.'

The Child's eyes closed.

'I think she's already translating,' Markson offered.

One of the monitors above her, upon which the constant flow of changing numbers usually streamed, started to glow with a new light. Green lines formed, pathways of data reaching out into the network via the plugs in the back of her skull and into the world beyond the bunker. Markson stared, mesmerised, as the lines divided and branched and became at once both more complex and more recognisable. The pattern forming became smaller as the data became concentrated and the scale adjusted to reveal the whole shape.

'London,' Bambera said triumphantly.

The lines pulsed, bright dots passing down unseen cables leaving glowing trails in their wake. Some of them, when blocked, turned back and found another pathway, dividing again and rejoining beyond the barrier. Markson was reminded of brain scans and the electrical impulses needed to sustain life itself.

Then he noticed that Rachel had closed her eyes too. 'Command... activate...' she whispered, repeating Bambera's words from moments before. 'Restore... power... defend...' The Child's eyes were darting behind her eyelids, and her mouth, still leaking liquid, was curling into something almost like a smile. 'Command... activate...' Rachel repeated the words like a mantra.

The lights in the chamber dimmed suddenly, then returned, brighter than before. Rachel's eyes snapped open at the same moment as the Child's.

'This is London,' came a voice suddenly from the radio, making Markson and Bambera jump in unified surprise. *'We repeat, this is London. Power has returned. This is London. Power has returned. You are hearing us from London. News bulletin imminent. This is London.'*

Markson checked on Rachel and the Child one more time before he stepped into the antechamber and joined Bambera.

Rachel was once again applying cream to the Child, having

noticed new irritation around the points where the coding mesh was slicing into her delicate skin. It had heated up while she had done her work to restore the power to London, but now she was paying a price. Her head had lolled in exhaustion, her eyes unfocused again. The occasional twitch suggested she was in even more discomfort than usual.

Bambera stood by one of the ventilator panels, smoking a cigarette. Markson smiled to see him try to blow the smoke directly into it, as if he might guide it out of the bunker without anyone knowing. 'Mind if I join you?' he asked.

Bambera offered him a cigarette, which he took. The two men breathed the tobacco in deeply, seeking the soothing nicotine.

'If only we had that second implant,' Markson said eventually, unable to shift his thoughts from the suffering of the Child. 'We're causing her pain. We likely will do each time we use her.'

Bambera looked away from him. 'Needs must, Professor Markson.'

'What's the plan now? It wouldn't be too late for you to go back?'

'Events have been set in motion that can't be undone,' Bambera said, still not turning to look back at him. 'My family will have been moved somewhere safe and my position taken by my replacement. We've defended ourselves against the first major attack, but there will be more. My sources tell me the Association is openly attacking Jewish targets. We can't wait any longer. The Naebbetold network is fully active now. There will be retribution.'

Markson shivered. He noticed the way Bambera stamped on the remains of his cigarette, crushing its glowing end into a smear of ash.

'Professor Jensen will want guarantees about the Child,' Markson said carefully. 'There are limits to the suffering she'll allow.'

'If the rumours are true about the remaining artefacts, it won't be her suffering, it'll be the Association.'

'What do you know about them exactly?'

'We don't know where they've been stored, or even if the rumours are true. That's what Gilmore and the Order are for.

But if we're right, the Child will be able to overcome her current limitations. Just like she's been able to reach out mentally through the power network.'

Markson pondered his meaning. 'She's still reliant on physical connection to the systems though. The effort to reach London from here was enough. It scorched her. Push her too far and she'll burn.'

'That's why we need the remaining artefacts. She will become... mobile.'

It was Markson's turn to extinguish his cigarette. He fought the urge to ask for another. 'I need to know what you mean, Bambera,' he said. 'If I'm to convince Rachel, you first have to convince me.'

Bambera offered him another despite not being asked, as he himself lit up again. 'The government is bound by the Auderly House Accords, so there's a limit to the new defensive equipment they can publicly fund and produce. Not without sharing with the Chinese, and therefore risking raising tensions with the Soviets. Besides, we're talking about defences for use in a civil conflict, not the hot foreign wars we've fought in the past.'

'A new Civil War? Is that really what's at stake?' Markson could barely believe the words could have meaning here in the 1970s. Even as he spoke them, he felt their archaism, images of Roundheads and Cavaliers holding them back in a safe and distant space of stories and legends.

'The riots were just the prelude,' Bambera explained. 'Woden and the prospect of Whateley in charge gave them a focus. Our democracy doesn't preclude the possibility of divides so great they spill into power grabs and civil militia. Ending the Woden threat has just made the real power behind them more vicious.'

'You spoke of forbidden weapons,' Markson reminded him, unsure as to how much he actually wanted to know.

Bambera nodded. 'In order to make the Child mobile, able to defend us wherever an attack comes and take the battle to them, we'll need a weapon currently on the Auderly House Accords' prohibited list.'

'Another reason why you resigned?'

Bambera nodded.

'What is it exactly?'

'A tank. For her.'

Horrific possibilities flashed through Markson's mind. 'What kind of tank?'

'Both kinds. Firstly, in the sense of a heavily armoured vehicle. Auderly House didn't just give us the Accords. It gave us more remains from the race that built the Child. We have a prototype tank based on that technology, fully mobile, impenetrable, able to connect rapidly to any systems we need it to.'

'And in the other sense?'

'This depends on the remaining artefacts. If we're right, they will allow her to be suspended inside, painlessly, totally integrated into its systems.'

'She still needs to breath,' Markson said incredulously.

Bambera shook his head. 'Not if Gilmore and the Order find what we need.'

'Rachel won't accept this. What you're turning her into...'

'She could be the one weapon we need to end the Association threat for good. They have the technology too, remember. Ratcliffe inherited it from the Shoreditch Event just like we did her. He has connections to powerful sources of assistance. His two lead scientists, Hareward and Carstairs, and now Atkinson too of course. Rumours of a connection within government itself, someone who signs off each escalation. Through her we can avoid civilian casualties and target them directly.'

'But *her* suffering... It's inhuman.'

'That's the beauty of it,' Bambera said, his eyes shining with zeal. 'We know her real suffering comes from a disconnection from the technology she was originally integrated with. Dr Williams' findings confirmed it. We've never been able to replicate the stimulus of those original implants. They were feeding her data from the history of a race so far beyond ours. She was being drugged every time she solved one of their problems for them, some kind of pleasure stimulant that we haven't been able to recreate. That's why she ended up like she did, seeking out the same kind of buzz from our inadequate efforts. First her own drugs, then our data. She's an addict, and we're running out of things to give her to feed her needs.'

'You're saying this tank will *help* her?'

'Professor Jensen wants her to have quality of life, to find peace. The only place she'll find that is back with the technology we separated her from.' Bambera finished his second cigarette and ground it, like the first, into the floor with his heel. 'She's going home,' he said. 'Back where she belongs.'

The bunker felt empty without the bulk of Bambera overseeing everything and making pronouncements. He had left them a little while before, saying he needed to return to London to 'mop up' loose ends.

Markson sat in one of the soft armchairs that had been set up in the corner as a space to rest. He did not feel restful. The comfort of the chair felt at odds with the tension he felt in his very bones.

'I need to get out for a bit,' he told Rachel, who was still hovering around the Child, unwilling or unable to leave her for long.

'It's not safe out there,' Rachel protested. 'We're targets, remember.'

Markson thumped a fist onto the arm of the chair. 'I'm sorry, Rachel,' he said firmly. 'I'm willing to risk it. This place... I just need some air.'

He hadn't told her what Bambera was planning, but the knowledge of it had thickened the atmosphere in the chamber, making it feel even more airless than usual. The smell of singed flesh lingered, mixed with the antiseptic scent of the cream Rachel insisted on applying to the Child. He felt sick.

When she nodded reluctantly and turned back to her true focus, he climbed up the metal steps, gave stern insistence to the guards and, finally through the heavy, multi-locked doors, he exited the bunker.

Reaching cold night air, he breathed as deeply as he had the cigarettes, exhaling clouds of steam as thick as their smoke.

He turned into the main street, watching students pass on the other side of the road, oblivious to what was going on beneath their feet. The news from London had made them giddy and over-excited and they wobbled along on inebriated legs, holding each other for support, singing. What would they do if war really did come here? The younger generations were already softening without the threat of a direct conflict in which they would be asked to fight. What side would they choose against people from their own country? What lengths would they go to, to protect those the Association wanted to remove? However liberal their proclamations, would they really risk their own lives in defence of their foreign friends?

Markson passed Magdalene College and Chesterton Lane, crossed the deserted Fellows' Gardens, and found himself on the banks of the river. It was too cold for the usual walkers and wanderers, and he felt grateful for the peace.

It took a moment to register footsteps, quicker than an ordinary fellow walker, approaching from behind. It took another to realise something was pressing into his back. But it took only seconds to recognise the voice that whispered, 'Don't move,' into his ear.

He allowed himself to be turned so that he faced his assailant, and looked Professor Neville Atkinson coldly in the eyes.

CHAPTER FOURTEEN

Friday – Whitehall, London. 9.10pm

AT FIRST, the striding confidence of the policemen did not cause Gilmore concern.

He supposed that officials and security forces had been enacting long-planned-for evacuation plans, taking the government and royalty to safety, and securing their premises. Downing Street, gated with extra metal grills, was silent and dark. A mere three decades since the city had been under daily attack from the air, the prospect was not so strange.

It was when the approaching steps of the policemen became more of a swagger, a strut, that he worried, and gripped Dillon in one hand and his Browning in the other.

'We have company,' he warned the others, who quickly took defensive positions behind the Cenotaph.

'We'll draw them away and deal with them,' Saunders offered, his body already adopting the confident poise that had so surprised Gilmore in the tunnels. Bes was moving likewise, low in the darkness.

'But Dad, they're police,' Dillon pointed out, his face puzzled and frightened.

'We can't rely on that anymore, son,' Gilmore told him. There was no time to think of a kinder way to soften the blow that the supposedly immovable structures of British culture were breaking down fast.

Before he could stop them even if he wanted to, Saunders and Bes had emerged from their hiding place, arms up in false surrender, adopting a nervous and wounded gait that allowed them to get close enough to the police to enact a lightning-fast transformation into the warriors they really were and swipe the threatening side-arms. The two assailants seemed initially as confident with their fists as they had been with their weapons, and they jabbed back at Saunders and Bes with force.

Trevor and Allison leaned in closer alongside Gilmore, continuing to shield Dillon from the sight of the vicious fighting.

'They need help,' Trevor whispered to Gilmore, moving again to block Dillon's panicked look in their direction at his warning.

Gilmore felt the cold of the air and the fear of leaving Dillon freeze his limbs. Even with a decisive pledge to save the academics, he didn't think he could make himself move away from his fragile cargo. In that silent moment, he had never felt more useless.

As more dark figures flooded into the area around the Cenotaph from the direction of Trafalgar Square, the feeling of uselessness sank naturally and quickly into a resignation to their fate. The darkness of police uniforms merged in a blur with other figures in less identifiable garb. Gilmore found himself blocking out the sounds of fighting, the aggressive challenges, muffled thumps and gasps of pain, to stare directly into Dillon's face, as if by this alone he could block out the world for a last few precious seconds. Dillon stared back, his eyes wide, unblinking.

If it had been anyone other than Trevor to let them know when the danger had passed, Gilmore wasn't sure he would have believed it. Continuing to shield Dillon from the sight of fallen bodies and the black-clad figures that stood triumphantly over them, he looked around in confusion.

One of the new arrivals, a muscular and lithe Chinese man, strode over to Gilmore and saluted.

'They're with Bambera,' Trevor explained.

'We're Naebbetold,' the man announced. 'Association agents have infiltrated the police. We've been watching and waiting for them to break cover.'

As if in harmony with the turning of the tide, lights came on confidently, filling the buildings and the streets, transforming the dark winter sky with a sodium glow.

'Things have changed,' the Chinese man continued. 'Bambera has broken cover too. He's no longer Minister for

Defence, but your mission in his name must continue. We'll prevent you being followed from here. He will join you back at the Order's base.'

Gilmore's head was swimming and he felt giddy with the release of tension and the continued falling away of any stable structures. Chains of command, uniforms of authority, titles and badges were all dissolving into a muddle he could not make sense of.

As Saunders and Bes rejoined them, he looked around at their small circle, at them and Trevor and Allison, and Dillon, nestled between them all. However it had happened, they had formed a unit he could just about trust. Feeling the barrier of the newcomers at their backs, he followed Saunders and Bes as they led the way back into the tunnels, where the Great War Archive awaited them.

The academics led the search along rows and rows of documents and dusty objects.

They had switched seamlessly once again from fighters to thinkers, moving through the archives and tracking the catalogue references as calmly and gracefully as swans on a lake. Gilmore remembered, from experience, how quickly swans could turn too.

Gilmore drew alongside Trevor, who he was relieved to see, looked as confused as he did by the hunt for the correct corridor, row, shelf and box as indicated by the catalogue reference. Allison hovered close by too, somewhere between the two distinct teams. She was showing Dillon some of the other treasures of the archive; letters, photographs, maps.

'Those fighters,' Gilmore whispered. 'What did they call themselves?'

Trevor answered with a quickness that surprised him. 'Naebbetold.'

'You know them? You know the name?'

Trevor nodded, and for the first time Gilmore felt a distance between them.

'Well?' Gilmore prompted, unwilling to let secrets taint what he hoped had become a friendship, forged through the mutual instinct to protect Dillon above all else.

'I guess if Bambera's broken cover, I can say,' Trevor said, as much to himself as to Gilmore. 'He's been preparing a private army. Just like his work with the Order, he's been playing a very long game. If the Association are the hunters, we're the ones who will turn the tables.'

Gilmore decided to be direct. 'Are you one of them?'

'I didn't give Bambera my answer. He kind of assumes, if you're like us, that you wouldn't think of turning him down. I think he assumes I am.'

'Like us?'

Trevor smiled ironically and indicated his face. 'Pay attention, Group Captain,' he said, not unkindly.

'An army based on ethnicity?'

Trevor nodded. 'Seems so,' he said. 'That's what put me off. It's a bit black and white for me.' He laughed to himself bitterly.

'And Hannah?'

'Same as me. Just wanted to get on with things, keep people safe, no matter what colour. Good or bad, it goes beyond all that, right?'

Gilmore sensed Trevor was seeking his agreement, and he nodded, genuinely. 'For now, at least they're providing us with some needed defence I suppose. Although unofficial militia on the streets of Britain, no matter the race or reason, can't end well.'

The two men fell into silence, browsing seemingly endless rows of remnants. Turning a corner, they almost bumped into Allison. She had allowed the boy to wander further off, while she had seemingly chosen to read through a pile of handwritten notebooks. Gilmore glimpsed lewd drawings and the cheeky graffiti of the young soldiers who had filled it just before she snapped it shut in surprise at their presence.

Gilmore looked at her, feeling yet more suspicion crowd into his already muddled mind. 'Found out anything interesting, Allison?' he enquired casually, purposefully watching her reaction. *Were you listening to us?* his eyes asked.

'Not yet,' she replied, holding his gaze.

'We've found it!' came a call from further along the long corridor. Bes was moving back down towards them, holding a large tin box aloft. Saunders followed from behind, a contented grin on his face.

'Back to base then?' Gilmore asked as Dillon gave a huge

yawn, reminding him how late it must be and how much they'd been through for one day. 'We stick to the tunnels. Hopefully the power will last out this time. Who knows what's going on up there.'

Taking his son's hand, which was gripping back only gently, like he did when he was exhausted, he allowed the others to go first. Feeling a shared tiredness and a lingering worry that this team of his was still so unknown to him really, he watched their backs as they led the way, grateful that he could keep them all in his sights.

Dillon felt as if he were floating by the time they arrived back at the base below the Library.

His tent was there, and it seemed to him as welcome as his own bed at home. That ornately patterned cloth, thin though it was, would block out the chaos he had seen. The past and present were jumbling up in his mind; in the shadows he could see his old familiar soldiers from World War One crawling through mud with the survivors of the concentration camps, while behind them stalked skeletal machines with blank eyes and exposed silver bones. He knew they were all waiting for him to sleep.

He trudged, exhausted, to his tent. The others were already clustering around the box, keen to expose the treasure within. His curiosity was drowned by tiredness.

'Dillon,' came a quiet voice, hooking him still before he reached the entrance to his sanctuary. Bes had separated from the group, and was looking between them and him as if she didn't want to be seen.

'I have to sleep,' he slurred.

'I know,' she said, leaning down to him. 'And you will. You have your bullet?'

He nodded, knowing it was there waiting for him.

'The Unknown Warrior will protect you from your fears,' she told him. 'When you need him, call him up. You have the bullet he needs to end the nightmares.'

'I... don't under...' he tried to say, but he was already laying down, and she was covering him with his blanket and placing his bullet in his hand for him and closing it over. Besides, in those moments as he sank into sleep, he felt that somehow, he *did* understand anyway.

Allison held the box reverently.

Gilmore and the others leaned in, watching with expectation. She pulled on the lid and after some resistance the box burst open, letting out a breath of stale, chemical-tainted air.

What she pulled out looked exactly as described in Keisel's notes. Gilmore had visualised them with help from the suggestions of similar structures that adorned the walls and glinted coldly in the candlelight, and now something almost exactly the same was there, physically in front of him.

Saunders held a hand out, and touched the artefact gently, tracing his fingers across the enclosed lozenge-shaped chamber at the top, along the thin metal capillaries and around the rubbery structures that had to emulate the lungs themselves.

'The transcendence of human breath,' he said, awestruck.

'We still don't know why this would be useful for the Child,' Gilmore noted, cutting through the admiration towards what he saw as a monstrosity. 'It's too late to call the bunker now, but first thing in the morning we'll need to confer with Rachel and Markson. I'm guessing Bambera will want to get this to them as swiftly as he can, so we should expect his visit any time.'

'There's a warning here too,' Allison added. She was clutching a scrap of paper that she had pulled from beneath the artefact. The paper was stained brown with age.

'What does it say?' Trevor asked.

'*Long-term pain threshold problem insurmountable,*' she read.

Gilmore sighed. 'So, whoever uses it would need the pain control implant too. Remember what Keisel warned; the agony would render any benefits useless.'

'But the Association have that,' Saunders said. 'So maybe it's enough that we keep it from them.'

Allison held up a hand to get their attention, the paper still held aloft in her other where she was tilting it to the light. 'There might be another way,' she said, straining to read something. '*Longest successful experiment used Fusion Gel AM1791. Access restricted by Order of HM Govt. Further research recommended if restraint eased.*'

'Fusion Gel,' Saunders repeated, looking at Bes. 'Our holy grail.'

'What is it?' Gilmore asked, looking between the academics, unwilling to let either of them get away with more obfuscation.

'I'm guessing it's the oldest and last of the artefacts Bambera is hoping we'll track down. It's the panacea of human-machine synthesis, a formula for a gelatinous liquid that bridges human flesh to metal and allows the flow of information, electricity, nerves, commands, between the two. It overcomes the body's natural instinct to reject the alien material and the resultant infection, pain and ultimately, failure. It's a legend we've been chasing for decades. Add it to the other artefacts, or use it with our existing tech, and you'd have the advantage. A Child with access to all of that would become powerful beyond measure. Any system in the world could be fed into it and through it with no barriers. And, likewise, the other way around. Whoever controlled a Child with that power could manipulate those systems as they wished.'

Gilmore could tell Saunders' words were sinking in. Trevor and Allison looked aghast at the artificial lungs, while the expression on Bes' face was more inscrutable than ever. 'As epic as that all sounds, is there anything we can practically do now?'

The group were silent.

'Then we wait for Bambera,' he instructed, mustering the command he knew he still exerted even in these distorted circumstances. 'We've reached a dead end, and the most useful thing we can do is sleep. From tomorrow onwards, who knows when we'll get chance to do so again.'

Perhaps from exhaustion, perhaps recognising that barrier and the rightness of his words, the group quietly started to drift away. Whether they or he would achieve sleep despite their efforts would remain to be seen.

Gilmore woke with a start, feeling a hand squeeze his arm and an urgent voice in his ear at the same time.

'Ian, we have a problem.' Allison crouched next to him, a piece of paper from the tin box in her hand. He could smell its unnatural scent. Behind her, Saunders and Trevor loomed, worry etched on their faces. He propped himself up and rubbed his eyes.

'Something had been nagging me, stopping me from sleeping,' she explained. 'I went back to the box and looked again. There was another sheet,' she said, pointing at the corner of the paper where a rusty staple held the torn corner of something that had been removed.

'And?'

'Our sheet. It finishes with "see att.", as in "see attached".'

'So, there was another sheet, where is it? What was on it?'

'It could have been the location of the Fusion Gel,' Saunders explained.

'Hang on,' Gilmore said, standing to join them and looking about. 'Who had the box before we opened it? And where's Bes?'

'Exactly,' Trevor said with finality. 'Only Bes spent time with the box before we opened it together. She said she was going to remove the catalogue label to preserve it. And now...'

'She's gone,' concluded Allison. 'And with her, the clue to the location of the final artefact.'

CHAPTER FIFTEEN

Friday – Northern outskirts of London. 11.40pm

THE LIGHTS of London had not yet coalesced into their orange concentration, but Markson knew they soon would. The car sped through the darker density of Epping Forest, nature's last encroachment on the city before concrete and tarmac became dominant.

The faint light thrown back inside from the headlamps allowed Markson to make out the reflection of Atkinson's face in the window. The man's stiff body sat on the back seat next to him, pressing against the door and looking away even as the gun remained trained in his direction. Was distaste at a potential injury pushing him to expand the limited distance between them, Markson wondered, or distaste at the man himself?

The car slowed, the gentle pull of gravity moving the two men forward slightly in unity.

'Badgers,' the driver said gruffly.

Markson felt a hysterical chuckle bubble inside his chest, and he thought he saw a flash of embarrassment in Atkinson's eyes. 'Wouldn't want to harm any defenceless creatures now, would we?' he said, his urge for a sarcastic barb needing to be satisfied even if it risked retribution.

Atkinson took the bait. 'The natural world is important to us,' he said tartly. 'There's little natural about you, Professor Markson, if some kind of hypocrisy was being implied.'

Markson breathed deeply, taking the insult into his mind as he did so often, whether it be directed at him or just something overheard; some slur, some intentional or unconscious offence against him and those like him. Leaving it there, hanging, stinging despite his years of mental defence, he turned away.

The car pulled off again, gathering speed and cutting its path of light through the darkness.

Atkinson continued to look ahead, not turning back to the window as he had been, perhaps grateful that dialogue, however cruel, had been opened. 'You'll be telling us everything you know, you do realise that, don't you?'

'Have you been learning gangster-speak from your new friends?' Markson shot back before he could stop himself. 'If so, you need some practice. It's a little stilted at the moment.'

Atkinson grimaced in a combination of amusement and disgust. 'Enjoy your capacity to speak while you can,' he said. 'I can only imagine the plans Ratcliffe has for you.'

'He scares you, doesn't he?' Markson again allowed his instincts to speak before what was left of his good sense prevented him.

Atkinson, against his expectations, replied swiftly in the positive. 'He terrifies me.'

'Is that why you're doing this? In fear of him?'

'That, and I sympathise with his goals. This country has compromised itself, fatally. We're bloated with immigrants, services stretched to breaking, while women and children...'

Markson heard a catch in his voice.

'Professor Jensen used to excuse your behaviour as a result of your grief,' Markson said gently, the performance of his earlier efforts stripped away. 'I think she knew, as I do, that grief can distort us completely out of shape.'

Atkinson was breathing heavily and quickly. 'Distortion,' he spat. 'An ironic judgement coming from someone like you.'

Another insult to hold, to add to the pile. 'Or maybe you were like this already. Bitter, bigoted, ignorant. Is that what she liked about you...? Your wife?'

Atkinson raised his gun, aiming it directly at Markson's mouth. 'My wife died because of them.' Each word was uttered as if through chest-tightening pain. 'Black doctors, black nurses.'

Markson closed his eyes in case his next utterance was his last. 'They didn't give her cancer,' he whispered.

'No, but they gave her the infection that finished her. Her and our child.'

'Surely you know that's not true. It's terrible luck, but infections can just... *happen*.' Markson heard the click of the gun in preparation and screwed his eyes tightly shut.

'Don't waste him,' the driver called back from the front.

'Ratcliffe said dead or alive,' Atkinson returned with determination.

'Imagine him dead *after* having betrayed his friends,' the driver added, quite cheerily. 'Much more satisfying.'

The inside of the car returned to silence, only the relentless sound of tyre on tarmac droning underneath them. It took a while before Markson felt able to open his eyes again.

A small audience had gathered around Ratcliffe, eyes bright despite the late hour, fuelled by the potential for more violence.

Their urgently babbling voices echoed around the corrugated iron of the walls of what was unofficially known as 'the conference room', even though the connotations of discussion and democratic decision-making were evoked in irony only.

Enclosed within the bigger space of the Shoreditch warehouse, those who were allowed to enter it knew that while it permitted them a certain kudos among their fellows, it also put them at risk of punishment for failure. The group was, essentially, Ratcliffe's lieutenants, those he had noticed as being marginally brighter than the others, their intelligence often resulting in a more creative type of cruelty.

'I started tonight impressed,' Ratcliffe said, quietly enough to force the noisy men to pipe down. Speaking over him, they knew, never ended well. 'Now you're telling me we've encountered targeted resistance?'

The men remained completely silent in response and then, as if functioning autonomically as a collective, they pushed one reluctant representative of their number forward as a mouthpiece for them all. How and why they had selected him in particular, Ratcliffe was unsure. Was it that they perceived him to be the strongest of them and more confident to speak up, or perhaps the weakest and therefore the most obvious to sacrifice?

'Tell me exactly what's happened,' Ratcliffe commanded, fixing the proffered lieutenant in his gaze.

'Some of the Bolts, Boss, they were dragged away.' The man, a Scot called Iain, returned his stare bravely, clearly framing his report with an edge of outrage he hoped would save him. 'As soon as they'd done the shop windows, some of the blacks, and the Japs, they seemed to come together and they just... took them.'

Ratcliffe kept his interrogation quiet and level. 'They were co-ordinated?'

'Boss?'

'Did it look planned? Organised?'

'To be honest, yeah,' Iain admitted.

'As if they knew that the Bolts were co-ordinated too...' Ratcliffe allowed his thoughts to be heard.

Iain shuffled, nervous at providing more bad news. 'Did you know how they were when we found them, Boss?'

Unwilling ever to shake his head in the negative in front of a subordinate, or to reveal he knew less than them, Ratcliffe stared until the man told him anyway.

'We found nine of them... Their bodies... arranged.'

Ratcliffe held his face firm even though he was intrigued, excited even at the level of challenge this potentially offered. *Bambera's forces?* he wondered. Were they really declaring war?

'Three lots of three,' Iain explained. 'In each set of three there were two arranged at angles, one horizontal, joining them up together in a—'

'Lightning bolt,' Ratcliffe concluded. He asked no more on the matter, instead dismissing them and telling them to get rest in readiness for the battles to come.

As they filed out to leave him alone in the room, he felt an unfamiliar shiver of uncertainty. So used to feeling like the apex predator, the thought of other hunters out there, as bold and devious as he, was paradoxically worrying and thrilling. That those hunters were supposed to be his prey raised the level of the new possibilities to intoxicating heights, and he grinned, giddy with tiredness and the dawning of new thoughts.

From nowhere, he remembered the little black boy in the playground, robbed of the torch, robbed of his playmate. He remembered the glint in the boy's eye as he had been brave enough to look directly at the man who had brought reality crashing into their fantasy of friendship. It had spoken of pain, that bold stare, of the recognition of an old enemy, even though he was so young, and it had promised, one day, revenge.

Markson stared, aghast, as the toll of the London power cut became clear.

People were still milling about in the streets aimlessly, mostly youths who felt brave or foolish enough. They stepped through the broken glass of shopfronts and the litter of disorder. The streetlights shone down on it all, the power returned, but what the darkness had spawned was not so easily dissipated.

He wondered if anyone was able to sleep, despite the early hour of the morning.

The car started to take right-angled turns into smaller and smaller roads, threading its way through the capillaries of the city. Eventually it pulled up in front of a large, bland warehouse, corrugated iron and metal struts giving it the air of the temporary structures built during and after the war that were still clinging to cohesion long after their intended lifespan. It was streaked with rivulets of rust-coloured staining and studded with small windows through which only faint light shone.

The driver now doubled as a crude and forceful escort, presumably saving Atkinson from the indignity of having to bundle his bulk into the warehouse and allowing the grim-faced figure to stalk alongside, the gun still pointing towards Markson.

'Not bothering with a blindfold?' Markson asked, mustering what he knew could be his last attempts to annoy his captors. 'I'm not adverse, you know.'

'That would suggest we might be worried you might escape and reveal our location to someone,' the driver replied as matter-of-factly as usual, 'as opposed to the reality, which is that you're unlikely to be leaving here alive.'

Take it in and hold it there, Markson told himself, even as he felt a wave of quivering terror take him over. Whether the driver could feel it or not, he couldn't tell; he was pushed further ahead, arms held behind his back painfully, Atkinson by his side.

Having passed through more layers of internal iron barriers, deeper into the honeycomb structure of the giant warehouse, they eventually reached a plain door at which Atkinson knocked, tentatively. *This must be it*, Markson thought, noting the change in his captors as if they themselves were almost as nervous as he was.

'Enter,' came the command from within, and Atkinson nodded to the driver to open the door.

Markson, despite himself, was struck by the man's looks.

Tall, broad, with dark, swept back hair and piercing blue eyes, he was the epitome of 1960s film-star handsome, preserved from the randomly scruffy colours and louche fashions of the new decade. His suit was immaculate, his black shoes shiny. Only the shadows under his eyes gave away a crack in the armour, the tell-tale sign of days without proper sleep that Markson often saw among his students.

Thinking of them, of the university and of Rachel, opened a chasm of homesickness in the pit of his stomach. He was thrust forward into the room by the driver, who took his chance to escape whatever might follow, and closed the door, sealing them in together.

Tommy Ratcliffe rose from the desk. 'Professor Markson,' he said politely. 'Albert.'

Markson was surprised by the pleasant charm of the man he suspected would kill him. 'Mr Ratcliffe,' he said carefully.

'And Professor Atkinson,' Ratcliffe said, still friendly. 'You've done well, bringing one of them to me. Both would have been ideal, along with their Child.'

'The bunker's on full lockdown. This one was stupid enough to leave.'

'And what about your preparations? Given what's happening out there, we might need to be ready. The threat might bring some calm.'

Atkinson's eyes took in Markson before they settled on Ratcliffe, and there was a flash of shame or embarrassment in them. 'I've brought what I can from my lab,' he said quietly.

'Like most weapons, it's the plausibility of the threat that will hopefully do the job. They're starting to see what we can do to the power. We can make our demands soon. But it looks like even if the government give in, certain elements have gone rogue. Your weapon could be our solution to them.'

Markson didn't need to think too hard to work out what they were referring to, and he remembered his last proper encounter with Atkinson, back when his proposal for the study of ethnicity-targeting biological weapons was rejected by the funding panel led by Rachel. He perceived the tangle of a pattern months in the making, and a sickening feeling of inevitability joined the dread inside him.

Ratcliffe turned and studied his face, looking for a reaction. Markson didn't give him the satisfaction, but swallowed involuntarily. 'We don't mind talking about all this in front of people who won't be leaving,' he said, echoing the certainty of Atkinson on the journey. 'So much easier than dancing around with code words and the like.'

The need for clarity suddenly panicked Markson's mind too, and he found himself blurting out, 'What do you want from me exactly?'

'You're going to help us with our Child,' Ratcliffe explained. 'You're going to tell us what we need to know about Bambera's plans for the other one, and how we can defend against it. If you're good, we'll let you assist our expert. If you don't tell us what we need, or work against us in any way, the tortures you will suffer will leave you begging for death. Do you understand?'

Markson could think of nothing to do other than to nod, obediently.

Ratcliffe led the way to the Child's chamber, telling himself this would be his last act of the night. Seeing it, remembering its potential, would sooth his mind he was sure.

The two professors shuffled along beside him. Ratcliffe smirked to think of the gun still being trained on Markson by Atkinson, the petty bitterness of the man fuelling the atrocities he was capable of. Minimum effort was needed; this collaboration would manage itself. Markson was a weak, indulgent specimen, used to the pleasures of the world and of the flesh. His ample bulk spoke of years of it. Any slight threat to that would easily be magnified into a terror that would ensure co-operation.

Ratcliffe unlocked the final doors and eventually, there it was before them.

He noticed the intake of breath from Markson upon seeing the Child.

'It's a boy,' the professor said pathetically, as if announcing the birth of a son.

'An appropriate counterpoint to yours,' Ratcliffe said,

enjoying the clarity of the binaries he had decided upon long ago. 'And a timely reminder that the male will always be superior.'

'Who is he?'

Markson had stepped forward and was leaning down to look upon the boy's sleeping face. Behind the thin lids, his eyes danced in unknowable dreams. Blue veins pulsed beneath the pale skin, snaking around the red wheals where the wires and cables were pushing into his flesh.

Ratcliffe was tired, and thought about turning to go, leaving the question unanswered. But something stirred in him, a desire to make the strange beauty of it known.

'When we found him, he didn't have a name,' he said. 'His mother was using him to beg for money. She gave him to us happily for enough to keep her fed for a year. He's the product of a broken country, Professor Markson. Imagine a culture that allows a single one of its children to live like that, let alone hundreds, thousands. Look at the colour of his skin. He is one of ours. We offer warmth and shelter to *them*, while neglecting so many of our own.'

He found himself stepping towards the Child and cupping its chin in his hand. He felt it respond, very slightly, like a cat leaning in for a stroke. 'He is any of them,' Ratcliffe said, unsure where the words were coming from within his exhausted mind. 'He is all of them. All the forgotten and abandoned ones. He is the Unknown Child who will fight for them all and *win*.'

CHAPTER SIXTEEN

Saturday – Beneath Cambridge. 6.20am

RACHEL WOKE with a start, not knowing where she was.

The echoes of a dream fled her mind, leaving only an impression of metal grating, of circles and spheres, and a scent of static and warm flesh. Banks of equipment, the beeps and low buzz of power eventually took the place of wherever she had been in her sleep.

Swivelling too quickly, hurting her neck where it had become stiff in the unplanned slumber, she checked the Child. Judith was awake too and looking in her direction. She shook her head to try to clear the muddle, avoiding the Child's unfocused gaze, but still feeling the tendrils of connection that had intermittently returned since their first joining and which now seemed to be strengthening through proximity. Her issuing of Bambera's command, received and understood so clearly by the girl and her systems, had only bound them even more closely together.

Are we sharing dreams now too? Rachel wondered, shivering. 'God, I need a coffee.'

Footsteps on the metal staircase descending into the bunker made her turn uncomfortably again, and she saw the head of security, who she knew only as Adams, fully uniformed and armed, his face set in concern.

'He's still not back,' he said.

'Albert?'

Adams nodded grimly. 'We shouldn't have let him go. Bambera's gonna go mad.'

'Never mind Bambera. Have you searched? He might have sat

down somewhere and just passed out from exhaustion, like me.'

'The guards have been out since four. No sign at his quarters or any of the university offices he tends to use.'

Rachel felt a swell of regret build. She had been so obsessed with the Child, she should have made him stay. 'He's a grown man,' she said, as much to herself as to Adams. 'We're not in a police state, yet. He was always free to come and go to maintain our cover here.'

'Not a good idea at night though, you have to admit. I'd better get on to Bambera. And talking of police state, I'm guessing you haven't heard the news yet?'

Rachel shook her head, bracing herself for the next shock and wishing she had managed more than just a few hours' rest.

'The government has enacted some emergency powers in the light of last night's cut and the violence.'

'Violence?'

Adams paused, as if nervous to go further. 'There was a spate of attacks, Professor. Shops, businesses.'

Rachel froze. 'The targets?'

'The pattern seems to suggest... an antisemitic motive.'

Her heart thumped hard in her chest. The implications... for her family, for Dillon...

'But the government has acted. Martial law zones have been activated across London. Dispersal orders are in place around particular hotspots. A special taskforce has been set up to focus on the energy problem and they're promising to have a solution by the end of the weekend.'

Rachel appreciated his efforts in sounding hopeful. 'But where do we fit in to all of this? Bambera resigned. Is he part of this government response? Are you?'

'I've sworn my loyalty to Bambera.'

'In addition to your previous work, for the government I presume?'

Adams shook his head, looking slightly confused as if she should have known already. 'I've never worked for the government, Professor. None of us have. We're employed directly by Bambera.'

Rachel turned away, processing the implications of this simple admission. 'A private army...?' she breathed, looking again at Judith and sure that she was returning the look of concern.

*

Gilmore allowed time for what he guessed would be an early start for Rachel, and at least two coffees, before he picked up the phone to make contact.

The rest of the group had settled after a period of aimless milling around. Trevor kept Dillon occupied, the boy reluctantly sketching in his book, his face creased in concerned concentration rather than the peacefully enthusiastic way of old. Allison and Saunders sat at the main desk, staring at the artefact and the remaining paper as if scrutiny alone would reveal its missing twin.

The phone didn't have to ring for long before the familiar voice answered, 'Hello? Ian?' The sound of it flooded him with a desire to see her. It had only been a few days, and yet events had distorted time so that it felt like so much longer. His voice caught in his throat as he thought of her seeing their son again, wondering whether he was the same boy she had left or whether the things he had seen and heard had changed him irrevocably.

'My dear,' he replied, any ability to maintain a professional persona gone.

'Ian, tell me you're both safe.'

'We are. We're back at the base, Dillon is with me.'

'I don't know where to start.'

'Me neither.'

'Markson's—'

'Bes, one of our researchers, has—'

Their speech overlapping, they both coincided with the word 'gone'.

'You first,' Rachel instructed. 'What do you mean, gone?'

'She's abandoned us. Taken what might be a clue to the location of some ultimate artefact or other.'

'Ian, I need you to be clear. What artefact? What more have you found?'

'We've got hold of some kind of breathing apparatus, like artificial lungs.' The silence coming from the receiver told him she was processing this. He could see her puzzled face, her mind working fast through the connections to find the pattern. 'They're too painful for anyone to use though, without help. We lost the first pain reliever to the Association as you know. We think that's how they've been able to launch this bigger attack on London. But there's something else out there.'

'Something else that could ease Judith's pain?'

'Saunders says its discovery would be like a key to unlock the full potential of the technology. A fluid, a gel, that means pain-free fusion of flesh with machine parts.' Gilmore felt his empty stomach churn at the thought.

'And that's what this Bes woman has gone off to find?'

'Saunders is bereft. They've been working together for decades. He can't understand why she'd go alone, and he can't believe she'd betray this Order of theirs. Tell me about Albert.'

He heard Rachel sigh. 'He talked with Bambera and left. Late last night. No sign of him since. The guards have searched, but nothing.'

'If he's fallen into Association hands...'

'You don't need to say it, Ian. He wasn't designed for this life. If they torture him...'

'Does Bambera know?'

'He does now. He's on his way to you, and his chief soldier here is waiting for instructions. There's talk of movement to some kind of back-up location.'

'For whom?'

'I don't know. Ian, he's no longer part of the government. And it seems he's been building up his own army for some time, preparing for this battle.'

Gilmore remembered the bodies on the ground, the police uniforms worn by traitors and the new defence force, the Naebbetold, striding across London with some authority beyond his understanding.

'Darling, I know this is going to be hard for you,' Rachel continued. 'Chain of command means everything to you.'

'I don't know who I am any more,' he found himself saying before he could hold it in any longer. 'Chasing about these tunnels and archives, bodyguard to academics. Ex-pilot, now well and truly grounded. Terrified dad. Spare part. I can't work out where I fit in and what I'm supposed to do next.'

He held out a hand instinctively, as if reaching to her across the distance.

'I heard one word in there that told me who you are, Ian,' she said with certainty. '*Dad*. There's only one role you really need to focus on now.'

He closed his hand around hers, even though it wasn't there.

*

Dillon finished his drawing, but when Trevor leaned in to have a look, he closed the sketchbook firmly to make it clear he didn't want it seen. The imagery lingered in his mind's eye as his drawings always did; the Unknown Warrior, blank-faced, standing strong amid a hail of bullets and broken glass.

'Where do you think Bes has gone?' he asked Trevor.

The man looked towards the heavy door to the base, as if it contained the answer. 'I don't know, my friend,' he said. 'But maybe we will find out soon. Try not to worry.'

His dad joined them and ruffled his hair. 'Mum's fine,' he told him. 'She sends her love.'

'I wanted to speak to her.'

'She was called away, son. But you will do soon.'

'Soon, soon, soon,' he repeated impatiently, feeling the need to be alone and stomping off away from them, half-regretting it even as he did it.

He drifted near to the radio, from which the announcer was repeating the update they'd heard numerous times now. Normal programming had been suspended and between scripted reports, serious music played.

'The government is reminding Londoners to stay calm and advising them to stay in their homes across the weekend. An update on securing power supplies is expected later today. An emergency reshuffle has seen several key positions filled by those the Prime Minister has described as "best placed to deal with the current crisis". The Ministers for Energy, Defence, Health and Universities are among those replaced. Details are expected to be confirmed as part of the official update. The rest of the country is being advised to be vigilant and to preserve power supplies where possible. Areas of London particularly affected by the new martial zones include Westminster, Holborn, Farringdon, Islington, Soho, and Shoreditch. Notices are being posted and residents advised to obey all instructions from armed forces. Restrictions are expected to be temporary.'

The words coalesced into a pit of worry in Dillon's stomach. The seriousness of the voice, the earnest music playing in between, was transmitting a grown-up world of fear he didn't think he would ever be able to understand. Even the pips, which had once brought him comfort and familiarity, were now just countdowns to more fear. *Six, five, four, three, two, one...*

He closed his eyes and tried to focus the way Bes had taught him. He counted upwards and cast the circle around himself that no one could enter unless he let them. Then he drew the figure of the Unknown Warrior once again. Free of the limitations of the pencil on the paper, he was huge, and moved, three-dimensional and turning in his mind's eye. His face wasn't just blank. It was flickering, changing, racing through the possibilities of all the men he could have been. His eyes were cycling through blue, green, brown, grey. His skin darkened through every possible shade to black and paled again, back and forth between all the colours of the human race. The Unknown Warrior looked down at Dillon, and no matter what face he wore, he smiled.

Kofi Bambera, ex-Minister for Defence, entered the code and pushed the heavy door open, entering the Order of Albion base and immediately sensing the mood of its occupants.

First up, as expected, was Gilmore. The man stalked towards him, his eyes wide and his sharp features set in barely suppressed agitation.

'At last!' Gilmore exclaimed with sarcasm. 'Are you going to explain what on earth is going on? Rachel tells me you've resigned. So, what are you now?'

Bambera held his hands aloft, his palms open in supplication. 'I need you all to listen. And I need you to stay calm, Group Captain Gilmore.'

'I'm still a group captain, then? Air vice marshal as was, if you recall.'

'Your military title is far more than something that can be given and taken by a government, Group Captain. It's part of who you are.'

'Don't patronise me,' Gilmore snapped back. 'Just explain what's going on.'

Completing his headcount as the others gathered around the main table with him, Bambera asked, 'Where's Bes?'

'Gone, like Markson,' Gilmore said, almost sounding satisfied at being able to deliver information that Bambera himself didn't already have. 'With our latest lead, leaving us stranded here, useless.'

Bambera picked up the silver artefact from the desk. 'Not

useless, it seems,' he said. 'You found it. We've been searching the archives for this for years. It's going to save time, and lives.'

To his shock, he felt Gilmore's hand grip his wrist, and he let go of the device. 'Not until you tell us what's going on,' the man growled.

Bambera pulled his hand away and looked in the faces that stared expectantly at him. Even the boy was staring at him, as if daring him to defy his father. *I might need to get used to this*, he thought. 'Very well.' He indicated that they sit. When they did, he continued. 'We're withdrawing from all our existing bases. The Cambridge bunker is compromised if Markson is with Ratcliffe.' He watched the faces of Gilmore and Allison carefully, noting the flash of shared recognition that passed between them, but unable to tell exactly how much they had shared and guessed between them in his absence.

'We're leaving too?' Saunders asked, sounding more sad than worried.

'Not just leaving, but scorching the earth in our wake. We can't leave anything for the Association to pick over. Everything we need, we take with us to our new base of operations. It's been prepared for this and is now at the centre of an exclusion zone from which we can launch our counterattacks.'

'And Rachel?' Gilmore asked.

'And the Child?' Allison added swiftly.

'They'll be joining us there. Together, from there, we'll launch our final stand.' Again, he watched their faces carefully, seeing how far he could push them, how likely they were to follow without too many questions.

'You've been pulling all our strings for quite some time now,' Gilmore said, calmer now, but just as intense. 'If you've resigned, who exactly are we working for?'

Bambera took a deep breath, hoping he would only need to say this once. 'You work for me, assisting the Naebbetold. For the duration of this conflict, the government will oversee the safety of the people, while we have the freedom to eradicate the enemy, by any means necessary. We will match their Child with our own, using all the resources at our disposal. We will hunt them down and take them out. The Association must be ended before they go too far.'

The members of the group were looking at each other,

wondering perhaps if any of them were going to object.

'You two,' Bambera said, nodding at Gilmore and Allison. 'Your work with the Counter Measures Group always sailed close to the boundaries of government approval. You know how these things work.'

The pair were silent. They shared another look of recognition and shared history.

'You, Mr Gordon,' he said, catching Trevor's eye from where he had been watching the boy with concern. 'Your work with MI6 has always included the possibility of stepping beyond sanctioned activity. And you, Dr Saunders, have lived on the fringes of society all these years, preparing for precisely this. I've funded you when all others have turned away and mocked you. I'm the only one who shares your goals.' He could see the logic and persuasion working in the eyes of the men.

It was Gilmore, perhaps predictably, who raised his hand to ask another question. 'And afterwards?'

'What do you mean?' Bambera said, careful not to let his impatience shine through.

'What guarantee do we have that we won't be held accountable for what happens next. If there are fatalities...'

Bambera nodded. It was a fair question. But he wasn't ready yet to lay down the pathway that would follow once the Association threat was ended. 'We stand completely outside the government for now, and wherever power lies afterwards... they are only going to thank us. Believe me.'

'Back with the government, one presumes?' Gilmore asked pointedly. 'Where power will lie afterwards, I mean.'

Bambera kept his gaze level. 'Of course. Now, the quicker we evacuate here, the sooner you will be reunited with your wife.'

He noticed the boy look at his father with eager relief. Gilmore returned the look and nodded. Seizing the moment of distraction to seal the deal, Bambera asked, 'Are you all with me?'

Gilmore nodded again, and the others, one by one, did too.

Bambera smiled in triumph.

CHAPTER SEVENTEEN

Saturday – Beneath Holborn, London. 9.40am

'**BOY, AM** I sick of tunnels,' Gilmore complained as another turn brought them into a dark and dripping cavern. 'Aren't you, Dillon? I swear, after this is over, no more tunnels for me.'

'I kinda like them,' the boy replied, taking this new one in with his keen eyes. 'Where are we now? This bit's older than the others.'

Bambera turned back from his position at the front of the group. 'He's observant,' he noted, with an admiration that riled Gilmore. 'We're now under the Old Bailey. And just to reassure you all, that means we're nearly there. This part of the network was used by priests to travel to provide last rites to prisoners about to be executed, so they could avoid the crowds.'

'Executed?' Dillon asked, his innocently questioning voice making the word sound at odds with its meaning.

Gilmore placed a hand on his shoulder protectively. 'We'll talk about it later.'

'He means killed, doesn't he? Why were there crowds?'

Gilmore sent Bambera a cross look, but the man just swept onwards, leading them to their destination and seeming to enjoy the anticipation a little too much. How to explain the gruesome urge to see death for real? Gilmore had seen enough of it to last more than a lifetime, the piles of bodies upon which peace had been built. He had never understood why anyone would want to add more to their tally. Death seemed so embedded in London's foundations, perhaps it was no wonder the city couldn't shake the habit.

How much longer can I protect him from it? he thought. He forged onwards through the damp darkness, remembering that every step was taking him closer to a reunion with Rachel. She'd know what to say.

'Bes would have explained,' Dillon said quietly.

Gilmore swallowed down a sense of injustice, tinged with what he didn't want to admit might be jealousy. As concerning as the disappearance of the academic was, he couldn't help but be relieved that her influence on his son had been put on hold.

Trevor fell into step with Gilmore and ruffled Dillon's hair in reassurance that he hadn't been abandoned. 'He mentioned priests. Another church?'

'He's enjoying the mystery, that's for sure. But a church as a base? Surely not.'

With a gathering sense of inevitable confirmation, they stepped up chilly stone steps, cut into the ground into a narrow spiral.

'I think you're going to be impressed.' Bambera's voice drifted down grandly from the top. 'Welcome to the Church of the Holy Sepulchre.'

Against his instincts and spurred on by a gasps of 'wow' shared by both Dillon and Trevor, Gilmore stared in awe at their new surroundings.

They were standing at the top of the stone staircase, which had opened out into one of the grandest churches he had ever seen. At first sweep his eyes took in the vaulted roof, rows of strong stone pillars, and the windows containing restrained stained-glass saints and holy figures, glinting in a weak winter light. It was when his eyes settled on the altar that he realised what Bambera had meant by 'base'.

A black and silver throne sat waiting. He knew it had been made ready for the arrival of the Child. Cables and wires splayed outwards from the ornate chair in a half-circle, running over the back of the altar like the exposed roots of an ancient tree. They connected to banks of equipment that merged into the stone alcoves. Metal and electronics twitched and twinkled incongruously amid the varnished wooden shelving.

He wasn't a religious man, but Gilmore felt the instinctive wrongness of the adaptations. He had felt the same when he had first seen the Child itself; something natural and beautiful, distorted out of shape under the onslaught of wires and tubing. A word floated to the surface of his mind as it attempted to name what he could see. *Blasphemy*.

'What have you done?' he whispered.

'Needs must,' came the confident reply as Bambera looked around at his creation. 'Once all this is over, the church will return to its original purpose. Until then, it makes the perfect fortress.'

'Why this one?' Allison asked.

'We've been clearing this area of Association influences for some time. The proximity of the courts has helped; they're instinctively allergic to the concentration of legal power next door. We have the Holborn Viaduct from which my men will defend our position to the west, and we've got another barricade at St Paul's to the south. And finally, we have the hospital.'

'You're expecting casualties?'

'We've secured its power supply for the purposes, given the recent attack on St Thomas'. The beds at St Bartholomew's have been cleared in readiness.'

Gilmore looked at Bambera who, although still wrapped in his khaki army uniform, stooped slightly as he held his chest. His presence, which had filled the Order's base and the tunnels beneath the ground, seemed diminished now he stood in such a grand space. Not for the first time, Gilmore wondered about the sense in trusting the man. 'And where are these men? How many do you have?'

Bambera looked at his watch and smiled. He held up a hand to suggest they wait. The seconds ticked by.

As the church bell began to toll ten o'clock, the main door of the church opened and armed, black suited figures poured in. They lined up in formation all along the back and sides of the church, stretching downwards to form a guard of honour towards the throne.

Gilmore couldn't help but be impressed by the grandeur of it. Bambera had found the ultimate theatre for his achievements.

Last to enter came a short, grey-haired woman who walked imperiously between two Indian men wearing traditional long silk coats, fawn coloured and adorned by military awards and badges. They carried swords and rested their hand on their hilts as they stood surveying the church and its transformed, electronic-gothic beauty.

'Ex-Minister for Universities, Jacqueline Grove.' Bambera bowed in welcome, and the woman tilted her head curtly in reply. 'Leader of the Naebbetold.'

Gilmore had the distinct feeling that Bambera was expecting him to bow too. So, he very resolutely did not.

Gilmore insisted that the new arrival gave him some time and attention, despite the woman's efforts to appear as a visiting governor, inspecting troops and equipment, nodding in magnanimous approval.

'I've heard much of your contributions to our cause,' Grove said as she indicated Gilmore should join her on a pew. 'I'm glad, too, that we've been able to keep you safe. Without us, I have no doubt you would have fallen in the first wave of attacks.'

Gilmore had to concede this was true, but he noted the conscious attempt to combine the thanks with a sense of binding obligation and duty towards her and her cause. 'I just need to know where this is all going. I've been a military man for most of my life, so I'm finding this... overturning of order... a little confusing.'

'I can understand that,' Grove said, seeming to want to continue to walk a line between power and equity with Gilmore. 'I was brought up in India and saw a certain amount of "overturning of order" as a result of this country's actions. I saw my father's casual superiority, based merely upon the shade of his skin. I see such *stupidity* everywhere, inviting chaos, bringing pain where it doesn't need to be. And here we now sit, together, defending our common purpose.' She indicated her guards. 'Imagine what we can do when the best of us work together.'

'I can understand the need to finish the Association,' Gilmore explained, trying to get closer to what he needed to know. 'But the Naebbetold. Your private army. Your separation from the government. It concerns me, I have to be honest.'

Grove fixed him with a cold gaze. 'Another white man worried that others might be rising above their station, Group Captain?'

Gilmore scowled. 'How dare you suggest...?' he exploded, feeling his hackles rise. He shook his head, took a deep breath. 'You were a respected politician. This has nothing to do the race of anyone, but the chain of command—'

'Is changing,' Grove completed. 'When the dust settles, a new structure will be in place, one that will prevent a threat like the Association from rising *ever* again. Do you understand what that means? An end to fascism and the racism that feeds it. For good.'

'I admire that goal, of course. I fought in the last war.'

'You will understand the wider pattern of history then, Group Captain. You've seen it, on your travels under this city, which buries its past but not quite deeply enough. This one city, a crucible for all the horrors of the last century, one event leading to the next to the next, history repeating, cycling around to the same disasters time after time. We will end that cycle.'

Gilmore could feel the woman's passion bringing what he needed closer. 'And what will follow?'

Grove paused, her grey eyes staring into him, assessing him.

Gilmore weighed his next words carefully. 'I just need to know what I'm fighting for.'

'Meritocracy,' Grove said, her zeal unleashed. 'The best and brightest from around the world. Every race and colour. The establishment of a system that will start here and spread, soon enough, around the world. Power in the hands of those who know how best to use it. Decisions made only by those intelligent enough to understand the implications of their choice.'

Gilmore kept his face level and prompted further. 'So that's what you've been preparing with your universities' portfolio? A new elite? And how will we establish and sustain this new structure?'

'The Child will show us the way. Technology does not recognise racial difference. As we merge with the machine, all sense of difference and otherness will fall away.' She fluttered her fingers through the air as if suggesting the gentle fall of snow.

All Gilmore could see, looming in his mind, was the blank-faced mask salvaged by the Order of Albion, and the very thing they had been warning against.

He looked over at Saunders, Trevor and Allison, wondering when they would realise they had all been used for this purpose, and he looked at Dillon, wondering not for the first time what kind of world his son would have to take his place in.

*

Rachel mopped Judith's mouth as the truck bounced over more rough ground.

She didn't seem concerned by her relocation into the darkness at the back of the vehicle, any more than she ever seemed very concerned about anything. But Rachel felt her vulnerability for her, and she cursed as she bumped her head once again as she tried to tend to the precious cargo.

The temporary life support system hissed and wheezed like the one that had been used to transport her to Jura. Where these systems were effective in keeping her alive, they did little for her mental inputs, so longevity was not an option.

Rachel tried to make up for it by talking to her softly, hoping that the coding net still crowning her scalp was converting her words of comfort into something useful. It seemed to be working; her almost-transparent eyelids were flickering as if she was drifting into sleep, and her heart rate monitor steadied into a slow, regular beep.

Taking the opportunity to gauge their progress, Rachel crawled forward to look out of the front window. 'Where are we?' she asked the driver, a young Malaysian man who had been friendly enough, politely looking away from Judith to preserve her dignity when they installed her and having provided occasional updates on the journey.

'Poplar,' he replied, attempting a Cockney accent. 'Proper East End, right?'

Rachel couldn't help but smile. 'And you still won't tell us where we're going?'

'Soon we won't need words. Your eyes will tell you. I think you will be impressed.'

The black clad guard next to him felt for his rifle, raised it, and scanned the road ahead.

'Expecting trouble?' Rachel asked.

'The route has been secured. Straight through to base. Best to check though. Bambera wouldn't forgive us if we didn't make this delivery.'

'Now I feel like a parcel,' Rachel said, feeling her head for bumps.

'Apologies, ma'am.'

'That's very respectful. Professor is fine, if you must use titles.'

'In the new order, that title will afford you great power,' the driver said with a curious reverence.

'The new order?' she repeated. 'I'm not sure I like the sound of that. Orders, new or otherwise, don't often sit well with me.'

She caught the guard give the driver a look that suggested he shouldn't say any more, and the cabin fell into silence.

The road itself was eerily quiet too, especially for a Saturday morning. Occasionally a figure could be seen standing guard on the roadside, dressed in black like the guard here and those that had protected the bunker. They would nod gently as the truck passed by.

Rachel focused on the view through the tinted windows to try to suppress the uncanny feeling gnawing in her chest. They drew alongside the Thames, its wide swell rippling beneath a leaden sky. They passed the docks, the boats paused in their journeys as if waiting for the tide to turn. They passed some of the poorest streets of the city, still scarred by war, and their freshly built replacements, constructed by the hands of Ratcliffe and others like him, aiming to shape the city into their image at the same time. They drove down Cable Street, site of an earlier battle in this seemingly never-ending war against intolerance.

She saw the Tower of London approaching, its walls and turrets impassive in their elegance, unconcerned with the new conflict unfolding around it.

As the truck paused near the Tower, she asked, 'Not there, surely?'

'No, ours is better. I just wanted to look.'

Then they sped on, passing more guards, whose presence thickened as they passed the looming concrete towers built amid the ground that had suffered some of the worst of the bombings. Rachel saw the proud dome of St Pauls, then the earnest front of the courts of justice, and then their destination.

'The Church of the Holy Sepulchre, ma'am,' the driver announced.

The building sat amid the city with a quiet pride at having survived so much. Its tower, which three centuries ago would have looked out at the burning city and prayed for deliverance, a watch kept once more only three decades past, now stared out over a strangely silent London. Its pale stone had become streaked with the liquid grime of pollution, but it had not lost its underlying beauty.

'I think you're right, this is definitely better,' she told him. 'And it looks like they're ready for us.'

A line of men in the now-familiar black suits were lined and ready to escort the Child inside to safety. Some were poised to carry her while others had taken up defensive positions, watchful for any sign of potential attack. She allowed them to do their duty for her first, keen for Judith to find some greater comfort in this new home than she had endured in the bunker and on the journey here.

Entering the church itself, she was unprepared for what she saw.

Machinery had colonised the altar, and the throne that had been prepared for Judith was the grandest she had yet seen; sleek black, studded with silver bolts, the cables ready to integrate her into the systems of the city reaching up into the dark spaces as if connecting her to the heavens. Lights flickered on banks of equipment like candles.

As she took that in, she felt rather than saw the tight hugs from her husband and son. They held her between them, and she couldn't speak. Her voice caught in her throat and a tear made its way down her face.

'Rachel, my dear,' Ian kept repeating, his own burden of the past days pressing against her. 'It's not right,' he whispered, so quietly that not even Dillon would hear. 'It's not right.'

So, she hugged them tightly and watched as Judith was installed into the machinery on the alter.

When it was done, Judith sat, arms grasping the sides of her new vessel, looking down upon the men who had placed her there. Rachel could see Bambera among them, and a small woman with iron-coloured hair flanked by men in beautiful Indian robes. Bambera and the woman stood with their heads bowed, as if they hoped to receive a blessing from the arrived goddess of this strange new age.

CHAPTER EIGHTEEN

Saturday – Shoreditch, London. 10.30am

PROFESSOR ALBERT Markson watched the consequences of his confessions unfold.

From his position in the doorway, covered by guards on either side of it, he could see the panicked bustle outside as Ratcliffe's men cleared out equipment ready to evacuate and see the calmer, more precise work being enacted upon the Child.

Ratcliffe oversaw this work, occasionally glancing over at him with a satisfied smile, like an eagle eyeing a corpse, knowing that he could feed upon it whenever he chose.

Markson tried to rehearse the story he had started to tell himself as the late dawn had broken over the warehouse, visible only through tiny, slatted windows in the room in which they had tortured him. *I had no choice*, he repeated to himself. *No one could have expected me to endure that much pain without talking. Everyone would have done what I have done.*

Then he remembered Rachel's resolute face, and he knew he was lying to himself. Strangely, with that acknowledgement came hope. In the same way that she would have withstood the pressures or found some way out, she would be able to sort out the mess he had created by revealing Bambera's plan for the Child. He knew that with certainty. And while he would never forgive himself for betraying them, and for being stupid enough to have left the bunker in the first place, he would find some small way to help her. He had to.

For now, he watched. The expression of defeat that had settled over his face since he had talked, now gave him the perfect mask with which to observe. While he could still be a help to them, he was certainly no threat. Ratcliffe seemed to enjoy having him there as a trophy and a reminder that the exercise of physical pain on another was sometimes the only power worth having. Markson thought of his qualifications, of the intellect that had borne developments in medicine that would save lives. In another time, perhaps that intelligence would provide some kind of defence. Against the threat of more broken fingers and torn out nails, it was worth nothing.

Hereward and Atkinson stepped back from the Child with a sense of finality.

'Is it ready?' Ratcliffe asked.

Hereward nodded. 'The new systems are installed. Mobility is still limited, but from what our friend here told us about their Child, that shouldn't be a problem.'

'And the overrides?'

Atkinson turned to Markson as he replied, to remind him of his role in the development of this potentially game-changing advantage. 'They're ready too. It will need to be fairly close to the other Child, but when it is, the access codes and the translation mechanism on her will be like an open door. He'll be able to step inside and take over. Then when we get close again, we can take control of both.'

'As it should be,' Ratcliffe said, a look of peace falling over him. 'Her moment is past. The male is ascending. We'll control the power systems once and for all. With that, we can issue the ultimatum. Refuse to obey, and we let the final sanction loose.'

Markson thought Atkinson turned a little paler than he already was at this.

'Let's clear out,' Ratcliffe commanded. 'We leave enough men to make the defence of the Child look convincing.' Then he turned to the little boy.

Since the final adjustments had been made, his face had become more determined, as if he knew his powers had grown and that soon he would be able to use them.

'I'll see you on the other side,' Ratcliffe told the boy with what sounded like genuine affection.

Then he pulled one of the plugs out from the back of the boy's throne and watched as the dials registering blood gas levels started to sink down towards the danger zone.

As Ratcliffe swept from the room and the others marched after him, Markson took a last look at the dying boy. He hoped Bambera would reach him in time, even though he knew that could mean Ratcliffe's ultimate triumph.

Gilmore waved Saunders over to him from where the academic sat, desolate on one of the pews.

Bambera and Grove seemed content to let them gather, arrogant in their control of the situation. He watched the way they moved up and down the aisle as if empowered for a holy mission by the building itself. For now, he needed to gather the collected thoughts of his team and form some kind of plan.

Dillon was resting, tiredness overcoming his small frame after their early start, having been soothed by his mum into a reluctant doze.

Rachel hissed into Gilmore's ear, 'Look at them. Who the hell do they think they are?'

He smiled at the correspondence of their thoughts. 'We're in church don't forget, dear,' he hissed back, preparing himself for a gentle slap.

'Not my religion, so I'm exempt.'

Saunders sat down beside Allison. Gilmore noticed that he was still clutching the paper they had retrieved from the artificial breathing artefact. He made a mental note to address that, but first he had to speak from the more urgent part of his mind.

'How much of their plan did you know?' he asked, sweeping them all with intent eyes and watching for signs of mistruth.

Trevor replied first, with a sigh. 'I knew Bambera had plans, but had no idea what. He's talked of a "protected status" in return for loyalty to him above MI6 command structures. I've kept my replies vague. All I care about is protecting you, and Dillon.'

Gilmore nodded, having seen this to be true so often over the last few days. He turned to Saunders. 'And you?'

'The Order is sworn to protect humanity from its drift towards the machine,' he replied, giving voice to a belief in which he sounded utterly convinced. Gilmore could believe how a lifetime of service to that goal that shaped him completely, at the expense of a family, friends, and much sense of normality. 'Power structures come and go. Conflict cycles around, but we stay separate.'

'Floating above it all?' Rachel said, a little harshly.

Saunders met her gaze, matching her fire with an icy certainty. 'No. Buried beneath the ground, rooting around in the mess you all leave behind. Willingly, for the protection of your child, and all the children to come.'

Gilmore saw the words sink in, and Rachel lowered her eyes from him. Then he braced himself as she fixed them on Allison. 'And what about you?' she asked coolly.

'I've had my suspicions for a while,' Allison replied. 'Whatever threat they pose themselves, they're our way of finishing the Association. That *has* to be a worthy goal.'

'Are you sure you're not tempted by their promise of an intellectual utopia?' Rachel loaded every syllable with disdain.

'After all these years, you still don't really know me.'

'First Woden, now this? Can you blame me?'

Gilmore risked leaning in between them. 'So, where do your loyalties really lie?'

Allison met his gaze with a steady force, calling to mind the shared moments of danger and uncertainty they had faced so many times. 'With you,' she said. 'Beyond any group, any network, any structure. My loyalty is to *you*. I trust you to make the right decisions when it comes to dealing with the Association, and whatever comes in its wake. I always have.'

It was enough for Gilmore, and while Rachel did not reply, he noted her small nod and knew that it was enough for her too, for now at least.

'The question is,' he stated, 'how far do we allow the Naebbetold to go in order to defeat the Association? Are we enabling something we'll come to regret?'

'Look around, Ian,' Rachel said. 'They're already on their way. Their battle is playing out whether we like it or not. It's just like last time. Imperials and Renegades, remember?'

Gilmore shivered at the words and looked over at the Child in its black and silver throne. 'Last time we had a special kind of help,' he reminded his wife.

'Yes, but he counted on us... So, just like last time, we can find a way through it, protecting what really matters for whatever comes next.'

Gilmore noticed the group shuffle and straighten, as if to

attention, and he guessed correctly that Bambera had neared.

'We have word of their location,' he announced. 'They're pulling out, so we're going in now. Whatever they've been preparing there, within the next two hours it will be ours, or it will be destroyed.'

He didn't wait for a reply. Gilmore recognised the swell of power behind his words. He wasn't seeking approval or co-operation anymore; he was content with silent acceptance of his new authority.

Allison drew closer to Rachel once more. 'If the Association do have a Child of their own and they capture it, they'll bring it here. They'll have two of them. With that much power...'

Rachel reached out and took her old friend's hand despite everything. Gilmore saw her look around at their team, her gaze binding them together better than he had managed. 'Above all else, no matter what, we protect the Children,' she stated, and they all nodded in acceptance.

The sound of gunfire broke the uncanny silence of Saturday lunchtime.

Bambera was pleased to see that the combination of government warnings and their expanding exclusion zone were keeping the public safely inside. It was another cold, wet day; they were probably grateful.

Keeping himself back behind three rows of his guards, he watched the focus with which the Naebbetold attacked the Association men with admiration. While Ratcliffe's forces were slightly more numerous, they were panicked and emotional, firing off wildly and hoping for a victim rather than working with precision. One division of Naebbetold guards had divided and disappeared into the buildings around the warehouse, appearing as snipers perched high amid the bricks and gangways like owls picking off mice.

Nonetheless, Bambera was careful not to get too close to the front line. He had suffered enough discomfort recently and another bullet, even a stray one, would be one too many. Instead, he watched the three-dimensional gunfight from his position at the back, close to the lead van that had led the convoy through the deserted streets to Shoreditch.

The guns fell silent, and he wondered if it was too soon, if it had been too easy, if this was a trap. The guards, their distinctive Naebbetold training telling them to likewise be wary, held their positions.

Another round of gunfire, which through its random blitzing took out two snipers in the nearby printworks, was met with an equally deadly reply. The silence that followed was even more total.

After some final occasional shots and an agonising wait for definitive news, one of his lieutenants emerged with a report. 'No sign of Ratcliffe or Markson, sir,' he announced, controlling his breathing but clearly heightened by something. 'But it's in there. Their Child.'

Bambera controlled his own reply. 'Is it alive?'

'Barely. Looks like they tried to finish it off, but it's hanging on.'

Warnings flickered from his subconscious. *Too soon? Too easy? Trap?* But Bambera decided that these were echoes of his earlier fears rather than heralds of new ones.

'Bring it to the van,' he instructed.

Grove and her guards continued to receive radioed reports and made notes on a map of central London pinned against one of the pillars, ignoring Gilmore and his friends. Occasionally one of the Naebbetold guards looked over in their direction, but they seemed of little interest.

The focus was still on protecting the area from attack and preserving the Child at the centre of their expanding web. She sat on her throne on the altar, a look of contentment having settled over her as she stretched out along whichever new pathways the church's cables and wires were giving her access to.

Gilmore beckoned Saunders more closely in once again, and he held out the paper from the artefact unprompted. To Gilmore's surprise, it had been scribbled on vigorously. A sheen of graphite was obscuring the original faint writing.

'Dillon's not been at that has he?' Gilmore asked.

'Darling, Dillon doesn't scribble any more,' Rachel reminded him.

'Oh, yes, well, what's happened to it?'

Saunders held it up to the light from one of the stained-glass windows. Filtered through the blue of a saint's robes, it shone on a particular spot at which he angled it, tilting it gently back and forth. 'Palimpsest,' he explained. 'The words from the sheet above have scored the one below. We can see what was written on the paper Bes took.'

'What does it say?' Gilmore was forced to ask, as even while squinting he couldn't make out the spectral writing.

'Poland Street,' he said, as if it was the most obvious thing in the world.

'Significance?' asked Rachel.

Saunders smiled sadly. 'The likely location of the Fusion Gel. Potentially the most helpful or dangerous of all the artefacts. The bridge between human and machine, hidden somewhere so obvious that none of us thought to look there in all these years.'

Gilmore frowned. 'I don't understand.'

'Bes was always better at the origins stuff than me. I was more focused on the future, on my curiosity about our developments and potential. She was far truer to the Order of Albion. She understood its creation and its true purpose. She said it had been handed down to her by generations from its beginnings on Blackfriars Bridge.'

'You're going to have to get to the point,' Rachel urged, nodding at the increased activity at the church's heavily guarded entrance.

'Our founder,' continued Saunders, 'was a man called William Blake.'

'Not the poet?' Rachel asked.

'The very same. He watched the Albion Mills burn, salvaged the experiments that had started there, and set up the underground network so that others would continue to guard against such progress beyond him. The base was made from its ruins as a reminder. I should have realised when I saw the code for the gel. AM1791. Albion Mills burned down in 1791. He took the most important of its relics back home, to Poland Street, in Soho. The Fusion Gel must be hidden there somewhere.'

Rachel's eyes glinted. 'If we could get that, it could give us the advantage. Keep it out of the hands of both sides.'

'Maybe that's what Bes wanted,' Saunders said hopefully.

'Either that or she's sold us out to one side or the other,'

Gilmore added.

'I've known her for most of my life. I think she knew we'd be able to find her.'

'And Dillon was singing her praises,' Rachel added.

Trevor and Allison had leaned in, sensing perhaps that decisions were being made. 'One last mission underground then?' Trevor asked. 'I reckon they'll let us if they know what's at stake.'

'Let's not give them the option,' Gilmore suggested as the action at the entrance became louder and more frantic. Guards were running from other stations around the church to join whatever was happening.

Rachel caught him by the shoulders. 'Ian, take Dillon,' she insisted. 'I don't like the way this is going. Keep him with you and Trevor. I don't want him near the Child. Especially if there's another on its way.'

Gilmore kissed her, then swiftly rounded the edge of the church while guards flowed past in the other direction. Trevor roused Dillon and they hurried towards him. He ushered them into the side passage that led to the steps and the tunnels.

With one final glance, he turned back to see Allison gripping Rachel's arm as a second throne was carried through the entrance with urgency. He didn't want to waste time watching any more despite his curiosity. It was clear enough that the second Child had arrived.

CHAPTER NINETEEN

Saturday – Beneath Soho, London. 1.00pm

DILLON WANTED answers.

He still felt the shadows of sleep curled around him like a shroud, and the competing energy in his limbs that told him he must be awake, alert and keeping up with his dad, Trevor and Saunders. He felt the shock of the change in temperature from the warmth of the church to the dampness of the tunnels. He felt a word growing inside that he wasn't able to contain.

'Stop!' he bellowed. He heard the echo, *Stop! Stop! Stop!* bounce and return and was surprised at the commanding pitch of his own voice. He froze, his mouth open, in shock at his own strength.

The others pulled to a halt too and his dad turned quickly in panic. 'Dillon? What on earth?'

Dillon reached out, feeling as if the tunnel floor was turning to water beneath him.

His dad took one arm and Trevor took the other, but he shook them off angrily, choosing the unsteadiness as his own rather than the constant reliance on someone else to provide solidity. 'What's going on?' he demanded. 'I'm not coming with you unless you tell me what's going on.'

He saw the way the men looked at each other, lightning flashes of eye contact that communicated in a language he couldn't understand. It made him angrier and, added to his frustration, he could feel a wetness on his cheeks. His own body was betraying him.

His dad crouched down so their faces were level. 'Dillon, we don't have time for this, son. I promise, I *promise*, we will explain everything as soon as we can.'

'Why couldn't I stay with Mum? Who was the woman in the chair? Why did she look like that? Why are all those soldiers there? What was coming through the door?' The questions tumbled out of him.

Trevor crouched down too, his kind eyes locking on to his. 'Dillon, man,' he said softly. 'I know this is frightening. I feel the same. But hey, you were the one learning all the cool stuff from Bes to help us through, right?'

'But where is Bes?'

Another silent exchange between the three men flashed in their eyes.

'That's what we hope to find out,' explained Saunders. He didn't crouch, but he towered between Dad and Trevor, his worried face at odds with the confidence of his stance. 'We're trying to find Bes. And when we do, everything else should fall into place.'

'It might take a while,' Dad continued, an unexpected honesty lacing his tone as if in reply to Dillon's own deeper pitch. 'It might still be frightening for a while. I can't promise that it's going to be easy, but we will get through this, and soon enough, we'll be back at home complaining about your mum's breakfasts and trying to find your games kit at the last minute and dozing off with our books.'

Dillon felt a rush of calm flood through him as the images of the familiar rose like spectres in the darkness of the tunnel. His old friends, the soldiers he could bring to mind, those who had died so that he could live an ordinary life, flickered around the edges.

'Every frightening moment is a step back to our old lives,' Dad concluded. 'You coming?'

Trevor rose first, inviting Dillon to walk on. He nodded and, shakily, did so. Saunders drew alongside, and dad rose and followed them. This time as the men met eyes in the darkness, he was included. Silent nods of resolve passed through each of them, and the four continued on their way, Dillon's unseen companions around them.

Gilmore's heart continued to hammer long after Dillon's call for them to stop.

He knew events were taking a toll on his son. Rachel had been shocked by the change in him. Gilmore just hoped that the change wouldn't be too great by the time this was over, and that they could indeed return to the ordinary life he now craved perhaps more than he ever had.

The country's going to have to look after itself after this, he thought. *Or others are going to have to take my place.*

'We're almost there,' Saunders said with anticipation, though for the destination or for a potential reunion with Bes, Gilmore couldn't say.

The tunnels were old and rancid here, more so than at any point during their subterranean journeys. They stank of the thick cigarette smoke of pubs with their undertones of stale alcohol, and the sewers seemed close too. It was as if the walls dividing the people from their chemical and biological realities were breaking down.

'Tell me about this Poland Street,' Gilmore instructed, keen for distraction from the smell.

'Blake lived there around the time he set up the Order,' Saunders explained, 'but the belief was always that he had left everything we'd need in the base beneath the Library. The Order has treated Poland Street like an abandoned shrine ever since, somewhere to visit to dedicate or re-dedicate to the purpose, to connect to the mission, but nothing more than that.'

Trevor held up the tatty map and pointed. 'And it's just around the corner.'

Holding up their torches, the three men stepped forward carefully.

Embedded into the wall and encrusted with calcium deposits and mould, was a wooden door. Saunders produced a key, which to Gilmore looked comically old-fashioned. The man at least had the decency to look a little apologetic as he placed it in the lock and turned it. *The strange rituals of the Order and their lonely existence must suddenly seem embarrassing now outsiders were seeing,* he thought.

The sight inside the room was equally poised between awe-inspiring and bizarre. Candles had been lit to bathe the walls in their golden glow. Upon the walls were painted murals; surreal designs of human forms in geometric exoskeletons, landscapes turned brown and black from the churning output of giant factories, bare trees turned into chimneys and antennae, demonic forms falling from the sky and angels rising from the depths.

'Blake's unseen prophecies,' Saunders breathed reverently. 'I've only seen them once before, when Bes brought me here for my initiation.'

Gilmore watched as Trevor and then Dillon entered the space. While Trevor looked as disconcerted as he did by the imagery, Dillon took it all in with wide eyes, awe-inspired, as if he recognised instinctively what he was seeing. Not for the first time since this had all started, Gilmore wondered whether his son's imagination was becoming more powerful than the practical realities he tried to instil in him. He felt the need to talk with Rachel, as they so often did while drifting off to sleep, about their hopes and fears for their boy.

Saunders moved through the small, brightly coloured space towards another door. 'Through here,' he indicated.

Pushing this door open, Gilmore heard their objective being reached before he saw.

'Bes,' Saunders said, the single syllable laden with concern.

Pushing ahead for a look, Gilmore saw the woman, folded compactly on the ground, her arms wrapped around herself and her head down against her knees.

When she lifted her head to look at them, she only did so to the level of Dillon, and she fixed him with a look of utter relief.

'He's here,' she said in a voice animated by fervour. 'The child is here.'

Gilmore shivered.

Dillon tried to control his urge to run forward to join the woman in the centre of the small chamber.

Dad raised his hand in warning, but even that didn't feel enough. Only Dillon's shock at seeing the previously dignified figure so changed prevented him. Her hair was dirty and dishevelled, and she had taken off the overalls of her Order to cope with the heat, remaining in only a stained shirt and long shorts.

Bes' eyes remained fixed on Dillon. It was as if the others weren't there. He felt a strange privilege, as if he was special at last, but at the same time a competing discomfort and the need to retreat into that promised normality of his old life.

Saunders stepped forward and broke her gaze, standing in front of Dillon as if he himself wanted to be the special one. 'Bes,' Saunders said, crouching down to meet her face to face as Dad and Trevor had done to Dillon in the tunnels. 'Why did you leave? What are you doing here?'

Dillon moved around to see her clearly and her eyes followed him and locked on to his once again.

'I found it,' she said, still in that altered state of awe. 'It was here all the time.' Without breaking his gaze, she pulled a large jar from behind her and held it out to them. It was filled with a greenish substance that glowed queasily in the strange light of the flickering candles.

'The Fusion Gel?' Dad asked Saunders.

The man nodded in reply. 'Got to be.' He leaned down to Bes again. 'But why didn't you tell us? Why lead us here?'

Bes started to shake her head, left to right and back, her face creasing in concern. 'Can't trust the others,' she muttered. 'None of them. The child must be protected.'

'Ours or theirs?'

The shake of the head became more vigorous, but somehow her eyes remained locked onto Dillon's. He felt his stomach lurch as she confirmed what he somehow suspected she might say.

'Neither. Him. This is the child we need.'

Gilmore watched as Saunders held Bes and she tipped the flask back and drank down its contents. She spluttered and he helped her recover. The drink seemed to accelerate her return to relative normality, as if some kind of hallucinogenic was loosening its hold.

'It's not a drug,' she said suddenly, making Gilmore snap out of his thoughts and aware of how much his face may have been communicating without him realising.

'Then what?' he asked in reply, hissing so Dillon couldn't hear. Trevor was showing him more of the murals in the other chamber while Bes recovered. 'You seemed pretty far gone. And the things you were saying about my son...'

'There's an advanced state of perception,' Saunders

explained. 'Blake taught his followers to adopt it in order to see the patterns in things. He called it fourfold vision, in which the symbolic reality underlying all things becomes clear.'

Bes nodded, grateful for his explanation. 'I used it to find the gel, to follow the codes in the murals to its hiding place within the walls themselves. It took the ultimate faith, to deface one of his works to retrieve it.' She shook her head as if trying to dislodge something. 'It's not a good idea to remain in that state for long. Reality fuses with imagination, and you stop being able to distinguish between the two. Or worse, you stop wanting to.'

'Sounds like drugs to me,' Gilmore muttered crossly, his patience wearing thin. 'I don't like the way you scared Dillon. I want you to stay away from him.'

'By bringing him here, you've kept him safe. Grove and her people cannot be trusted. What they offer is a different kind of horror to the Association, but a horror nonetheless. Intellect over imagination. The prioritising of science and technology at the expense of art, literature, music, emotion. I had to get you away from them and I knew if I came here, Saunders would track me down.'

Gilmore saw how she patted Saunders' hand, and they looked back at him together, unified in their decades-old mission. 'So, what do we do now?'

Bes struggled back to standing with Saunders' help. 'We fulfil our mission. Prevent either side using their Children to establish themselves in power.'

Gilmore could feel something worrying lurking, building. He could hear Dillon chattering away to Trevor in the other room. 'You looked at Dillon and said he was the child we need. What did you mean?'

Bes looked at Saunders and he nodded in assent. 'When you hear this, you must remain calm. Out of all of Bambera's network, you were the very best. Not just your skills and the connections of your family, but because of him.'

'Dillon?'

'In order to stop their Children, we need a Child of our own.'

Gilmore's blood ran cold, and he could not think of a reply or be sure that he could utter it even if he did. At the back of his mind, a thought flitted away as his horror at her plan push it out. *How does she know about Grove?* Images of Dillon being integrated into the throne of a Child filled his mind instead.

'He's one of the most powerfully imaginative children I've ever encountered,' Bes continued in admiration. 'As our own weapon against theirs, he is perfect.'

CHAPTER TWENTY

Saturday – Fitzrovia, London. 2.00pm

RATCLIFFE SURVEYED his new, smaller empire with mixed feelings.

He swallowed down the sense of indignity he felt at having to crawl inside this workmanlike set-up. It was a dark room which, like many of Hareward's dwelling places, was packed full of whirring, blinking, humming equipment.

The scientist himself squeezed past Ratcliffe, bending carefully back and scraping against the door so as not to touch him. It was that kind of respect, combined with his usefulness, that had kept him alive longer than most of his previous collaborators. Only Carstairs had lasted longer, and that was mostly due to the distance he kept.

When Atkinson joined them with Markson, Ratcliffe could smell the air change as fear filled the room. The vast collective intelligence in that small space was still beholden to him through the crudest of controls.

'The defence perimeter is set up,' Atkinson confirmed.

'My general too now, are you?' Ratcliffe shot back quickly. Atkinson lowered his eyes in deference then prodded Markson with his pistol, obviously feeling the need to pass on the slight to the lowest in the pecking order. *So predictable*, Ratcliffe thought, shaking his head in disappointment.

Hareward busily rearranged connections, yanking plugs out of sockets and replacing them with his own additions. 'We should be ready in about ten minutes,' he hissed around a screwdriver held in his mouth, while his hands danced amid the blur of wires and cables.

'You're really going ahead with all this?'

Ratcliffe turned slowly to stare at Markson, noticing the others do the same, perhaps a little impressed by his boldness. Atkinson jabbed him again, probably embarrassed that his control over his old colleague didn't extend to his tongue. Hareward shook his head and returned to his work, as if getting ready to block out what might follow.

'It would be a bit pointless without this bit,' Ratcliffe replied drily.

'Am I allowed to know where we are?' Markson asked, emboldened by the indulgence. 'As I told them earlier, I'm not adverse to the practice, but the blindfold rather impeded my vision, and I do so like sightseeing normally.'

'Your vision will be rather more impeded when I remove your eyes,' Ratcliffe said, his tone as level as before, Markson visibly recoiling as the hierarchy was restored. 'A street away is Broadcasting House. Hereward has been getting this place ready for about two years now. My father rebuilt the shell of the building from the rubble, so I feel a sense of ownership, you know?'

Hareward tutted as he flicked a switch on and off with no result. 'It's harder without the Child,' he muttered.

Ratcliffe bent down to inspect the work. 'Problem?'

'It could be that they've built in extra protection given the situation. We're right on the edge of the exclusion zone, and they must have known Broadcasting House might be a target.'

'Make it work, Hereward. We need to make that broadcast today. Speaking of the Child, any signal?'

Hareward shook his head. 'Not yet. It must be there by now, but there are no signs it's interacted with the other one.'

Ratcliffe stood back up, stretching to his full height. He caught sight of himself in a silver panel on the wall. He tried to push a loose strand of dark hair back into position with the rest, but it fell down towards his eyes. A distortion in the panel made his face look simultaneously pinched and bulbous. His distance from the Child and the thought of finally issuing his ultimatum to the people crashed in together, and he felt a swell of nerves for the first time that day.

Come on, boy, he silently urged the absent Child. *Don't let me down.*

*

Rachel felt Allison's hands squeeze her arm tightly, but did not ask her to pull away. She needed that contact, taking her back to the start of all this, so long ago now.

Together they watched as another Child was wheeled into the church.

'It's dying!' Bambera called in uninhibited desperation. 'Help it!'

Rachel and Allison rushed to the little figure, which seemed to be curling back into its throne as if desperately tired and ready for sleep. He was panting, the wires and cables threading from his scalp rising and falling in time with his laboured breath.

'Clear the area!' Rachel commanded, only just aware that the soldiers were recoiling from her, perhaps in reaction to her demand or perhaps in horror at the new arrival. Instinctively she performed the checks she had perfected while caring for Judith, while Allison, experienced from her work on Cerburus, moved fluidly around her doing the same.

'He's fading,' Allison confirmed. 'The life support systems are the same as hers, but some master component is missing. He's rejecting every implant all at once. His body is realising what's been done to it.' She stifled a sob, her hands at her mouth.

Rachel paused, looking between the little boy and Judith. They were at opposite ends of the black-and-white checked aisle, which now formed a clear path from one to the other. She repeated Allison's words over once more. 'The life support systems are the same!' she cried. 'They can share!'

Allison stared at her in puzzled hope.

'The primary support system,' Rachel clarified, aware of the echo of her voice around the church. 'We can divide the central jack. It's always providing way more power than needed in case of more cuts, so we just need to divert that spare energy down a secondary cable.'

Allison looked hopeful for a moment, but her face quickly clouded again. 'But the pain. We don't have time to dial it up gradually. The shock will kill him.'

Rachel looked closely at the little boy's features, following a hunch. Amid the chaos of his arrival and through the filter of her own disgust she hadn't acknowledged it before. But he looked peaceful. His eyes were flickering, dark globes behind tissue-thin lids, as if he were dreaming. The skin of his face, while grey and pallid, was smooth, not creasing in discomfort. His lips, tinged with blue, were flickering gently into the briefest of smiles, as if the dream was a kind one.

'He's not in pain,' Rachel breathed, almost laughing as she made out the silver tracing across his patchy-haired scalp glinting in the candlelight. 'They've used the implant. He won't feel it. We can save him!'

Together they pushed him along the chessboard pattern of the aisle towards the altar.

They worked in perfect synchrony, deftly disconnecting parts of Judith's systems and linking them to the boy. Rachel was aware of a feeling of pure instinct, as if she too were becoming part of the consolidated mechanism they were building. The thicker cables felt like extensions of her arms, and she separated the wires into fingers to form handholds, binding the two lives together into a network of synthesis with the machine.

The final connections were made, and they sat back, exhausted and relieved, watching the boy's chest breath more gently, the blueness of his veins dimming back to dull grey. He was sleeping peacefully.

Judith, meanwhile, stared. Her mouth opened slightly as she fixed her gaze on the new companion she now shared her life essence with. Rachel had never seen her eyes so wide, or so beautiful.

'And we're in,' Hareward announced with pride.

Ratcliffe felt the same rush of nerves he had felt earlier, but he kept perfectly still, conscious that any movement might betray him. He would have to exact some pain after this was over, he knew, to balance things out. Markson's time was coming. The thought of that kept him warm against the chill of anticipation.

Hareward moved the microphone into position. 'You have access to the frequencies of the main radio stations. If they follow their own protocols, they should switch the television channels on to the broadcast too. Public safety, breaking news, they'll broadcast you. I don't know what they'll say or do afterwards, but the message will be out by then.'

Ratcliffe cleared his throat and swallowed. He fumbled in his pocket for his notes. The tightly folded paper had become crumpled during the frantic evacuation of Shoreditch and the journey here. He left it where it was and took a deep breath.

'Residents of London,' he began, trying to ignore the shake in his voice. 'You are aware that a State of Emergency has been declared in response to recent events. You are being kept in your homes for your own safety by a government that is acting out of sheer terror. This terror it has brought on itself. Years of open borders and uncontrolled immigration have swelled the numbers and corrupted the potential of our great nation.'

He paused. He didn't need the notes after all. He could picture the words he had carefully inscribed on the page, bold black ink on the whiteness, and he tapped directly into the place they came from. He imagined his father, watching from somewhere close by, proud at last perhaps.

'I will keep this simple. A new governing force is ready to take control. We have an Association of Shadow Ministers preparing to take power. Unlike your current government, these are drawn from the very industries they will oversee. Each one has a primary goal in order to restore power and control to the British people. The *original* British people. Our borders will close immediately. No more arrivals, no more refugees we don't have room for. The invasion of our lands ends today.'

He took another breath, allowing the new reality to sink in, for each step to settle before he led the people by the hand to where they wanted to be.

'More than that. Population control measures will begin immediately. Resources are scarce. Only those of pure British origin will be able to access them. Food, fuel, medicine. *Support*. By trying to share with *everyone*, we haven't left enough for those who *matter*.'

Ratcliffe felt the urge to let go, to continue on, to let a lifetime of hate pour outwards through the wavelengths into the hearts and minds of people who would understand. These were the earliest words and phrases he had learned. He had listened while his father had intoned them to a succession of young men. Not quite old enough to be of use, he had watched while others became his father's favourites. And he had listened, and heard, and felt.

'It comes down to this. Outsiders must leave now, one way or another. You have two options. Either you do it, or we do it for you. We have prepared an immediate deportation plan and have allies on the continent who are waiting to receive them. Camps are ready to make use of them. Assist us in their removal. Gather on the streets and make your feelings known. Make no mistake, this is a coup. Remove the sitting government from power and we will take their place.'

He looked at Atkinson, who could obviously feel his own moment approaching.

'If you fail to do so, we will take matters into our own hands, as we have done over the past week. The power cuts will continue until you comply. If you continue to resist, we have a final sanction ready to be deployed. Foreign groups will be targeted, one after the other. Those you could send to the camps alive, will instead be... exterminated.'

The final word hung in the thick, sweaty air of the room. Hereward and Atkinson looked aghast, as if they had woken at the end of a train journey and found themselves somewhere they hadn't quite believed they would reach. Markson was shaking.

'We require no official response,' Ratcliffe concluded, suddenly exhausted. 'Your actions will speak louder than your words. Broadcast ends.'

Feeling behind himself for a chair, he slumped back. The burden he had carried all his life had been released, and he felt strangely light and dizzy. Whatever happened now was not in his control. The people would decide. *Democracy at its purest,* he thought, his mouth curling into a smile of utter relief.

The room was silent until a small, insistent beep started from one of Hareward's contraptions. Ratcliffe didn't even have the energy to ask what it was.

'It's our Child,' Hareward told him despite his silence. 'It's activating.'

Bambera drew closer to the altar. Rachel hadn't seen him this tentative before. It was as if he recognised that this operation required components way beyond his understanding, and despite his intricate planning, control was slipping from him.

Grove hovered among the pews at the front, presumably unwilling to become involved and keeping herself clean for her planned ascent to power. Rachel made sure the woman recognised the distaste in her glance before she turned to Bambera.

'Is it safe?' he asked, staring at the cables that now connected the two seated forms.

'We had no choice,' Allison stated firmly. Rachel couldn't help but smile in relief at their shared achievement. For too long they had been divided by the complex lines fracturing the government and its agencies.

'It could be a trap,' Bambera growled.

Rachel stepped between them. 'One problem at a time,' she said, echoing Allison's earlier sentiment about the Naebbetold and appreciating it anew. 'We couldn't let him die.'

Bambera paced around her, circling Judith and the new Child, stepping over the cables that connected them to the pulsing energies of the church's equipment. 'I want precautions taken. If they wanted us to bring the boy here, they might have a plan to use it against us. Either way, I want it loyal to us, like the original.' He beckoned to some black suited guards, some of whom Rachel had noticed coming and going from a sealed off chapel to the right of the altar. 'Deploy the tanks,' he told them.

Rachel looked at Allison and found her quizzical look reflected. 'Tanks?'

Bambera stared her down, regaining some of his lost confidence. 'The ultimate destination of the Child,' he said. 'Or Children.'

'You were anticipating more?' Allison asked.

Grove stepped up to the altar now, her small frame magnified by a sense of entitlement that swelled her. 'They must be mobile *and* protected. When we establish control, the Child will be needed to integrate with the systems around the whole of Great Britain. It will need assistance from others. The Association has given us the first.'

Rachel felt another lurch into fear, a vertiginous topple from her earlier triumph. 'You can't be serious,' she said, almost laughing in disbelief. 'This is ridiculous.'

Then she saw movement from the direction of the chapel.

The guards Bambera had sent away were returning, each carrying a panel of studded metal. They were the darkest grey, almost black, with round silver bolts, similar to the base of the Child's original throne, which itself had been based on the... invaders from all those years ago.

Rachel swallowed down the instinct to be sick.

'We can seal them inside and afford them independent motive power,' Grove said. 'There's room for basic life support and a radio interface so they can move freely from their connections for short periods of time. With further work on the artefacts, we will be able to totally submerge them in the equipment. They will be free to do our bidding.' She directed the guards to take the panels onto the altar. 'Put the boy inside first. Make sure any external connection to his old masters is cut off.'

'My god,' Allison breathed.

Rachel was about to agree with her, a tirade about the inhumanity of the plan building, ready to be unleashed. Then she saw what Allison had seen. While they had been focused on the arrival of the tank panels, Judith had moved, and so had the boy.

He was now upright in his throne, his eyes wide open and staring at the woman sat opposite him. She meanwhile had stretched out a hand, her eyes not just staring but alive with joy. They were both reaching forward, his spindly arm rising and reaching out to hers in reply.

'What are they doing?' Grove demanded desperately, control slipping once more. 'Stop them!'

Rachel watched in awe, realisation dawning after months of suspicion. 'I couldn't if I tried.'

Grove held a hand up to pause the arrival of the guards. 'Arms,' she commanded, and they raised their weapons in the direction of the Children.

Rachel and Allison moved to block the Children from the guards. 'Fire at us and you lose your advantage,' Rachel said coldly. She looked at Bambera, urgent appeal in her eyes, but he just watched impassively, as if he was content to watch how things played out rather than directing them.

Grove frowned, moving an outstretched arm downwards in a signal for the guards to lower their weapons.

The rest of the church was still. Rachel was dimly aware that the Naebbetold forces were watching the altar intently. Mentally dismissing them all, she focused on Judith and the boy. Allison stared too, already mesmerised.

They continued to reach out to each other until their fingers were inches apart. They paused, nodded. Then their fingers interlinked, sending a pulse of energy through the cables into the machinery, sparks flying and light flashing up and into the arcing columns of the structure.

Rachel felt herself thrown back by the burst, and held on to Allison as they tried to stay standing. The guards sank into defence crouches, guns raised again.

As the sparking stopped, the final flares falling and fading from the ceiling, smoke drifting all around, she could just about make out the two figures. They stared at each other in wonder, hands grasped together, fused.

CHAPTER TWENTY-ONE

Saturday – Church of the Holy Sepulchre, Holborn, London. 3.00pm

THE SCHOOLGIRL froze amid the snow.

Her whole world had been white for so long that she was surprised when colour started to leak in falling streaks across the infinite landscape. She assigned a numerical value to each different colour and danced through the calculations as each new flake appeared.

Somewhere deep inside herself she knew that it was the snow that was meant to be white, bleaching out the colours where it landed, and that this was the reverse. The usual rules had never really applied to her, she knew that above all else, and so she accepted it and enjoyed the new stimulation of the numbers as they drifted down.

The recent accumulations had formed shapes, to which she could attach words. As long as she went via the numbers, each letter having its own value, she could find the names of things.

Glass. Wood. Stone. Church.

Even despite her new perception, she knew that things had not really changed. She was still suspended in the empty space with only the numbers to comfort her. Some pathways brought her little bursts of pleasure, in that they reminded her of the greater pleasures from before, when she contained centuries inside her head instead of mere decades. Other pathways brought her pain, and she withdrew from those even when the strange gravity of the outside tried to drag her there.

The only other change had been the return of the face she recognised from those times before, the times that gave her such pleasure-pain that she shied away from them on the whole. The face skimmed the edges of the space, and the mathematics needed to find the words to describe it was complex.

Familiar. Frightening. Frightened.

Concern. Care. Kindness.

Rachel.

She had joined her in the void at one point, asking for her help.

Satellite. City. Firing sequence. Please.

Then she had returned after however-long and had given her instructions.

Command. Activate. Restore. Power. Defend.

The words had been spoken, translated into numbers and taken her down strange new pathways, networks that were alive with crackling colours and jagged equations. She had chased her way around blockages and found the way to make the formulas flow.

That was when she had first sensed something old-new, unlike anything else since those days gone by. She had spent whole seconds afterwards playing with numbers and letters to find the combination that suited the presence, which was somehow a combination of both of those elements.

Two. Plural. Too.

Another.

It was there, but distant. It was a shape on the other side of the blizzard, something exciting-frightening that might approach or recede, she knew not which.

Now she knew. It was here.

So, she froze, shy, looking at him.

'Hello,' he said.

'Hello,' she returned.

Then her arm unfroze and started moving, whether she wanted it to or not.

Numbers of her own were finding satisfying reflections in numbers of his, equations balancing and resolving and blossoming into new formulas.

Approach. Connection. Interface.

Before she knew it, they were holding hands, and everything that followed seemed the most normal thing in the whitespace.

'Want to play?' she asked.

The little boy smiled the most ginormous grin, as if it had been infinite-time since anyone had asked him that, and as if he had stored up hundreds, thousands, millions of games ready for them to enjoy. 'Oh yes,' he replied.

Still holding hands, they ran into the snow to play.

'This is *obscene*.' Rachel had never said that word with so much certainty that it was the correct one before.

Now she said it with such force that Bambera and Grove couldn't help but lower their eyes in shame. It echoed around the church, each iteration giving it more space for her dismay.

Allison drew close and she allowed herself to take deep breaths. 'This has to stop,' she said slowly. 'Look at the precedent we've set. By continuing to use Judith, others have taken her as a model for the future.'

'I hope you aren't likening me to Ratcliffe,' Grove spat.

'It seems like it doesn't matter,' Rachel told her. 'Your side or his, you're both abusing these children for your own ends. You both think you have the better system for running this country and will use the powers you've squirreled away to force it on the rest of us.'

Rachel noticed that Bambera was staying silent, his eyes still sensibly downcast.

Grove on the other hand, looked emboldened. 'I'm surprised at you. You're one of the most intelligent women in this country. You could have all the power you deserve in our new order. Instead, you allow yourself to be wafted and cajoled by the men in your life, who you know, deep down, have only a fraction of the talent you have. Yet another woman debasing herself, holding herself back so as not to offend their hypocritical moral structures.'

Rachel felt Allison's arm holding her back before she realised that she was pushing forward to march up to the woman and... she didn't know what.

'Rachel, the Children,' Allison urged close to her ear.

Remembering the real victims, Rachel turned back to them, away from Grove.

'We are where we are,' Bambera announced. 'We need to assess the damage. Is there a way of finding out what's happened to them?'

In that, Rachel had to admit that her curiosity was too strong to resist. She studied the way the two figures now leaned towards each other, their eyes fixed on each other, their hands still intertwined in a bizarre handshake.

'Are they communicating?' Allison asked.

'I'm sure of it,' Rachel replied.

'But what are they saying? If they're from opposing sides, are they arguing? Or are they combining forces? And if so, whose side will they take?'

Allison had verbalised all of the burning questions in Rachel's mind.

'The boy could be enacting a pre-prepared set of instructions. I know we couldn't let him die, but we might have delivered them a victory.'

'He's so small,' Allison whispered.

Rachel couldn't find the words to reply. The name 'Child' had been somehow safer for Judith because she had an adult's body, as emaciated and deformed as it had become. To see an actual child hooked up to the cables and wires, his thin limbs pale against the darkness of the machinery in which he sat... She had never felt so certain that, somehow, this all had to end. This pathway of science had to be terminated.

Bambera was suddenly looming between them, staring at the children with a look of concerned distaste. 'You communicated with her before, when she restored the power. Could you do it again?'

Rachel focused her mind, unwilling to give him the satisfaction of her consent, and instead reaching out to Judith. Ironically, between communicating with her or Bambera and Grove, it was Judith who seemed the more human and appealing.

There was nothing. The usual trace of a connection, that drift of strange and alien thought, was absent. She shook her head.

'You have to try,' Bambera urged.

'I am,' she hissed back scathingly.

Taking a deep breath, Rachel reached out towards the joined hands of Judith and the boy. She focused her consciousness on her fingertips, aware that the waves of electricity and energies that had pulsed from them before may still be live.

Again, there was nothing. She placed her dry hand on theirs, but the touch was merely physical. Judith's thumb was rough where it had been scuffed against an edge while the soldiers had handled her during transport.

Barely aware of what she was doing, Rachel reached into a pocket and pulled out the cream she had been using to sooth Judith's skin. Scooping a little from the pot, she gently started to apply it in tiny, looping circles over her thumb.

The joined hands moved slightly. Judith tilted her thumb away to position the boy's in its place. Mesmerised at the delicate adjustment, Rachel continued to apply the balm, which became warm as it melted and disappeared into his skin.

Rachel raised her head and closed her eyes, letting her hand become one with theirs, the cream binding them together through the softest of touches.

It took mere moments to receive the impression she needed.

She drew her hand away and stood, slowly turning to face Allison, Bambera and Grove, who looked at her probingly, waiting to hear what she had seen.

'Well?' Allison asked gently.

If any of the others had asked, Rachel suspected she may not have answered. So, she addressed Allison and let the others hear. 'They're busy,' she told her with a sad smile. 'They're playing.'

Judith and the boy rose and fell in turn, first one then the other, over and over again. Each was sat on either end of a see-saw.

They constructed the object together using their numbers and enjoyed the ways the sequence was now looping around to make Judith higher one moment, then the boy. There was a moment when the numbers equalised and they were level, but the momentum of the formula sent them upwards and downwards, one riding high on the positives and the other dipping into the negatives until they switched around again.

The boy's tousled hair waved in the breeze as he was lifted into the air. 'What's your name?' he asked.

Judith knew the answer to this one, and said, proudly, 'Jud-ek.'

'Judek?' The boy laughed. 'That's a strange name.'

Judith agreed. Not only was it strange, it wasn't the name she had meant to say. 'Hang on,' she said, thinking hard and checking her workings again. 'Not Jud-ek. Dal-ith.'

'Dalith?' The boy laughed again. 'I haven't heard of that one either.'

Judith frowned in puzzlement. Something had happened when she had tried to convert the numbers into letters, and they were now all jumbled. Two equations were fighting for space. She needed to separate them. 'Jud-ith,' she said finally. 'My name is Judith.' That felt right. The other equation, excised, seemed to hover nearby, seething. The spare syllables, now joined, drifted away like a passing storm. She thought about saying them, but the word they made frightened her more than anything. Speaking it might bring the storm back.

'Judith,' the boy said in confirmation, and she felt better.

'Anyway, what's your name?' she asked.

The boy thought about this for a long time. She could sense him testing out the numbers to find the solution, but it was elusive. Possibilities resolved themselves briefly then floated away, discarded.

Child. Boy. Scum. Boy. Child.

'Hmmm, I'm not sure,' he said eventually.

'It's all right, you don't really need one anyway,' Judith told him. She was older than him, although by how much she couldn't quite tell. But she knew it was by enough to be able to reassure him and help him if he became worried. She tested this unfamiliar feeling and enjoyed the chemical rush it produced. She had been alone for so long, with only the numbers for company, a sum with no answer.

The boy nodded, accepting this, but then he turned his head as if hearing something from far away. Judith wondered if it was thunder from the storm, and she shivered.

'We might have to stop playing soon,' the boy said seriously.

Judith felt her earlier rush of happiness dip as she descended and he rose. 'Why?' she asked plaintively.

'There was something I was supposed to do,' he replied.

Then she rose, high above him once more, looking down at his tiny form. 'Like what?' She tried to keep the disappointment out of her tone. She didn't want to frighten her only friend.

When he rose again, he scouted the horizon, trying to see what he had lost. Failing, he shook his head as he descended again. 'It's gone,' he said. 'I can't remember.'

Judith felt contentment. She was aware of the snow still falling, little flakes of reality against the white. For a moment her hands felt very warm, and she thought she saw Rachel again. She wondered if they were in trouble, her and the boy, but if that had been Rachel, she hadn't seemed cross. She had seemed pleased.

'Well, let's not worry about it,' she told the boy. 'Let's enjoy the game.'

The boy nodded and smiled, but Judith watched him closely. Whenever he rose to his height his eyes scanned the horizon keenly as if still searching for his lost instructions. Judith hoped that in time he would forget them.

She hoped they could play this game always, rising and falling, one after the other in perfect balance, and forget the snow and the lingering storms that rumbled and raged in the distance.

CHAPTER TWENTY-TWO

Saturday – Beneath Soho, London. 3.30pm

GILMORE RESISTED the urge to push Bes into the chair and demand the truth with the full force of his protective instinct. Irritation and confusion warred in his mind and made every muscle tense.

Instead, knowing that either Trevor or Saunders would hold him back if he lunged forward, he let her take her seat. She still looked exhausted, and while physically she would be no match despite her fighting prowess, he sensed that her stubborn will might close up even further if pushed too hard. Dillon was sitting in the corner, silent, aware that something serious was happening and drinking it all in through wide eyes.

'Explain,' Gilmore instructed through gritted teeth.

She met his gaze levelly. 'The boy was chosen for his potential, and he's more than realised it. We always knew it might come down to a battle in her territory, and that we would need our own Child.'

'Her territory?'

'The original Child's. Judith's.'

Gilmore remembered the climax of the Cerberus threat and Rachel's account of what happened when she met Judith in the mental landscape in which she dwelt. Rachel had become misty-eyed when she talked about it, in the way he had seen religious folk describe spiritual moments. That in itself was so unlike her that it had troubled him, and he was relieved when her rational side had returned and she explained the process in scientific terms that he understood even less.

'The Children will decide the outcome of this conflict,' Bes stated in that same, awe-tinged way as Rachel had spoken.

'What do you even know about them?' Gilmore snapped back. 'Rachel and Allison have spent hours working on that poor girl's systems, trying to stabilise and improve her quality of life. What do you know?'

Bes smiled gently, irritating him even more. 'She is exactly what the Order of Albion was set up to understand. In scientific terms, she is the most dangerous living fusion of humanity and machine. We are pledged to prevent the distortion spreading. We've spent our lives understanding the inventions and experimentations that threaten to consume us if left unchecked.' She looked at Saunders, who nodded his allegiance. 'But we also understand what this is really all about.'

'Don't tell me,' Gilmore spat. '*Imagination.*'

'Whether you decide to see that as mystical nonsense is up to you. Choose the scientific route if you must. It doesn't matter. What matters is that with our guidance, Dillon can safely enter the conflict and help us end it for good. We have the means.'

Gilmore looked at his son. The fear he felt was not reflected in that young face. Instead, there was something else, familiar from the mirror. It was the recognition of duty, the same look he gave himself when assigned a mission, when he would psych himself up to go back out and do what was necessary, and afterwards, as cities burned, when he told himself it had needed to be done.

'You said safely,' he said, aware that with the question he was leaving the door of possibility open just a little. 'How on earth can you be sure?'

Bes held the jar of pale green gel up to the candlelight. 'Blake recorded that the biggest danger of this material was that it worked too well. It could facilitate the fusion with machinery they were using in the Albion Mills to speed up their work, but it could also allow the complete removal of the parts and the recovery of the subject. Children would fuse with the machines in the morning and eventually, when allowed, sleep free of them at night. Only after over-use would the skin be unable to heal itself.'

Gilmore let the implications unfold hypothetically in his own imagination. The goal of returning to their utter mundane normality still beat strongly in his heart. 'What about while he's in there?'

'Admittedly, that's where faith comes in,' she replied sheepishly.

Gilmore rolled his eyes. 'I thought it would come in somewhere. Faith in what exactly?'

'In him.'

Gilmore's breath caught in his throat, blocking any comeback.

Saunders stepped forward and took over the explanation, allowing Bes to sink back in exhaustion. 'He can deliver a message on our behalf. Bes has been training him in the mental techniques and he has been a model student. The nature of the message depends on him. On how you've raised him and shaped his understanding of the world. We're being given a choice out there. Ratcliffe's Association and the base level nationalism of white supremacy. Or Grove's new intellectual elite, multicultural but with power concentrated on the brightest few and guided by the kind of technology we're battling. Which would Dillon choose?'

Gilmore looked at Dillon, and even without asking, he knew the answer. He didn't say it, but he recognised it and thought it in a single word, clearly.

Neither.

'Exactly,' said Bes.

'His mother...' Gilmore said, feeling that same door of possibility widen even despite his fears. 'She succeeded before. She connected to Judith and together they stopped death raining down from the Cerberus satellites. Why can't she do it again? Or better, me?'

He saw Bes and Saunders lock eyes in a mutual understanding he felt excluded from.

'There are unique properties in the mind of a child,' Bes explained. 'Mind or brain, take your pick as you prefer. The rate at which his synapses are developing with every new experience gives us a narrow window in which to deploy him at the height of his powers.'

'But Judith is technically an adult now,' Gilmore countered, 'despite the moniker she can't seem to shift.'

'It's more than a moniker. She's been suspended in the

child-state, but *artificially*. That's what most of the brain implants are doing to her, emulating the evolution of an adolescent brain, slowing some processes down, reversing others to begin them again. She's a Child in a loop, and there is a huge price to pay for such a distortion to the natural order of development. Your son is perfect because he's just *there*, at that precious point, and that makes him powerful.'

'Somewhere between innocence and experience,' Saunders added, indicating the murals all around them and their mythic depiction of the eternal struggle of humanity against its own worst instincts. 'He's poised in the doorway.'

Gilmore could see through that doorway in his mind's eye, an image again of Dillon wired up to the same mechanisms as the Child, cables forcing their way into his scalp and his eyes staring no more at him but at an entirely different world.

'His mother will never allow it,' Gilmore said, conjuring Rachel as a shield of protection around them both.

'And if you can't ask her? What about you?'

Gilmore went to speak, but couldn't find the words again. He looked at Dillon, who stared back with one thought clearly in mind, that word they had spoken of so many times, as explanation for his absences and in the stories of warriors past, as the origin of courage itself.

Duty.

Ex-Minister for Defence Kofi Bambera sat on one of the pews, wondering whether it was time to start praying.

He edged along the bench so that he could feel small beneath one of the towering pillars. He looked with envy at one of the Naebbetold guards, black suited and helmeted, anonymous in their conformity.

'Have you seen the ultimatum?' A hard-edged voice interrupted his brief moment of respite, and he turned to see Grove edging her way along the pew towards him. She was clutching a typed transcript of the radio broadcast.

He nodded. His own copy sat on the pew next to him, the formality of the type giving a chilling authority to the sentiments it contained. He had dealt with verbal racism all of his life, the muttered insults and disapproving noises that floated malignantly through the air as he passed through it up the steps of power and into government. To see it in written form felt different, as if the hatred had manifested and forced itself onto the paper of its own accord.

'Our old colleagues are in quite the palaver,' she said conspiratorially. Bambera recognised the attempt to consolidate their alliance. 'Police presence remains strong outside the exclusion zone, which we still control. The people are cowering, as they tend to do, taking shelter from the storm.'

Still, he did not speak as her own words ran out. The church itself was asserting its own attempt at calm, the electronic burble of the Children and their technology soothed by the sound of the wind buffeting the tower and pressing against the stained-glass windows. Even Rachel and Allison had stopped their frantic checking of readings and outputs, slumping in the larger chairs at the front usually occupied by priests.

Grove looked at him plaintively. 'What do we do now?' she asked with the desperation of someone who had no idea themselves. 'We've come this far. We cannot stall now.'

Bambera roused himself to reply, the small movement of turning feeling like great effort, as if he were a huge ship in the ocean arcing around to port. 'If that Child does start acting out whatever orders they've given it; we lose control of the power of the City. If the people don't act in the way the Association hopes, the murders begin. Deportation or death. What will they choose when they know it's serious? Which race will be chosen as the example to be set for the others?'

Grove's face fell under the barrage of questions.

'For all your collective intelligence and gathered forces, you're remarkably short of ideas,' he stated in scathing judgement. 'Maybe there are limitations for even the brightest of us.' He called to the nearest Naebbetold guard and requested a map.

Once provided, he smoothed it down on the pew between them and scanned the patterns. New lines had been inscribed in bold colours, rewriting the city in the space of a weekend: borders, clusters, weak spots, supply lines. From this angle, it was a city at war.

'We need to negotiate,' he stated, noticing Grove recoil at the prospect and ignoring it. 'It's the last thing anybody will be expecting. To break a stalemate, you have to take radical action.'

'What on earth could we give them that would go anywhere near their goals?'

'Oh, nothing,' Bambera conceded, his mind already racing ahead to new possibilities. 'But maybe they can be convinced that a way out might be better. This ideology of purity. How deep does it really run? A young man in charge, his views inherited second-hand from a disappointment of a father.' Bambera paused, as an image of his own son rushed into his mind... His estranged son. Estranged for very different reasons... He shook it away, focusing back on the problem at hand. 'They're just a hook on which to hang a grab for power. If we could offer him something even more appealing than being in charge of a country full of angry whites, would he take it? Or will he risk his life for his beliefs?'

'I would have thought your services' psychological profiling might have given you some clues to that already.' Now it was Grove's turn to accuse.

'Oh, they've done an adequate job,' he said, piecing together the fragments of reports and photographs he'd been studying for years. 'And what they found was someone who had one significant interest above racial purity. Cruelty. He enjoys exerting pain and doesn't mind what colour the skin of the victim.'

'How does that help us?'

'It tells us that for all his talk of fairness and care for his own people, concern that they don't have enough resources because they've been somehow stolen, it's all just an excuse to exert personal power over individuals. That gives us a way in.'

Grove frowned, just enough to suggest she may be listening.

Bambera pressed home. 'We only need time. If they broadcast the ultimatum from close to Broadcasting House, then they're also near the forces you've built up at the university. We can offer them a space to negotiate and herd them... here.' He pressed a finger onto a point on the map exactly halfway between Broadcasting House and the Church of the Holy Sepulchre.

'Russell Square?'

He nodded. 'We need to break this deadlock. We convince him he still has the power to go through with his promises, but we bring him here. Reunite him with his Child. And together, we end it, once and for all.'

'He'll never agree,' Grove said, as if daring Bambera to argue.

He didn't reply, but smiled, knowing that there were things he could offer Ratcliffe that would ensure that he did.

Ratcliffe stared at the green light as if it were salvation itself. It ceased its blinking and shone steadily.

'Hereward,' he growled, desperate for some kind of meaning to be assigned to its new state.

Hareward studied readings on the bank of equipment connected to the box with the shining light, where dials twitched and other displays pulsed.

'Just a moment, Boss,' he said, his eyes flicking to Ratcliffe nervously for any sign that he was overstepping a mark.

Ratcliffe allowed him his time. The man had not let him down yet, and having seen many of the punishments Ratcliffe had been forced to deliver, Hareward knew what would await him should he go too far. The biological curiosity he claimed as the excuse for his presence at those events had at least instilled a complete understanding of the vast potential for pain stored in every inch of the human form.

'The Child is active,' he said eventually, 'but frozen.'

The brief rise in hope made the crash of the final word feel bitter. 'Frozen?'

'It seems to be caught in some kind of loop. The light indicates action over a period of a minute or so. While there are signs of mental activity, it's rising and falling in a way that produces an average of... well... nothing.'

'Nothing?'

Hareward visibly flushed at the second repeat. The signs of an outburst were there, building.

'It's as if he reaches wakefulness for a moment then collapses into a deep sleep. In terms of conscious usefulness to us, it amounts to zero. I'm sorry, sir, I can continue to try to prompt it out of whatever it's caught up with.'

'Is it the other Child?' Ratcliffe asked, jealousy rising in his throat like bile.

'It could well be. Yes, I think it is.' Hareward sounded eager to apportion blame, as if he might divert the coming anger towards a common enemy.

Ratcliffe seethed. He could sense Atkinson and Markson watching him and knew that the latter would be gleefully enjoying any signs that his plan might be falling apart. 'Atkinson, take that freak to the basement. I'll be down shortly.'

The shuffling and amateur threats issued by Atkinson, receding down the corridor, told Ratcliffe that they had gone, and so instead of being looked upon, he fixed Hareward with a stare and became the one doing the looking. He immediately felt a little better.

'Any word on a response?' Hareward asked, perhaps seeking better news. If the ultimatum had the desired effect of course, the Child would not be needed, at least in the short-term.

'I'll go and find out. Come and get me if anything changes.'

Relieved to be free of Hareward's tentative presence too, Ratcliffe stormed out of the room and down the dark corridor, lighting a cigarette as he walked.

He found the wall-mounted phone, picked up and dialled the number from memory.

After only two rings, a click told him it had been picked up.

'Well?' he demanded.

The voice he heard was, as expected, filtered and distorted. 'Government paralysed,' it stated calmly. 'Debating emergency measures.'

'And the people?'

'Nothing yet. Staying home.'

Ratcliffe thumped the wall. 'Our forces?'

'Pinned down. Naebbetold.'

A chill ran down the back of his neck. A flash of panic like those he'd had as a child rose unbidden. 'No,' he countered, as if denying it would change the reality of it. 'Options?'

'Negotiate,' the voice grated. 'Buy time.'

Ratcliffe pondered the suggestion. The shivering stopped as the idea settled. If the government really was unable to act, then his group and the Naebbetold were now the powerbrokers. And if the Children were locked into some kind of stalemate too, maybe the only option was to offer a compromise. And then...

The voice completed his thought. 'Then strike.'

CHAPTER TWENTY-THREE

Saturday – Fitzrovia, London. 4.30pm

PROFESSOR ALBERT Markson stared into the darkness and pondered his options.

They narrowed into grim thoughts of ways in which he could ensure a swift despatch for himself as opposed to the lingering suffering Ratcliffe had planned. He wondered when Atkinson would return and what he could say to push the man into action.

He didn't have to wait long, and as the heavy door swung open and light spilled in, Markson wished he had had longer to plan and to look back over the pleasures of his life, just a few of them, just one more time, to prepare himself for the end. Instead, his mind felt as murky as the company he now kept. Despite the world telling him he was so, he had never believed it of himself, so to end in a way that validated their efforts gave him an anger that overrode his fear.

'You bastard,' he spat with force as Atkinson drew near to check the ties binding his wrists together. 'Your name will go down on the list of the worst, you do know that don't you?'

Atkinson did not reply, his mouth set in a clamped shut line.

'And by extension, so will hers.'

Atkinson froze.

'When the studies are done and the histories are written, contributing factors will be assigned. Driven mad by the death of his wife. Underlying prejudices fed by the coincidence of the colour of her doctors. Pre-existing sociopathy triggered into mass murder.'

He remained still. Markson couldn't even tell if he was breathing.

'Give it enough time and you'll end up in the textbooks. A-level probably. Not suitable for O-level, not complex enough for degree. They'll be drawing diagrams, those teenagers, with arrows from the causes through your name and to the consequences. They'll graffiti the photograph they chose to illustrate you. Which one will they choose?'

Markson felt something let go in his mind, a certainty that the stillness would end in gunfire, the swift exit he now desired more than anything. He'd spent years constructing amusing ways to assassinate character with his friends, his defence against the rejection he felt. He allowed that instinct to reach its apotheosis.

'Will they choose one of you smiling?' he asked. 'Or one of you grimacing, off-guard, more in keeping with your true nature? Will it be one of you and your wife? So they can see how pretty she was and how easily you must have been driven mad by her death. How pale her skin was, how *white*. How will they graffiti you? Devil horns and a little beard?'

He saw Atkinson's hand move, mechanically, to his pistol. *Go on*, Markson thought. 'They'll probably graffiti you both,' he said.

Atkinson lifted the pistol to his head and fired.

Ratcliffe wondered if he would ever sleep again.

The grey sky, thick with cold, drizzling cloud, was darkening to deep blue. Yet the prospect of night falling on that November Saturday seemed impossible to him. The thought of climbing into bed, his mind quietening into sleep... He somehow knew it just wouldn't happen, perhaps ever again. He had wound himself up so tightly, and he wanted the world to share it.

'Boss, we've had an approach.' The voice of one of his men made him jump, and he hid it by leaping off the stool he perched on and rounding on him.

'In what form?'

'They want you to make a call,' the man explained, his voice quivering. 'Direct to Bambera.'

Ratcliffe felt a welcome rush of adrenaline push away the meanderings of his mind. Direct action at last. 'Was it a response to our offer?'

'That's the weird thing, Boss, they had it before we even

made one.'

'They must have come to the same conclusion we have,' Ratcliffe surmised. 'Something's got to give, right?'

The man didn't reply, unused to being consulted by the boss himself.

'Well?'

'Err, yes, Boss, I guess.'

Ratcliffe frowned, disappointed not for the first time that no one could rise to the job of a decent lieutenant. 'Oh, get out,' he told him, and with obvious relief the man thrust the piece of paper with the phone number into his hand and exited almost at a run.

Returning to the phone in the corridor, Ratcliffe was about to dial the number when the sudden burst of a single gunshot echoed through the building.

'No...' whispered Markson down to the fallen body of Atkinson at his feet. 'That wasn't what I meant...'

The frozen stance of the man before his death had seeped into Markson's limbs, but as he started to shake, he could feel something dizzying behind him... A movement that shouldn't be possible... A motion that threatened to unbalance him entirely in surprise.

The ties that had been wrapped around his wrist had fallen away. Atkinson had not been tightening them, he realised. He had been loosening them.

He knew Ratcliffe would be on his way down. The building was small that it wouldn't take long. He would want to see whether Atkinson had finally broken and finished off the promise of torture he was saving for himself. There was no way Markson would be able to push past Ratcliffe and out. Perhaps Markson's own death was to be a quick sequel to his counterpart's.

The thing was, he realised as he tested the new freedom of his arms, that moment was passing. He wanted to *live*.

He bent down to the body, ignoring the mess of the head and checking the pockets. Questions flicked through his mind rapidly as he tried to make sense of the man's decision. Had it really been his words that had made it happen? Terrified it might be true, he searched Atkinson's pockets for anything he might have left that indicated otherwise.

He knew he had seconds. Ratcliffe would be close. So, when he felt the stiffness of a photograph, he grabbed it and placed it without looking in his own inner pocket and rose back to standing, placing his hands behind his back in the pose of someone still bound.

When Ratcliffe did enter, expressions cycled over his face with the same rapidity of Atkinson's decision and death. Markson watched, transfixed, to see which he would settle on. Wide eyes of surprise narrowed into anger, which melted into amusement. He shook his head, chuckling, looking between Atkinson's remains and Markson.

'Talking people to death,' he said, almost admiringly. 'I thought that was my trick.'

Blood pooled across the floor of the small basement room, and Ratcliffe struggled to take his eyes off it.

He liked a genuine surprise, so predictable were the people he usually associated with, so he felt an unexpected momentary gratitude to Markson for providing a twist to the proceedings. His initial fear that Atkinson would still be useful fizzled away as soon as he remembered that his main task had been completed. His weapons were ready and in place for deployment. They had been for almost a day. It was only his role as guard for Markson that held any use, and even that was tentative.

'Good job his work is ready to be loosed,' Ratcliffe said, confirming his disinterest in the man's continued existence aloud. 'Bit like that.' He indicated the dark liquid oozing over the floor.

He studied Markson. There was something different about the man. His bearing had changed. There was a new confidence, a new resolve, a light of challenge in his eyes.

'You know, I could work with poofs if I had to,' Ratcliffe told him magnanimously. 'In fact, I'm pretty sure I have, frequently. It's never something we'll be able to openly sanction in the new order, but there could be compromises. There's precedent, you know.'

The more Markson stared back defiantly, the more Ratcliffe felt a sense of potential in the man. Someone with a mind equal to Hareward and Atkinson, but much stronger in character.

Ratcliffe bent down and picked up Atkinson's pistol from where it had fallen. At what point after firing at close range would his hand have released it? He pondered the second-by-second possibilities of death with his usual curious morbidity. Most importantly, how many bullets had been inside? What had Atkinson been planning?

Checking and realising, he raised the pistol towards Markson. There it was again, in the defiance of his stare and the downturn of his mouth as if he was silently praying that Ratcliffe wouldn't shoot. The man wanted to survive this. That made him malleable.

'A life, not only free of pain, but full of your old favourite pleasures,' Ratcliffe purred from behind the pistol. 'It's possible. Ponder it.'

Concluding the exchange just before boredom set in, and fuelled ready for his next conversation, Ratcliffe turned his back on Markson and stalked back to the telephone.

The heartbeat quickened as he listened to the rings, wondering where this would take him, flattered and proud that he was attracting the attention he deserved.

'Mr Ratcliffe.' The deep voice said his name with calm respect.

'Mr Bambera,' Ratcliffe returned, the hint of a mocking accent in the bounce of the syllables. 'What can I do for you?'

'Formal negotiations,' came the reply. Ratcliffe could barely believe it and cautioned himself not to.

'How's my boy?' Ratcliffe asked, taking interrogative control.

Bambera paused before replying, perhaps deciding whether he could maintain his level of calm for long. 'He seems to have made a friend,' he said eventually. 'Not sure any of us were expecting that, eh?'

Skilful reply, Ratcliffe mentally acknowledged. The offer of a bridge of shared surprise in an attempt to build rapport. 'Stalemate then,' he replied, reaching the mutually frozen position they found themselves in.

'So it seems. There are some genuine concessions we can make as part of our own power grab.'

Ratcliffe let him continue, surprised to hear such a bold acknowledgement of their own treasonous plans.

'We presume your biological weapons are still primed,'

Bambera said, 'even if you can't control the energy supply while your Child is incapacitated. The power still lies in your hands.'

'Don't bother with the false flattery,' Ratcliffe snapped, irritated at the basic attempt to manipulate his ego. He was more than aware of its proportions and the dangers it posed to him.

'I'm stating fact,' Bambera countered. 'Meet us in Russell Square. Out in the open, where none of us need feel penned in.'

'It's inside your exclusion zone. You could slaughter us.'

'If we do, presumably we trigger the biological weapon.'

Was he actually bold enough to propose this as a plan? Ratcliffe stopped himself from being impressed; along with his changing attitude towards Markson, he was in danger of going soft.

'We can escort you using our troops from the university. They are close to your location already. The future of the city depends on your safe delivery. We won't risk you coming to harm.'

Ratcliffe probed the possibilities. 'And yet you risk yourselves? What's stopping us wiping you out when we get there?'

'If you do deploy your weapon, it will be because you've lost. Nothing and no one would let you survive after that. You do know that, don't you? I think you want power and control in life rather than a senseless death, even if you take thousands with you.'

'Don't pretend to know me,' Ratcliffe said. He could have been saying that to every person he'd ever met. 'You don't.'

'But I want to,' Bambera said, and it was hard to detect the slightest amount of deceit in his voice. 'Between us, we've ended this government. We've shown the people that faced with crisis, it's useless. But that's because they've been voted in by people who are equally vapid. We get the government we deserve. That's democracy. I think it's time for something different and I think you do too. That's the starting point we have in common. Once we've met in the Square, we can agree terms and retire somewhere more civilised, of our mutual choosing, and decide the future of this great country.'

Those words, with that accent not far away. Ratcliffe could tell that Bambera tried to hide it, after years in a public life that preferred him not to remind people too overtly of his origins.

The obvious was enough. But Ratcliffe could hear it. The nerve of the man both appalled and intrigued him.

'I'll be there,' Ratcliffe said, aiming to sound casual.

'We have another request. Bring Atkinson and Markson. They could be useful intermediaries.'

Ratcliffe chuckled. 'Whoops,' he said. 'Only one still stands. I'll let you find out which when we get there.'

Bambera paused, then said, 'Agreed.'

'You can bring something in return,' Ratcliffe added, serious again. 'I want to see them.' He let the request sink in, enjoying the silence it provoked. 'Bring the Children.'

When he was sure Ratcliffe wasn't returning, Markson pulled the photograph from his pocket. Predictably, it was Atkinson and his wife, frozen in monochrome, reunited now perhaps. Markson felt a swell of regret at the taunts he had put the man through before the end.

Then he remembered the new holocaust the man could still be responsible for, and he swallowed down the guilt. He remembered supporting Rachel in her attempt to prevent Atkinson from continuing his research using university money. Was that what had pushed him towards Ratcliffe in the first place? If they had funded him, could they also have kept a closer eye on him?

It was too late now. The weapon had been completed, presumably. Knowing the time these things took to test and confirm through layers of university bureaucracy, Markson guessed that Atkinson had already been close to completion when he had requested the funding. Weapons like those seemed to manifest inevitably, like the Children, and it became a case of ensuring they were never used. The nuclear bombs that had ended the Second World War had established that principal, and Markson could see it stretching ahead as a never-ending obligation.

He turned over the photograph.

'Lee Lockwood,' he breathed, reading the name on the back aloud. His mind raced. There was something familiar about the name. But why would there be a man's name on the back of a photograph of Atkinson and his wife?

Bit like that. Ratcliffe's words returned to his mind, and

Markson looked again at the pool of blood, which had already coagulated darkly on the concrete floor. *Liquid*.

'The River Lee runs to the Lockwood pumping station...' he whispered to himself, his enthusiasm building, reconstructing vague memories of a colleague involved in the epic engineering task of restoring the flow, and securing the city's water supplies after years of drought. 'If the weapon is waterborne, that's where it could enter the supply.'

He had to find a way to tell the others. What use was it speaking it aloud down here with only a dead body as audience?

He didn't have long to think of a way of escaping the building when opportunity arrived.

He snapped his arms back behind himself and sagged uselessly as one of Ratcliffe's guards entered and pushed him roughly to his feet. Luckily the man was in such a rush, he didn't notice that he was already free, and the rope fell to the ground near Atkinson's body, to be replaced by metal cuffs that were much more efficient.

'Where are we going?' Markson asked.

'Boss' decision,' the guard muttered, as if the whole thing was way beyond his comprehension and he just wanted to follow his simple orders so as not to incur any wrath. 'Some Square or other. Some kind of negotiation or prisoner exchange or something, I don't know.'

'Not Soho Square I suppose?' Markson asked hopefully, proudly holding on to his knowledge and ready to deploy it at the earliest opportunity.

The guard seemed to recognise the reference and smiled, either in cruelty or genuine amusement. 'No. Russell.'

So, thought Markson. *Russell Square. As good a crucible as any.*

CHAPTER TWENTY-FOUR

Saturday – Russell Square, London. 5.16pm

RUSSELL SQUARE was wreathed in fog when they arrived and transformed its tranquillity into barely controlled chaos.

Troops and equipment pushed the gently curling clouds out of the way, and they dissipated in frustration, gathering instead on its edges. Floodlights lit up whatever was left, casting a harsh white light where before had been soft, deep orange. The bare trees were sketched in jagged lines against the sky, their branches like frozen lightning. The pathways across the Square, symmetrically laid out to connect the corners of the green space and converge in the centre, shone in an almost too-overt invitation to meet in the middle.

Rachel knew as soon as she saw the place that this would be where it would end. There was a sense of theatre to the design, the stage on which the players would come together having hidden in their various wings around the city for too long.

The potential for a bloodbath was significant, she realised, which was perhaps Bambera's thinking. It would almost be too easy to unleash that pent up tension in a hail of bullets, but everyone knew that would mean mutually assured destruction. The depressing condition of the whole human race was writ small in that square.

I'm so tired of the fighting, she thought, not in words but in an ache that made it hard to stand as tall as she needed to be.

'The Children are here,' Allison told her, touching her shoulder, making her jump.

She turned to see and could only utter, appalled, 'My God...'

The Children had been manoeuvred together into the basic motive units of the tank systems, their own limited throne movement enhanced by tracks and wheels. Armour now rose above and around them to protect them from stray fire, and Rachel couldn't help but get a horrible flashback of the first sighting in Foreman's Yard back in '63. They weren't yet sealed in, but guards stood poised to defend their remaining visible flesh.

Rachel could just about see their faces. They remained impassive, as if elsewhere. Occasionally there was even the flash of a smile about their lips and eyes. She knew that out of sight, within their shared casing, they were still holding hands. It had become clear when they were briefly separated earlier, and barbed lightning had started to play threateningly around their implants, that to part them now would be disastrous.

'How can this end for them?' Allison asked, as awestruck as Rachel.

Rachel turned her eyes to the ground. 'When I connected to them earlier, I felt...'

Allison leaned down to try to pull her gaze back up. 'What?'

'I felt like it wasn't up to us anymore,' Rachel replied, fixing her old friend with a grim smile of resignation.

Guards continued to pour out of the trucks assembled along Southampton Row. Whether by instinct or instruction, they formed symmetrical patterns across the corner of the square designated 'Naebbetold' in the agreement with Ratcliffe. They followed the lines of the pathways and stood to attention as a guard of honour for their intended leaders.

Bambera himself, with Grove by his side, stepped into the Square only when the preparations were complete. He had donned an army overcoat, and his already impressive stature was only heightened all the more. As small as Grove seemed beside him, her short grey hair framed an expression of intense entitlement, her high-collared, dark blue coat with its large gold buttons gave her the air of a Naval officer.

Rachel regarded them, and wondered what world they would really make together, given the chance.

They took up position amid their guards, far enough inside the Square to await the arrival of their counterparts and to move to the middle when the time came, and close enough to the edge to retreat if the bullets came instead. The Children powered forward behind them, guards moving with them in perfect time.

The Square became quiet as the final manoeuvres ceased. The displaced fog, emboldened by the stillness, crept back in to join them. They waited.

'They've relocated to Russell Square,' Trevor announced as he re-entered the chamber.

Gilmore and Dillon, who were sat huddled together in a corner, looked at each other at the news. His son knew that this was the call to arms; Gilmore recognised that look.

'Did they say why?' Saunders asked.

'To break the deadlock, the guy said.'

Bes, who had remained still despite the delivery of the news, spoke without looking away from the murals above her. 'And the Children?' she asked.

'They've gone too. The two of them have joined together somehow. I don't know. This is way beyond me now.' For the first time, Trevor seemed to have run out of hope.

'The combined power they now share will be used by whoever dominates at the end of tonight,' Bes proclaimed. 'Or it can be nullified by us. The Children can be made safe. Both sides can be de-clawed. Without the Children, they will be small. Easy to end.'

Gilmore eyed her suspiciously. She had taken on the trance-like aura of before and the pretentious manner to go with it. 'I just want to get back to Rachel. We're not making any decisions without her.'

'Then let's make ready,' Saunders said. Gilmore wondered if he suspected Bes was going too far into her *fourfold state* or whatever they had called it, and felt the need to maintain some sense of practical use for their archaic Order. 'We have the gel and an interface module we can use...'

Gilmore stared at him coldly, his arm around Dillon tightening.

'If needed,' Saunders added carefully.

While Saunders helped Bes to her feet and gathered their equipment and weapons, Gilmore ushered Dillon ahead of him to the antechamber where Trevor was visibly trying to cool and calm himself down.

'You're troubled,' Gilmore stated as fact rather than question.

'I pledged to protect your son,' Trevor said, looking at the boy in fear. 'I can't do that if you give him over to this... process. Before that, I pledged to serve Bambera. I always knew he had big plans. Me and Hannah talked about it. We felt we owed him after he gave us a chance that others wouldn't. We felt loyal to him. But now...'

'All of our certainties have fallen away, right?'

Trevor nodded.

Gilmore wondered what was left when all of his had too. He didn't have to think for long. Rachel and Dillon. He believed in them both, and in the goal of being together. No more separate missions and obligations. Either in normality or, if need be, fighting their way through a strange new world, they would do it together.

'Whatever happens,' he told Trevor. 'You have a place with us. You can be certain of that.'

They shook hands warmly. Gilmore noticed Dillon watching them, nodding slowly, as if he was understanding something crucial for whatever was to come.

Ratcliffe surveyed the last of his men as they surrounded him, all facing outwards, alert to threats from all directions but oblivious of *him*, his importance in this moment.

They were men who followed orders without wanting or needing to know the rationale, or how their small actions would contribute to the turning of the tide of history.

Surrounded by these men, accompanied by Markson and Hareward, Ratcliffe felt utterly alone.

The sight of the Square therefore brightened him, and as the light of the floodlights began to fall on his tired features, he felt elevated in status, like the star arrival they'd all been waiting for. Which, in a way, he was.

He allowed himself a smile. Respect at last.

The Naebbetold guards outnumbered his, but that didn't matter all the time the threat of the biological agent was hanging over them all. He squinted through the foggy air to see the eyes of some of those guards. He recognised the tell-tale signs; they would be some of those chosen to fall in the first wave of biological attack. The potential of that horror magnified his forces severalfold.

His entourage remained fixed around him as they entered. None of the theatrical fanning out of Bambera's people, who now rose their weapons to meet the empty eyes of those trained back at them. Instead, his men moved forward as a crude collective, raw danger and unpredictability entering the symmetrical, ordered space.

There was Bambera, bold as brass, flanked as if head of state. Beside him, some jumped up female counterpart Ratcliffe half-recognised from the news. Her disdain was clear even from a distance. He would enjoy wiping that look off her face when the time came.

And there, behind them, were the Children. He allowed himself to peer above the heads of the layers of guards to try to see them more clearly. There was his boy, pale but alive, his eyes shining in a way Ratcliffe had not seen before. Next to him, the original Child. Not a girl, but not a woman. Something in-between and unknown. They sat together in a crested vehicle, its liquid tar blackness and round silver globes triggering some deeply held memory, one that felt like it stretched back somewhere before his own lifetime.

'Will we be close enough?' he whispered to Hareward, who nodded discretely in response. 'If I give the word, activate the override. They've borrowed our boy for too long.'

Together they advanced until within speaking distance. Naebbetold guns remained trained upon him, each one feeding his sense of swelling importance. He felt the power of the weapon in the water to the north and the potential of his Child just ahead of him. He felt invincible.

'Good of you to come,' Bambera announced.

'No time for niceties,' Ratcliffe returned, unwilling to dilute the dizzying sense of importance he felt and allow words to trickle deceit and doubt into his mind. 'What's your offer?'

Bambera nodded, perhaps relieved not to have to dance around the protocols of official negotiation. 'No less than an alliance. Together we've brought the government to its arthritic knees. There is a way we can unify our goals.'

'I don't see how.' Ratcliffe couldn't help but laugh. 'A black man and an old woman, dictating to us? I don't think so.'

'You want a country in which resources are prioritised for

your own kind,' Bambera responded quickly. He had prepared all this well. The woman next to him eyed him carefully, as if she herself was unsure of what he was going to offer. 'I get that. Believe it or not, I do too. We want control in the hands of the brightest. That clearly includes you and your allies, given all you've been able to achieve. The new elite, as we will be, will have free passage across the nations of the world. We will make the decisions that will ensure peace and security and resources for everyone. And if Britain, under your stewardship, decides to return to its original ethnic make-up, then so be it.'

Ratcliffe stared at the man for any sign of deceit, but he could see none.

Bambera stepped forward. 'I think the thing you hate more than those who are different to you, are those who are not as clever. Maybe, for whatever reason, you think that's the same thing. Have your white land if you want it, we don't actually care. The most important thing is that we guide our collective race towards its ultimate destiny.' He indicated the Children, who stared blankly back at him. 'That we continue to master technology to serve those who deserve it, to protect our species from those who would threaten it, and take our own place in the future as the superiors.'

Ratcliffe realised, too late, that he had been watching Bambera with something like awe. He shook his head a little to break the spell, but found that any idea of a reply was escaping him.

The Square fell silent. The eyes of the Naebbetold were upon him, and he could feel his own men wanting to turn, their heads inching slightly back towards him, to see what he might say.

For the first time, alone in the crowded Square, he couldn't think of anything.

So, he turned to Hareward, knowing that with the tiniest nod of his head, he could unleash a chaos in which all of them would be consumed. Better that than the continued silence of a man who had run out of ideas.

He remembered his father. He would linger around squares like this one. He would flatter young men, give them gifts while recruiting them to his cause. He would turn his own son away, put his arm around someone else and draw them into his army. He remembered the one called Mike, how his father had fawned over him, impressed with or jealous of his youth and good looks and desperate to own them for himself.

He looked at Bambera, who was awaiting an answer. He whispered the only one he could think of in response, the only thought in his mind, perhaps the only one that had ever been there, under every single other one.

'I don't want to share.'

He turned to Hareward and nodded.

Nobody saw Hareward press the button on the device in his coat pocket, but Ratcliffe knew he had done it. There was a look of terrible sadness and fear in his eyes, a sudden shock at a dawning reality. They seemed to say, *What have I done?*

Gilmore led his son and their companions gently through the ranks of Naebbetold guards.

Since their initial encounter with the outermost guards, it was clear that while Bambera had authorised them to enter the space, it was at their own risk, and that the slightest error could tip the finely tuned defensive barrier into action.

Although he would never admit it, Gilmore found himself borrowing some of the techniques he had picked up from Bes and Dillon, their shared ability to move smoothly through trouble as if confident in an invisible barricade around them.

They reached the Square just as Ratcliffe was arriving. The atmosphere was tense, the cloying fog chilling him after the warmth underground.

There, at last, was Rachel. Willing her to stay as still and steady as he was, he greeted her by taking her hand. Without even needing to look too quickly, she gripped it back, their old familiar touch uniting them even here.

'I need to tell you something,' he whispered, relieved that the attention of everyone was on the interaction between Bambera and Ratcliffe. 'But you need to stay calm.'

'You know saying that is the quickest way to the opposite of what you want,' she hissed back.

'I mean it, Rachel. If things go wrong and the Children become dangerous, Bes has a plan.'

'And what's that got to do with us?'

'Not us. Dillon.'

Rachel turned then with enough force to draw the eyes of

some of the nearby guards. 'Whatever you're about to tell me, don't,' she urged. 'He's done enough just by being here. No more.'

'But...'

'Where is he anyway? Where are they?'

In his focus on finding Rachel, Gilmore hadn't noticed that he was now the only one to have made it through to her. With rising panic, he realised that all of the others had gone.

'Ian!' Rachel's voice rose in desperation. 'Where is Dillon?'

Before he could lead her back through the guards to where the others must have diverged, a ripple of movement started to spread from where the Children sat, cloistered in their armour.

A message was being passed back through the guards.

'It's the Children... the boy,' Gilmore heard someone say. 'He's moving.'

The snowflakes that fell were now made of night and fog and the bare branches of trees. They drifted on the cold, damp air of a London autumn heading freefall into winter.

Judith and her friend recognised it and remembered. They shared tales of Novembers gone by. The girl told of the time before she changed into what she was now, of the warmth of a home the boy had never known. She tried not to think of *that* November, when it had all changed again.

They were spinning on a roundabout now, facing each other across the still-point in the centre and travelling at just the right speed for the momentum to be self-sustaining.

On the edge of her consciousness, Judith could feel a new cascade of numbers, descending from the air with the snowflakes and decreasing as they fell. It reminded her of the time when Rachel had joined her in the whitespace and given her the strength to divert the numbers from their fall towards zero. These numbers seemed colder and harder than the others and she wondered if she would be able to stop them even if she wanted to.

The boy, meanwhile, was also sensing something. She could tell because he kept looking at a point on the horizon, swivelling his head to try to see it even when the roundabout took his vision away from it. The motion was changing the equations and disrupting the balance, and she was having to adjust. Tiny, cumulative errors were building like a snowdrift in a doorway.

'I think I've remembered what I was supposed to do,' the boy said suddenly, causing the roundabout to shudder with the change.

Judith had a terrible feeling that their too-brief playtime was ending.

CHAPTER TWENTY-FIVE

Saturday – Russell Square, London. 6.05pm

DILLON ALLOWED himself to be led by Bes.

He stared ahead, remembering what he had learned. *Focus.* In his peripheral vision he could see people moving, a gradual dissolving of the patterns into defensive crouches and raised weapons.

He felt her hand around his, warm and dry. He could feel gently indented lines and the bones beneath her skin.

He could hear Trevor amid the growing shouts and calls from the troops all around them.

'You promise he'll be safe?' Dillon asked Bes.

And to him, she said, 'Dillon, if you don't want to do this, just say.'

Saunders was there too, holding Trevor away.

They stopped. Before them, encased in black and silver armour, were two figures.

Bes stood between Dillon and them and they met eyes. 'I never told you why I chose this name,' she said, and he could hear her as clearly as if there were no other sounds in the Square. The clicking of weapons and shouts of commands with their increasing edge of panic, faded away. 'Bes was an Egyptian deity,' she told him, so calmly amid the building chaos. 'Short, ugly, fierce. Just like me.' She smiled. 'Protector of households, and mothers. And children.'

She placed her hands on his head and he felt something warm encase his hair. The feeling spread like melting wax down over his ears and to the back of his neck. She pulled a silver rod from her pocket and held it out for him to see.

'Show them the world you'd like to see,' she whispered, before, lightning fast, she wrapped her arm around his neck and plunged downwards in a sudden motion.

He felt a coldness spreading from the point she had struck. The sounds of the Square faded even further. Snow seemed to be falling from the fog.

'Step away!' he could hear, an angry shout, but muffled. 'Step away from the boy or I fire!'

He could just about see Bes through the fog and the snowfall, but now she was fading too. She was still smiling. *Protector of Children*, she mouthed. She raised her arms, palms upward, lifting her eyes to the sky.

'Final warning, or I fire!'

Gunfire, far in the distance and right in front of him.

Bes fell to her knees. She still fixed her eyes to his, but her smile faded. She lowered her arms slowly and sank to the ground.

In the space where she had been, were the Children. They stared at him. The last thing he could see before the snow blinded him was their brightly shining eyes, recognising him.

Electricity danced around them all and drew him into a warm embrace.

Judith held on to her friend as he breathed heavily and tears leaked freely from his eyes.

'I can't... I can't hold it back,' he shuddered through sobs.

'Just a little longer,' Judith soothed. She could feel the rage building within his small frame. The rage wasn't his, it seemed so much bigger than his small life could have collected, although his sadness and the memory of cold gave it access, a channel through which it could pour. Soon it would be too much for her to hold down, and she would have to get out of its way or be ended by it as it swept through her, taking her with it as it rampaged and stormed and burned itself away to nothing.

She wished, briefly, for the empty days when her mind had not been capable of such concepts, before the new consciousness brought by Rachel. She wanted to return to those times of playing in the numbers endlessly, watching light move. The giddy heights of finding a friend were collapsing into a shared pain of his suffering, and to remove both would be easier.

Although...

A new shape started to appear amid the snowstorm. Another boy, older than her friend, but with a face just as kind. He brought with him a tension, an awareness of immediate danger, as if he had raced through a doorway and wanted to slam it shut behind him.

'Are boys always like this?' she asked no one, and wrapped a welcoming shield around the newcomer.

She felt him relax as the light surrounded him.

Judith could sense noise and chaos in the snowstorm; the flakes were jagged like daggers now, ice reflecting army green and gunmetal. She strengthened the field around herself and the two boys, wrapping it around them so the cold shards bounced off.

'I can hold this for a bit longer,' she told the new arrival. 'Between that and him...' She indicated the boy in her arms, still shuddering, his face contorted. '...We don't have much time.'

'What's the matter with him?' the new boy asked, approaching and looking with such compassion on her friend.

'He's been asked to do something bad, but he doesn't want to,' she replied, sensing the translation implant in her scalp straining and smoking as she tried to word the feelings.

'Can you stop him?'

'I don't know. Can you?'

The new boy paused, and thought, and smiled.

Gilmore and Rachel, hand in hand, raced to Dillon's side. As they neared, Gilmore felt Rachel stop suddenly and pull his arm, preventing him from getting too close.

Trevor and Saunders were standing back too, shielding their eyes from a light that seemed to surround their son and the other Children. Bes lay dead on the floor.

'What the hell...?' Gilmore said, aghast.

'He's in there with them,' Saunders offered in explanation. 'In the mental space they share. He can disarm them.'

Trevor moved towards them, scooping them into a protected huddle and holding his gun aloft to defend them. 'I couldn't stop them, Ian. I'm so sorry.'

Gilmore turned to Rachel, fearful of the wrath that could now be unleashed.

She was staring at the three Children, the light from their shield shining in her eyes. She seemed calm. 'Our boy...' she whispered. 'It's up to him now.'

Gilmore felt as if the ground were giving way beneath his feet. If Dillon were lost... His knees buckled, and Rachel grabbed him around the waist to hold him up.

'Have faith in him,' she told him.

The sound of gunfire echoed around the Square.

Gilmore saw Allison running at a low crouch across the grass between two of the pathways. Following the symmetry of the Square robotically, the Naebbetold guards were firing down their lines, and Allison wove through them swiftly. Rachel opened her arms to receive her and pulled her inside their huddle.

'It's all falling apart,' she gasped, her breath short and panicked. 'They're saying they've activated their weapons. The boy – the other Child – and the biological agent. Scorched earth. They can't take London so they're unleashing it all.'

Gilmore looked to Rachel. 'What can we do? Even if we leave Dillon to deal with the Children, we can't let Ratcliffe do this.'

Rachel scanned the Square, and he could see her mind strategising quickly. The blue light from the shield around the Children flickered across her face. 'The rest of you, get inside the shield. Ian, you're with me. We're going for Ratcliffe.'

'Rachel,' Allison said, incredulously. 'What makes you think they'll let us in?'

'If my son trusts you, you'll be let in. Go on. You can't afford not to.'

Gilmore watched as Allison seemed to muster all of her own faith, sharing a look with Rachel that spoke of a bond he couldn't comprehend. Allison nodded to her and stepped towards the shield. Light danced around her outline as she passed through and joined the Children in their shimmering haze. Saunders followed.

'Let me come with you.' Trevor was paused at the threshold, torn between his urge to protect both father and son.

'Stay with Dillon,' Ian urged. 'Please.'

Trevor nodded and stepped through the barrier.

With the others safely inside the shield, Gilmore took Rachel's hand once again and they ducked along the pathway Allison had taken, across the grass, conscious of the lines of paving along which the battle was being fought.

Gilmore took his own shots against two Association men who had peeled off from the main group to defend the sides. One man went down and the other jumped over him and along the line of the fence, firing back. Gilmore tried to push Rachel behind him, but she took out her own pistol and fired at the man relentlessly, her face carved into scornful judgement. Her bullets found him, and he fell.

From the side came Bambera, firing his own weapon and pushing Grove behind him.

'We need a moment of ceasefire,' Gilmore told him urgently. 'Ratcliffe might have unleashed the biological agent. We have to find out how to stop it.'

Bambera thought for a moment, breathing heavily.

'I order you to push forward,' Grove said from behind him. Her voice was sharp and cold. 'Remember your place,' she warned.

Gilmore watched Bambera react to her words, staring at her, his face transforming amid the continuing gunfire.

'And there it is...' Bambera said, as if seeing the truth of them both at the same time. 'Perhaps this is a good moment to let you know that you're under arrest, for treason.'

Grove stared at him, open mouthed. Even Gilmore felt frozen in shock. He shared a confused look with Rachel.

'Since I resigned from the government, I've been working for new employers. They're very interested in the stability of their member states and any threats to their democracies. They've taken my family into shelter and have funded this whole operation from the start.' Bambera sounded proud, standing despite the danger to tower over her.

'Who?' Grove shook her head, dumbfounded.

Bambera's expression was one of utter confidence, as if he knew he was supported by a network much bigger and stronger than any of the nascent, fighting ones of recent days.

'The United Nations?' Rachel asked in reply, and Gilmore felt the whole journey they had taken together fall into place.

'You're not Naebbetold?' Grove sounded almost childlike as the truth dawned amid the battlefield.

Bambera shook his head. 'I've simply brought them out of hiding. It all ends tonight. As a permanent member of the

Security Council, the United Kingdom cannot be allowed to fall into chaos.'

'You betrayed me,' Grove stated in outrage and disbelief. She looked to her ever-present guards, wielding their swords in a defensive posture, pointing to Bambera in an instruction to take him.

Together, they turned to point the swords at her. They nodded to Bambera in satisfied completion of their mission. Grove closed her eyes in appalled defeat.

Gilmore noticed that the gunfire was receding. The troops on both sides were running out of targets. Bodies littered the grounds and beyond the fencing some were running, to be met by other troops at the boundaries. 'We have to find Ratcliffe,' he insisted.

'He's here,' came a voice from the darkness of one of the corners not occupied by troops. The battered, hulking frame of Albert Markson staggered from the shadows, pushed onwards by a man pointing a rifle at him.

Gilmore saw the shadow of an older man in his looks, as if he had stepped from a photograph of his father from years ago. He was unmistakably a Ratcliffe.

He felt Rachel push him back away from the approaching pair, translating a fierce look that seemed to take in Grove and her sword-wielding guards and strategising a double-back.

'The Child is active,' he heard Ratcliffe confirm. 'The power will fail, and the biological agent will be released. You can do what you like to me. I've already won.'

Gilmore met the eyes of one of the guards, placing his hand alongside his grip on the hilt of his sword. After a silent communication of his intent, he allowed possession of the sword to pass to him and, as Ratcliffe focused on Bambera, he circled around through the darkness behind him.

Ratcliffe continued to point the rifle and it swayed between Bambera and Markson before settling on the former. 'Your kind will die first. Obviously.'

'It's at the pumphouse at Lockwood,' Markson said innocently. Gilmore saw Ratcliffe stare at the man in furious disbelief. 'Isolate the power supply there and it can't be released into the Thames.'

Taking the moment of confusion as his chance, Gilmore

finished his approach and arced the sword around to the front of Ratcliffe's neck while disarming him and pulling his arm painfully behind him in a fluid movement.

Bambera called one of the guards over and gave him urgent instructions. The man raced away. Bambera turned to Ratcliffe, who had almost sagged against Gilmore in some kind of exhaustion or acceptance.

Bambera stepped up to address Ratcliffe directly into his face. Gilmore kept the sword at just the right distance from his throat. 'Even if your Child attacks the power again,' Bambera growled, 'we'll make sure that agent never gets out. Sorry. Looks like "my kind" will be around a bit longer.'

'The Child cannot be stopped,' Ratcliffe hissed through gritted teeth. 'If he doesn't destroy the power systems of London, he turns that energy upon himself and all around him.' Gilmore could hear the grin return again despite Ratcliffe's proximity to death, or perhaps because of it. 'Self-destruct,' he said, laughing. 'Our little lad will bring us all down together. His revenge for the life he led. And mine.'

Across the Square, the light from the shield blazed, energy crackling from its dome into the air. The ground shook and Gilmore felt his grip on Ratcliffe and the sword loosen. Lightning defied nature to shoot upwards into the foggy sky.

The snow was falling upwards in the whitespace, scrolling reality into the air where it dissolved and rained back down as dead data.

Judith could feel the whole construct collapsing after all those years. She was happy-sad at the thought.

'I can't hold on anymore,' she said, surprising herself by sounding a little like the woman she could have been if things had been different. A teacher perhaps, in a school like Coal Hill. A mother, maybe. A mother to children.

She cradled her friend in her arms. His building power had been too much for his little body, and while it still built in him, the rage just too much to contain, his own self had drifted away a few moments ago. She remembered the passing thoughts as he left. *Thanks for the games. It was nice to play. Goodbye.*

'Whatever you can do, do it now, before the energy release destroys them all. It has to go somewhere. We need to send it to a safe place. Or the right place.' She looked at the new boy hopefully.

He hadn't wanted to play, not that they could have done anyway. He had wanted to show them a book instead. It was a battered old thing, bound with a metal spiral spine and full of pencil drawings.

Judith decided she would continue to look at the drawings as she let go. They were good. They seemed familiar; people and shapes she had learned about when she was a little girl. Some of the people were very sad, others full of bravery and hope. Some were all at once, like she was. So, with her final breaths of energy, she animated the drawings so that they filled the void, and the Children were joined by the monochrome ghosts from the pages.

She smiled, watching them weave and dance around her, until she closed her eyes.

Dillon watched in awe as his creations flickered across the whiteness.

There were his ancestors, freed from their chains, and they were pulled up by the strong hands of the soldiers who stepped out of their trenches to join them. More children poured in from the corners of the pages, faces dirty from the factories, their limbs sore but light now, and dancing too.

He could see Bes in the distance, nodding, pleased, and a heavy-set man with the kindest eyes that twinkled with firelight.

He knew his friends were near, and Mum and Dad. He remembered his Dad and Trevor shaking hands, and smiled. He let his mind relax into the focus as he'd been taught, and he let the horrors and wonders of history flow around him while keeping the image of that friendship fixed as a template for the future.

The Unknown Warrior, his face flickering between all the possibilities of who he might be, reached down to him, his blurring hand outstretched.

Dillon gave him the bullet. He had been holding it for so long that it left an indentation in his hand, and he felt lighter without it. He remembered where it had come from and what it had changed into. It had once been meant for killing, but now it brought him stories and bravery and hope.

He thought of the woman and how she had held the little boy so tenderly. He thought what they would like done with the power that had been too much for them.

He let the pips count down, the final flakes of snow, falling.

Six.

Five.

Four.

Three.

Two.

One.

The Unknown Warrior loaded the bullet into his rifle, aimed at the sky, and fired.

The sensation of shared thoughts, as gentle as a feather brushing her skin, pulsed from the lightning that arced across Russell Square.

Rachel closed her eyes and could almost believe that Dillon was there, pressing against her, holding on while the world went mad.

But it was Judith she could also sense, waving goodbye as she faded at last from the life she had been clinging to. The connection that had been forged by Cerberus and strengthened this last week frayed and split and was gone.

The lightning swept across the Square in a frenzy, each bolt earthing frantically and chasing others along the ground. Some unfortunate guards and Association gunmen found themselves in the path of one of the forked blue swords, and they fell. Some of the bolts met, joining forces and moving more slowly, consciously almost, as if seeking things out.

Rachel covered her eyes with her arm and crouched low, holding on to Ian, as two of the strengthened bolts came close. They hovered, lingering, assessing. She could see Bambera, crouching and shielding himself too, squinting as he looked into the lightning, his face almost accepting in case he was judged and executed in that moment.

The two bolts became one, and the last of the flaming tendrils gathered into it, one final expression of the remaining power from the Children. Rachel closed her eyes as it brushed against Grove, illuminating her from the inside as she screamed and fell. Moving purposefully away from Markson, it drifted towards Ratcliffe. His face was defiant in its blazing light.

A stumbling figure emerged from the bushes nearby in a desperate run for the gate in the corner. The lightning followed, calmly, tracing along the ground then up his legs to the middle of his back before a final pulse evaporated him completely.

'Hereward,' she heard Markson say.

The lightning had gone. Turning back to the Children, she saw tiny sparks dancing gleefully around their armour, illuminating smoke that rose and blended with the fog of the cold night sky. Standing, silhouetted by the dying light, was Dillon.

Without words, Rachel pulled Ian to his feet and they ran to their son. She crouched to face him directly and looked into his eyes. He stared blankly ahead, but then they seemed to focus on her, and his face creased into a sob. She held his head, feeling the gel that had made his hair slick and stick to his scalp, her hand slipping downwards to where something cold and metal emerged from the back of his neck. With a gentle pull it came away, and as she held him, she tested the area it had merged with. It was sealing already, the skin supple under the thick fluid and quickly closing over.

Gilmore had crouched beside her and was holding them both too, his broad arms enclosing them. 'Is he all right?' he whispered.

Rachel nodded, unable to speak. Their child was alive. Nothing else mattered at that moment.

Except that she could see, in the corner of her eye, the smoking remains of the Children, and she knew that they were dead.

She pushed against Gilmore's embrace, moving his arm so it was wrapped as tightly around Dillon alone as it had been her. Separated from them, she staggered, but stood. Allison was near, parting from her own huddle of companions, and she reached for Rachel. They steadied each other while stepping towards the confirmation they needed in silence.

As they reached the cradle of the Children, its black metal warped and its silver globes scorched and crushed, they looked around the Square at the devastation. Amid the bodies of guards whose names they would never know, and Association thugs who must have died with no clue of what they had become involved with, was the body of Grove. Bambera stood over her, looking around too, searching for something. Ratcliffe, alive or dead, was nowhere to be seen. Perhaps he too had been scorched into nothing in the Children's final act.

Then Rachel looked at them, the image burning itself into her mind where she knew it would stay, always. All of the technology had been destroyed. Most of it was almost entirely gone, cables withered into wires and implants into ash. But their skin, against her expectations, was not scorched. It was pale in death, smooth and clear. In those final moments their bodies must have rejected all implantation, ejecting it from themselves and from the world in which it did not belong.

They died as humans, she realised as she peered down inside the burned crust of armour and saw that they were still holding hands.

Bambera's underground office had been transformed in his absence.

Although the faces behind and around the desk were unfamiliar, they wore the uniforms of United Nations Peacekeepers, and those who didn't were emblazoned with logos and lanyards heralding their status. Bambera stood among them, suddenly one among equals instead of the embattled leader of a rogue army. Gilmore shook his head in disbelief, thinking back to his first visit here, wondering how many layers of deception had fallen away to reveal the man beneath it all.

'Did they get back safely?' Trevor asked, breaking his thoughts and the intense stare they were fuelling.

'What? Oh yes, they got back a little while ago. Dillon is sleeping, it goes without saying I suppose.'

Trevor seemed content at this, and he nodded a little sadly as if a job long held dear had come to an end.

Allison and Saunders drew closer to them, and Gilmore felt the strange familiarity of a team, forged in danger and darkness, even though he felt he knew some of them still only a little. What would they all do next, he wondered? What family might comfort them through the hard nights of remembrance to come?

He met eyes with Allison, her face tired and lined, his memory of her stretching back to the beginning of the story that had ended with the death of the Children.

'Will he be all right?' she asked tenderly. 'And Rachel?'

'Oh, you know them,' Gilmore replied confidently.

'Rachel will remain indomitable,' a new voice added. Albert Markson joined them, a glass of white wine in one hand and fresh bandages covering the other.

'How did you get that?' asked Saunders with envy.

'They're looking for ways to thank me for the information that ended the biological threat. They retrieved the solution and made the area safe. So, I suppose it was worth it in the end.' Markson trailed off, sounding haunted.

'Any word on Ratcliffe?' Gilmore asked, knowing that Markson had remained in the Square as the UN clean-up had started, to advise on the safe storage of the Children's remains.

Markson took a gulp of his wine at the sound of the name. 'Nothing.'

'And the other fellow?'

'Hareward? No remains. He was the main architect of the poor little boy's plight, so perhaps that's right and proper, given all he did. Perhaps Ratcliffe ended the same way, and we just didn't see. It was all on his orders.'

'What about the artefacts?' Saunders asked. Like Trevor, the man had seemed exhausted and deflated, without purpose now things had ended. 'We fought so hard to find them. All those bloody tunnels, for most of my life. The base is gone, Bes is dead, the Order of Albion might as well be finished. Blake's legacy, lost in fire.'

'The artefacts have burned along with the surviving technology of the Children,' Markson told them. 'Perhaps, given the potential for their misuse, that's the best Blake could have hoped for.'

Gilmore remained silent, until he saw Bambera separate from the officials he had been conferring with. 'Excuse me,' he said politely, 'I think I need to find one of those wines.' Then he stalked towards his target.

He reached Bambera and blocked his path. 'You've come out of this well,' he accused. 'Standing on a pile of corpses, victorious.'

Bambera turned, his face indulgent. 'I can understand how you—'

'Do not...' Gilmore shouted, pausing as faces turned, and

continued in a barely restrained whisper '...Do not presume to know. You know as much about me as I obviously do about you. And you have used me and my family for the last time.'

'Ian,' Bambera appealed, using his first name for the first time that Gilmore could remember. 'Surely you can see that what we did together was needed. The Association and the Naebbetold needed to be stopped. We needed them out in the open. We needed to know their potential and the potential of their weapons.'

'Those poor Children...'

'Have found peace. At last. And there can be no more Children like them.'

Gilmore shook, holding himself as still as he could as his rage abated, whether through exhaustion or because he knew Bambera was right, he couldn't tell.

'You gathered together the weapons that could have blighted generations to come,' Bambera continued, a hand resting gently, bravely, on Gilmore's elbow. 'And you finished them. Your son chose the best possible future because of what he learned with you. You should be so proud.'

'Did Bes know you were working for the UN?'

Bambera nodded. 'Of all my *allies*, only she knew. She knew my plans would bring the Order's mission to its conclusion too. She was instrumental in it all.'

'All the way back to Woden?' Gilmore tried not to feel envious of the amount of planning and counter-planning the man had achieved.

'I'm afraid so.'

'And now? Where do you fit into this new world?'

Bambera looked around at the busy officials. 'With them. My role can be made official now that I'm no longer government. Special envoy to the UN. Winifred and her mother are already in Geneva, and my son... Well, he's safe too. I'll continue to guard against civil and political threats to the stability of member countries, liaise with our agencies and taskforces. There are a few loose ends. One of Hareward's colleagues, and a potential government leak...'

Gilmore narrowed his eyes. 'You'll be in your element, I'm sure.'

Bambera held out a hand for Gilmore to shake.

'And what about them?' Gilmore asked instead of taking it. He indicated to the familiar faces of those he'd spent the last week with, who looked so out of place amid the officials and guards. He saw Trevor, in particular, looking pensively over to him.

'After de-briefing, it will be up to them,' Bambera said, withdrawing his hand. 'As it will be for you, Group Captain. There will be... opportunities... I'm sure. You may yet make a good team.'

Also available from Candy Jar Books.

BIRDS OF PASSAGE BY ROBERT MAMMONE

LETHBRIDGE-STEWART MEETS COUNTER MEASURES!

The Cold War is in full swing as the British Government, in partnership with Woden Armaments, launches the Cerberus satellites into orbit, transforming world wide communications.

But all is not as it seems. Retired Air Vice Marshal Ian Gilmore is reluctantly drawn into helping an embattled government. Despatched to a divided Germany, he soon finds himself on the wrong side of the Berlin Wall as he helps a Soviet engineer with a terrible secret defect to the West.

Back home, Professor Rachel Jensen discovers her work at Cambridge has been perverted by Woden Armaments. When the Cerberus launch team, including Allison Williams and Anne Travers, goes missing, Rachel begins an investigation that unearths a terrible conspiracy at the heart of the British Establishment – a conspiracy that threatens the entire world!